Desire After Affect

Desire After Affect

Marie-Luise Angerer

Translated by Nicholas Grindell

Foreword by Patricia T. Clough

For Michael Cooper
Georgetown Texas
6 February 2016
(PAIDEIA)

ROWMAN &
LITTLEFIELD
INTERNATIONAL
London • New York

Published by Rowman & Littlefield International, Ltd.
Unit A, Whitacre Mews, 26-34 Stannary Street, London SE11 4AB
www.rowmaninternational.com

Rowman & Littlefield International, Ltd. is an affiliate of Rowman & Littlefield
4501 Forbes Boulevard, Suite 200, Lanham, Maryland 20706, USA
With additional offices in Boulder, New York, Toronto (Canada), and Plymouth (UK)
www.rowman.com

British Library Cataloguing in Publication Information Available
A catalogue record for this book is available from the British Library

ISBN: HB 978-1-78348-130-9
ISBN: PB 978-1-78348-131-6

Library of Congress Cataloging-in-Publication Data

Angerer, Marie-Luise, 1958–
[Vom Begehren nach dem Affekt. English]
Desire after affect / Marie-Luise Angerer ; translated by Nicholas Grindell ; foreword by Patricia Clough.
pages cm.
Includes bibliographical references and index.
ISBN 978-1-78348-130-9 (cloth : alk. paper)—ISBN 978-1-78348-131-6 (pbk. : alk. paper)—ISBN 978-1-78348-132-3 (ebook)
1. Emotions. 2. Desire. 3. Sex (Psychology) 4. Psychoanalysis and culture. 5. Affect. 6. Mass Media. I. Title.
BF511.A5413 2015
128'.37--dc23
2014029841

∞™ The paper used in this publication meets the minimum requirements of American National Standard for Information Sciences Permanence of Paper for Printed Library Materials, ANSI/NISO Z39.48-1992.

Printed in the United States of America

Contents

Acknowledgments

My work on *Desire After Affect* drew on conversations with colleagues and students at various times and places. Although I cannot give an exhaustive list here, I am grateful to them all. I would, however, like to make specific mention of my discussions with Bernd Bösel, Michaela Ott, Anna Tuschling and Rolf Grossmann, who prepared and ran the international symposium *Timing of Affect*[1] with me. The workshop *Re-working Affect* at Berlin's ICI,[2] to which I was invited by Brigitte Bargetz, also encouraged me to rethink the political and societal dimensions of affect. I am grateful to Claus Pias and Martin Warnke, who in the winter term of 2013 invited me as senior fellow to the Institute for Advanced Study in "Media Cultures of Computer Simulation" at Leuphana University in Lüneburg, where I was able to begin my work on the final chapter. Thanks to an invitation from Chris Salter, Brian Massumi, and Erin Manning, I was able to continue this work at Hexagram and SenseLab in Montreal in the spring of 2014. My special thanks to Bernd Bösel for his "insistent close reading" of the final chapter and to Patricia T. Clough for her wonderful foreword. Paul Patton and Moira Gatens encouraged me to push forward with the project of an English edition, as well as established the contact to Rowman & Littlefield International. Thanks to Sarah Campbell, who supported the project with interest and commitment from the outset, and especially to Martina O'Sullivan, who managed the project within the Cultural Studies series. A big thank-you to Nicholas Grindell for all his work on the English version of the book, and to Stephen Zepke for his constructive copy-editing. Thanks, once again, to Michael Heitz of diaphanes for his support. And finally, the entire project with all its highs and lows was accompanied by Rolf Walz, whom I would like to thank here once again for his help and patience.

Marie-Luise Angerer
Berlin, June 2014

NOTES

1. *Timing of Affect,* international symposium, Academy of Media Arts Cologne, 31 May–1 June 2013, www.khm.de/nocache/aktuelles/veranstaltungen/veranstaltung/article/2654-timing-of-affect-internationales-symposium/nCall/136 (retrieved 8 June 2014).

2. *Reworking Affect: Queer-Feminist Engagements,* workshop, 27 June 2013, www.ici-berlin.org/de/event/512 (retrieved 8 June 2014).

Foreword

Patricia T. Clough

While the publication of the English translation of *Vom Begehren nach dem Affekt* is a welcome event, we might note, as Marie-Luise Angerer does, that the English title hasn't the complexity of the German, as *nach* has a double meaning, giving us *the desire for/after affect*. Certainly there has been a desire *for* affect across critical studies as the concept increasingly has been given a central place in cultural studies; literary studies; neuro- and bio-studies; cognitive studies; media and new media studies and studies of practices in performance, dance, music and sound. Angerer also tells us that the desire for affect is after desire, a psychoanalytic desire that was so central to critical studies, to a politics of representation, the deconstruction of the sovereign subject and the recognition of unarticulated or invisible identities. The turn to affect marks a time when critical studies are engaged otherwise; the focus is on the biopolitics of securitization, financialization and militarization—or what we have called neoliberalism.

While criticisms of neoliberalism at first focused on the withdrawal of the state and the demise of its civil society institutions, criticism soon would turn to the paradox of neoliberalism that distinguished neoliberalism from laissez-faire and recognized the permanent vigilance, activity and intervention of governance. A securitization of every aspect of life, a setting of every aspect of life to risk, turned criticism to consider again the relationship of the state and the economy, public and private spheres. Angerer rightfully proposes that we understand affect in terms of life itself or vitality in the context of neoliberal governance and sociality. This requires, she proposes, that we recognize the ongoing shift from a *dispositif of sex,* as Michel Foucault describes it, to a *dispositif of affect*, raising questions about our understanding of subjectivity, consciousness, and the body.

What, then, of subjectivity, affect and neoliberalism? Michel Feher[1] has offered a view of neoliberalism that focuses on subjectivity, arguing that we have not attended enough to the question of what type of subjectivity is being simultaneously presupposed and targeted by neoliberal policies. In addressing the question, Feher takes up Marx's free laborer, who, whatever else, is a sovereign subject who is free to dispose of his property, his hours or his energy, while he himself remains free: free in the private sphere as a self-possessed subject to pursue "love, spirituality and culture." In terms of these liberal conditions about which Marx is writing, love, spirituality and culture cannot be reduced to a calculus of interest. These remain incalculable—befitting the assumption that reproduction in the home cannot create surplus value, as such work is outside the market and its evaluations. However, by the mid-twentieth century, with the democratic socialist or Fordist–Keynesian social compact, a neoliberalism would be introduced that eventually would no longer yield successes as it did at first and would lead to the breakup of the Fordist–Keynesian compact. With this, subjectivity must be understood in terms other than that of the free laborer, and Feher suggests that we begin to rethink the subject in terms of human capital or what I would rather treat as affective capacity, where the labor power of human laborers is replaced by an abstract labor power of *affect-itself.*[2]

As such, the subject is concerned with its affective capacities and their continued modification. One speculates on the ongoing value of affective capacities, and one invests in oneself not only for earnings but more for future well-being—psychic and bodily. This is what Feher calls the "self-appreciating subject." As he puts it, "insofar as our condition is that of human capital in a neoliberal environment, our main purpose is not so much to profit from our accumulated potential as to constantly value or appreciate ourselves or at least prevent our own depreciation."[3] But the self-appreciating subject is not simply a disciplined self-conscious, unconscious individual but rather a subject subjected to the dynamics of an affective economy interlaced with technology, a digital technology of measurement and calculation. As Angerer suggests, affect is to be rethought as the capacity for self-measuring in bodies—not only the human body but all matter of bodies, all matter.

In his canonical text on affect, Brian Massumi[4] argued that affect is in excess of the human body, and as I and my coauthors[5] have suggested, the human body can no longer be understood only as enclosed in the organism. The human organism becomes a special case in a general definition of the body that crosses organic and nonorganic life. Affect calls for a rethinking of bodily matter that resonates with what has been called the new materialisms and their reconsideration of the bio-, nano-, and neurosciences—all now properly technosciences. From the perspective of these sciences, the liveliness of all things, of all matter of bodies, is beyond consciousness in a broader sense than affect's being a preconscious capacity of the human body. Affect also is nonconscious in that the technicity that allows us to know, or should I say measure affect, in all matter of bodies operates beyond human consciousness generally. Even when referring only to human bodies, affect is shot through with technicity. Whether it be a matter of the auto-affective circuit that allows affect to be registered as that "missing half-second" of preconsciousness or a matter of being abstracted by the digitized algorithms that parse so-called big data at great speeds, affect, as a capacity, has the capacity to measure itself, to modulate itself, and therefore it is open to technologies that intensify its self-measurement. Conceptually, affect deconstructs the opposition between nature and technicity as it does between organic and nonorganic life.

But what, then, of human consciousness? Recently Mark Hansen has proposed that the technologies or algorithmic architectures distributing and parsing big data can effectively repress consciousness by operating in technical time frames to which consciousness has absolutely no direct, experiential or phenomenological interface. As he puts it: "Consciousness is generated after-the-fact, as an emergence generated through the feeding forward of technically-gathered data concerning antecedent microtemporal events." While consciousness continues to experience its own narrow bandwidth reality through sense perception, "this experience is disjoined, both temporally and operationally, by the operational present of technology—where behavior gets shaped—independently of any conscious access or input."[6]

As consciousness continues to experience its own bandwidth, there also must be a subject of unconscious desire. But what of desire in the *dispositif of affect*, or what Angerer refers to as desire *after* affect—the second sense of *nach*. While the answer is not yet clear, Hansen's discussion of consciousness after the fact of data would suggest that the return of the repressed, the past overcoming the present, is being displaced by an expanded present, a feeling of a present never to be left, as data of antecedent microtemporal events are continuously being fed forward. Angerer turns to what Catherine Malabou[7] describes as the *cerebral unconscious*, known to us through brain imaging technology.

Arguing that the human subject cannot directly experience the functioning of its brain or nervous system, Malabou proposes that the brain and nervous system can and do experience themselves. The brain feels itself informed and ever changing and this, the brain's relationship to itself, its auto-affection, is what allows for the cerebral unconscious. The cerebral unconscious, Malabou suggests, deconstructs the self-possessed subject of liberalism even more than the psychoanalytic understanding of the unconscious did. The cerebral unconscious of the "neurological revolution," Malabou concludes, far from being a "mere scientific phenomenon that threatens philosophy" is rather the "fulfillment of the deconstruction of subjectivity."[8] Instead of the end(s) of subjectivity in the self-appreciating subject, in the cerebral unconscious, where embodiment no longer can be taken up as a site where diffuse data is processed to yield images or experiences, it is as if "microcomputational sensors" literally abstracted affective processes providing an affect-itself for technological intensification.[9]

Are we then also at the end(s) of affect? In the pages that follow, Angerer surely has given us a rich sense of the ends of affect. But what of its end? Recently Alexander Galloway has suggested that, against the prediction of the waning of affect, there seems to be more and more affect.[10] Books, journals, conferences and disciplines are devoted to it, as social media circulate "personal profiles, wants and needs, projected egos."[11] Yet, as Galloway sees it, this also is a moment of the "absolute rationalization of affect in software," showing that "when something is perfected, it is dead."[12] Perhaps this is too quick an estimation, or perhaps affect's "undead persistence," to use another of Galloway's descriptors, is more relevant in these times, both in the academy and beyond. Relevant because it signals the *for* and *after* of neoliberalism as it yields to a biopolitical violence, "where the source of life is mixed with its failure to sustain liveliness [. . .] the more of life, the more of death."[13] This is the *dispositif of affect* that Angerer details and thereby gives us warning of the necessity to intervene thoughtfully and affectively.

NOTES

1. Michel Feher, "Self-Appreciation; or, The Aspirations of Human Capital," in *Public Culture: Bulletin of the Project for Transnational Cultural Studies*, 21.1 (2009), 21–42.
2. Patricia T. Clough, Greg Goldberg, Rachel Schiff, Aaron Weeks, and Craig Willse, "Notes towards a Theory of Affect-Itself," in *Ephemera*, 7.1 (2007), 60–77.
3. Feher, "Self-Appreciation," 27.
4. Brian Massumi, *Parables for the Virtual: Movement, Affect, Sensation* (Durham, NC: Duke University Press, 2002).
5. Patricia T. Clough, "The Affective Turn: Political Economy, Biomedia and Bodies," in *Theory, Culture & Society*, 25.1 (2008), 1–22.
6. Mark B. N. Hansen, "Beyond Affect? Technical Sensibility and the Pharmacology of Media," paper presented at the Critical Themes in Media Studies, New York University, 2013.
7. Catherine Malabou, *The New Wounded: From Neurosis to Brain Damage* (New York: Fordham University Press, 2012).
8. Ibid., 210.
9. Hansen, "Beyond Affect?"
10. Alexander R. Galloway, *The Interface Effect* (Cambridge, UK: Polity Press, 2012).
11. Ibid., 12.
12. Ibid.

13. Samuel Gerson, "The Enlivening Transference and the Shadow of Deadliness," paper delivered to a meeting of the Boston Psychoanalytic Society and Institute, 3 May 2003.

Introduction

Although the discussion surrounding affect has diversified hugely since this book originally appeared in German in 2007,[1] two main trends can be identified, confirming my diagnosis of a "*dispositif* of affect" and supporting my initial theory that sexuality has lost its status as a benchmark of the modern subject.

My claim that the focus on affect highlights the similarities between man, machine and animal rather than underlining the differences (as had been the case since the "invention of man", with its emphasis on the uniqueness of language) is now clearly justified. In recent years, as well as finding expression in critiques of this hegemony of language (and of psychoanalysis), the *dispositif* of affect, combined with the phenomena of an all-pervasive digitization, now offers new possibilities for intervention (pharmacological,[2] technological[3] and epistemological[4]) in almost every area of life.

As introduced by Michel Foucault, a *dispositif* is a discursive structure within which power, law, and truth are intertwined in such a way as to be articulated in both institutional practices and in the desire of individual subjects. For Foucault, "sex" was such a *dispositif*. Today, the enthusiasm with which affects, emotions and feelings are habitually used to underpin arguments points to a *dispositif* of affect: In the discourses of philosophy, art, and media theory, as well as cybernetics, cognitive psychology and neuroscience, affects are being used to establish a new vision of human beings and the world they inhabit.

This book outlines the development of this *dispositif* of affect. In historical terms, it traces a development from the late eighteenth century (Foucault's *The Order of Things* with its "discovery of man") via nineteenth-century physics and physiology, Freud's "invention" of the unconscious, cybernetic regulation, Lacan's hegemony of the signifier, and the declaration of a posthuman age. It traces the shift from a "truth of the sexual" to a "reflex of the affective"; from the modern "fear of castration" to the postmodern "becoming animal and other"; from Lacan's "fear as affect" to Deleuze's "affect image"; from sexuality as "little death" to sexuality as biodigital cell division; from a desire that draws on lack, via a desire based on the superabundance of Being, to my proposal at the end of the book that desire be understood as pure movement in time.

This list of themes and topoi highlights the links between affect and the fields of digital technologies on the one hand and sexuality on the other. From the beginning, the networking of digital technologies (which have since become all pervasive) was associated with the promise of organizing the question of identity in new ways that would replace "modern" man with a post- or transhuman counterpart. Since the 1980s, however, when Donna Haraway introduced the notion of the cyborg as a way of thinking about such developments and intervening on a political level, we have seen the emergence of a very real "biomediated body" (Clough) whose data are calculated and stored in the administrative apparatuses of an increasingly apparent "biosociality"[5] (Rabinow).

Concerning the link between affect and sexuality, I argue that all of the territories formerly defined and connoted as sexual—the unconscious and the Real, the body and desire—are being replaced by affect or integrated into the system of affect (Tomkins). Freud's model of the life-and-death drives is transformed into a process of adaptation organized by the affects. The latest theories on the plasticity of the brain (Malabou) and affects located in the subcortical deep brain (Panksepp) further underpin my original assumptions.

These three dimensions—the affective, the sexual, and the digital—are not causally connected, but under specific conditions they intersect, creating a matrix that I examine here both syntagmatically and diachronically.

During the last third of the nineteenth century, sharing the euphoria of the time, Étienne-Jules Marey hoped that the new medium of photography would allow natural phenomena themselves to speak.[6] In the middle of the last century, Marshall McLuhan defined *media* not only as mere "extensions of man" but as the essence of what they communicate: "The medium is the message".[7] In this model, man is understood as being entangled in media that control perception and communication. At the close of the twentieth century, Derrick de Kerckhove, then director of the McLuhan Institute in Toronto, stated that, in the next stage of this technological development, media signals will reach the brain directly.

Between Marey's era and Kerckhove's present lie the emergence of psychoanalysis, its golden age and the waning of its influence. As a discipline, psychoanalysis stands for the link between sexuality and language, for the enthronement of the unconscious as based on language and the dream as a rebus, both posited by Freud as ideal ways of exploring the "truth" of the subject. Although Freud and Lacan did not ignore affect (as integral to sexuality and language), they focused primarily on its "slippage" (Lacan), not sharing today's interest in its immediacy and functionality.

Two main traditions of affect are currently under discussion.[8] First, the affect theory developed by Silvan Tomkins in the 1960s was rediscovered thirty years later for cultural studies by Eve Kosofsky Sedgwick. She contrasts Tomkins's theory, which is influenced by systems theory and cybernetics, with Freud's model of the drives, privileging the former on account of its greater degree of freedom. Today, Tomkins's theory figures primarily in research on "affective computing", a field of which many are highly critical.[9] The second tradition, linking Spinoza, Bergson, and Deleuze, has formed an alliance with neuroscience. Antonio Damasio, Brian Massumi, Mark B. Hansen, and Catherine Malabou can be cited here as examples of an intense if heterogeneous debate on the role of affect in dance and the media through to affective cognition.

These lines were already traced in the German edition of this book in 2007, showing how the two traditions intersect at the nexus of the "extinction of the sexual" that replaces the sexual with an "affective suture"—with extinction and suture understood both epistemologically and in terms of media technology.

Each chapter analyses the "*dispositif* of affect" from a different angle.

Chapter 1—"Affective Troubles in Media and Art"—examines the growing interest in affect in media and cultural theory, philosophy, and political science. Both film and art theory speak of a "somatic turn" that centres on and accords special importance to the affective body of the viewer. With Deleuze's two books on cinema, *The Movement-Image* and *The Time-Image*, and Haraway's *Cyborg Manifesto*, the concept of the subject defined in terms of signs and language, and thus the line between such a subject and animals/ machines, begins to break down. Instead of addressing the subject in semantic terms, the emphasis shifts to sensory experience; at long last, art is allowed (and expected) to produce emotions again in order to overwhelm its audience.[10]

Chapter 2—"Human | Posthuman | Transhuman"—analyses this breaking down of the symbolic dimension under the influence of life philosophy, cybernetics, neurobiology, and theories of digital media. For a long time, the human was defined in terms of a key difference based on language and the unconscious. Neither machines nor animals were supposed to think, to speak, or to feel. Today, we can observe an implosion of this difference, potentially causing the human subject (who opened up this difference through language) to disappear, leading at the same time to such questions as "Do machines think?" "Do animals feel and empathize?" "Do machines forget?" And if they do, what does this actually tell us about the difference of the human? A prominent role in this development was played by the Macy Conference, whose members did not agree on the question of subjectivity nor on whether it was linked to something like an unconscious. The chapter summarizes these steps from a human being barred by the signifier (Lacan) to a cyborgian agency driven by its affective suture.

Chapter 3—"Affect Versus Drive, or the Battle over Representation"—presents various theoretical approaches to affect, from Sigmund Freud to Silvan Tomkins, from Baruch Spinoza to Antonio Damasio, from Henri Bergson via Gilles Deleuze and Brian Massumi to Mark B. Hansen. Current reception of these writers in art theory and cultural/media studies, and the discovery of Spinoza by neurobiology, are not so much signals of a new rapprochement between the humanities and natural sciences as a general reorientation of the way the human being is conceived of. Over a century after Darwin, the human being is not only being put on a level with its animal neighbours but also compared with intelligent machines. In these processes, language and consciousness become negligible factors as the affective body takes on the function of providing orientation and perception of the environment. The role played by psychoanalysis here is ambivalent: While seeing its own strength in the fact that Freud himself wished for a biological underpinning of his theory of the psychical apparatus, it responds cautiously when its basic tenets (such as the mechanism of repression or the Oedipus complex) are translated by brain research into bold and simple neurological terms accompanied by joyful cries of "Freud was right!" In chapters 5 and 6, however, I show how this critical position within psychoanalysis is giving way to attempts to call the premises of psychoanalysis into question in the face of neuroscience's alliance with digital technology, which seeks out equivalents for psychical phenomena in neural processes.

Chapter 4—"Virtual Sex and Other Metamorphoses"—examines the "sexual charging" of the digital world with examples from films and net art. Films, such as David Cronenberg's *Videodrome* and *eXistence* or Kathryn Bigelow's *Strange Days,* and the online work *carrier* by Australian artist Melinda Rackham can be cited as reflections on a growing cybersexual narcissism. Like any new medium, the digital space, too, played on its sexual aspect from the outset, prefiguring today's situation where online pornography has reached far greater proportions than the heavily regulated consumption of porn via predigital mass media. A different narcissistic scenario is presented in *Strange Days,* where technical devices (the "squid" that sits on the user's head recording his/her "visual emotions") are used to save memory images as affects (which are, it should be stressed, always in motion) that are then sold to digital junkies as the latest hype. In the face of the totally uncontrollable range of sex-related content and services on the Internet today, as well as the brazen trade in (child) pornography, such early forms of cybersexual networking appear prophetic.[11] Rather than spectacular cyber-projects, however, I am interested above all in how their interpretation has reinforced a way of thinking in which similar shifts have begun to take place. The space of the net is described not only as a parallel reality in the sense of an additional space of agency but also as a space where the ideas developed by Gilles Deleuze and Félix Guattari in their "nomadology" have been realized. Their central concept—becoming (*devenir-femme, enfant, molécule, intense, animal, imperceptible*)—is painted as the basic ontological motivation for denizens of the Internet. Today, in addition to cyborgs, digital spaces have long since been conquered by multishaped agents and viruses who play out their loving relationships as mutually affecting movements, prompting discussions of sexuality as affection; as contagion; as biodigital cell division; as a prehuman, briefly human and now posthuman dimension. Rosi Braidotti, Teresa Brennan, Elizabeth Grosz, Eve Kosofsky Sedgwick, and Luciana Parisi (to name some prominent figures) have worked hard to install affect as the basis for a biopolitical desire. Brennan defines *affect* as the other of language that must be brought back into communication; Braidotti calls for a uniting of *bios* and *zoe*; and in Darwin, Grosz discovers first traces of the kind of fluid conception of female sexuality later developed in Deleuzian feminist approaches.

Chapter 5—"Sexualizing Affect"—gives a brief history of the concept of the unconscious, making clear that Freudian psychoanalysis had a very specific understanding implying neither a space nor a substance but quite simply a "different scene". This scene is the stage of the subject, where the id acts, "showing" itself in dreams and everyday language. In this chapter, I contrast this sexually connoted concept of the unconscious with two new models: first, the speculative vision of a nonhuman sexuality that has not only left behind its prehistory of sexual reproduction but that has also detached itself from human protagonists. While the glowing viruses circulate in Melinda Rackham's cyberlove stories, Parisi translates this image of amorphous biodigital sexuality into a cultural-evolutionary model of "abstract sex". In this model, unconscious desire is replaced by a "nanodesire" articulated as pure energy. Whereas Parisi's thinking centers on the digital development, Braidotti focuses on life, defining *desire* as *potentia,* as a positive power (or *conatus,* as Spinoza calls it) that drives bodies to become multiple. What Derrida refers to as "original deferral", introducing sexual difference as originally deferred difference, is replaced in Braidotti's model by qualitative shifts of subjectivity. At the end of the chapter, the interpretative struggle between desire defined in terms of lack (as found in psychoanalysis) and desire defined in terms of a superabundance of Being (as advocated by Deleuze and others) escalates into the race between the hare and the hedgehog. For according to Joan Copjec, Deleuze was once very close to the psychoanalytical viewpoint before distancing himself from it increasingly with his critique of its founding principles. In Copjec's comparative analysis of affect in Deleuze and in psychoanalysis, affect becomes a phase of movement in which a slippage occurs between representation and affect. In this model, affect is understood as the "out-of-phaseness" inherent in representation.

Chapter 6—"Postscript: A New Affective Organization"—is a new section written for this English edition in which I discuss the implementation of affect as a comprehensive reorganization of what *desire after affect* means under the conditions of today's media technology. Two approaches in particular are relevant here: one from media ecology that culminates in the definition of *affect* as a ubiquitous technology detached from the body as "radical relationality"; and one from brain research, with its talk of neuroplasticity, as discussed by Malabou, that not only undertakes a reformulation of the unconscious but also declares the replacement of the *dispositif* of sex by that of affect as a fait accompli. In this way, however, affect becomes a "relational organizing power" that controls both the auto-affective movement of the brain and the politico-economic organization of the emerging biomediated bodies. From here, the next logical step is to locate affect as the centre of a new libidinal economy that brings forth or makes necessary an "emotional self" (Malabou). Whether such a self is granted any scope for autonomous movements remains to be seen.

My interest in affect and in the question of what makes it so desirable goes back many years. In *Body Options*[12] I linked affect with my concept of an "empty body image", suggesting that media theory might approach the modalities of media and body images more productively using the instrument of affect—as "in-between time after before but before after"[13] —than via processes of psychological identification.[14] The current debates on affect, emotion, and feeling take a different direction, however, with *affect* often treated as a biological variable, *feelings* delegated to psychology, and *emotions* attributed to biographical data. The three terms are often used as synonyms with no regard for their respective historical and semantic connotations. As well as generating a vague "feeling for affect", this enables every issue to be linked with affect. In sometimes very obvious ways, *affect* is brought into play as an umbrella term for all that was formerly referred to as unconscious, metaphorical, or psychological. But my critique is aimed not only at this excessive use of the term itself but above all at the tacit agreement that it offers an adequate answer, that it might constitute a response to all open questions concerning the social, the political, and the psychological. That is what I mean when I say that the *dispositif* of sex has shifted and been replaced by one of affect, that a truth of the subject constituted via sexuality has become an "affective mood". Although I subscribe to the definitions of affect from Spinoza to Deleuze, they cannot become a homogenized catchall for all that can be neither said nor seen—hence my wish to examine those forces that express an interest in this affective *dispositif* and to inquire into why this model has become so attractive today and to what ends.

NOTES

1. See Marie-Luise Angerer, Bernd Bösel, and Michaela Ott (eds.), *Timing of Affect: Epistemologies, Politics, Aesthetics* (Zurich, Switzerland: diaphanes and University of Chicago Press, forthcoming); Michaela Ott, *Affizierung. Zu einer ästhetisch-epistemischen Figur* (Munich: edition text + kritik, 2010); and Melissa Gregg and Gregory J. Seigworth (eds.), *The Affect Theory Reader* (Durham, NC: Duke University Press, 2010).
2. See Bernard Stiegler, "Relational Ecology and the Digital *Pharmakon*", *Culture Machine*, 13 (2012), 1–19, http://www.culturemachine.net/index.php/cm/article/view/464/501 (retrieved 19 June 2014); and Jonathan Crary, *24/7: Late Capitalism and the End of Sleep* (London: Verso, 2014).
3. Gadgets for monitoring and control on and in the body, surveillance of private and public space, etc.
4. Angerer, Bösel, and Ott, *Timing of Affect*.
5. See chapter 2.
6. Marey dreamed of a "wordless science", one that "spoke instead in high-speed photographs and mechanically generated curves", images as the "language of the phenomena themselves" [quoted from Lorraine Daston and Peter Galison, "The Image of Objectivity", in *Representations* 40 (1992), 81–128].
7. Marshall McLuhan, *Understanding Media: The Extensions of Man* (New York: McGraw Hill, 1964).
8. Gregg and Seigworth proposed this reading of the affective turn in their *Affect Theory Reader*, shaping subsequent debate in the Anglo-American world.
9. Ruth Leys, *From Guilt to Shame: Auschwitz and After* (Princeton, NJ: Princeton University Press, 2007); and Anna Tuschling, "The Age of Affective Computing", in Marie-Luise Angerer, Bernd Bösel, and Michaela Ott (eds.), *Timing of Affect: Epistemologies, Politics, Aesthetics* (Zurich, Switzerland: diaphanes and University of Chicago Press, forthcoming).
10. From Documenta in 2007 to the Cannes Film Festival in 2014, the affective, emotional power of art has once more been celebrated. Roger M. Buergel, artistic director of Documenta XII, attributed this development in art to the theory-aversion now faced by artists. In the name of sensuality and beauty, he claimed, art that deals with complex themes is rejected as being overly theoretical. And in 2014, under the headline "The Now in Pure Intensity", Frédéric Jaeger reviewed Xavier Dolan's film *Mommy*: "I was in tears. The screen had a radiance all of its own. I loved what I had learned to hate. I was seduced and captivated and I didn't want it any other way. If I could explain it, if I could understand cinema and reveal its secrets, then I would probably no longer be a critic" (www.critic.de/film/mommy-6705, retrieved 23 May 2014).
11. One need only recall Stahl Stenslie's *CyberSM* project (1993–1994), http://www.stenslie.net/stahl/projects/cybersm/index.html (retrieved 19 June 2014).

12. Marie-Luise Angerer, *Body Options: Körper.Spuren.Medien.Bilder* (Vienna: Turia & Kant, 1999).

13. Brian Massumi, "The Bleed: Where the Body Meets Image", in John C. Welchman (ed.), *Rethinking Borders* (Minneapolis: Macmillan, 1996), 18–40, here 29.

14. This was/is important in the light of remarks concerning the dangers of identification and imitation in the context of computer games and the frequent blaming of shooting sprees (among other things) on the related inability to distinguish clearly between fiction and reality.

ONE

Affective Troubles in Media and Art

Media Emotions,[1] *Cinema Feelings,*[2] *The Cultural Politics of Emotions,*[3] *The Power of Feelings,*[4] *The Inner Touch,*[5] *Affect and Emotion,*[6] *The Affect Theory Reader*[7] —The picture painted by these book titles was matched over the same period in the field of exhibitions: In 2004, the Art Center in Hasselt, Belgium, presented *Feel: Tactile Media Art*; in April 2005, Antwerp's Museum of Modern Art (MuHKA) staged *Emotion Pictures*; and over the last decade, one show after another—to name just two of the most recent, *Real Emotions* at Berlin's Kunstwerke in spring 2014 and *Affekte*[8] in Erlangen, Belgium, and Holland. The academic community also got involved, organizing symposia and conferences on the emotional and affective turn in media, art, and the humanities, from *Thinking through Affect*[9] to *Timing of Affect.*[10]

In their foreword to *Kinogefühle*, the editors write, "It is striking that the turn towards the emotions is being accompanied by a crisis regarding models in social and communications theory that are based primarily on the potential of rational discourse."[11] Whereas Jonathan Crary, in his book *Techniques of the Observer,*[12] identifies a turn at the beginning of the nineteenth century that focused attention on the body as crucial to the functions of perception, one could adapt this for today by saying that emotion and affect are now viewed as crucial to cognition and communication.

With this focus on affect, the long history of classical western dichotomies, especially that between mind and body, seems to have become surmountable. Affect theory brings a new picture of consciousness, of thought, of mind and of language that no longer accepts division, placing the emphasis instead on the fluid intermingling of matter and nonmatter. Since Descartes formulated his famous "I think therefore I am", there has been an ongoing debate on body and mind, soul and matter, reason and emotion, which has also shaped (and continues to shape) the categories of masculine and feminine, public and private. This debate had its high points and latent periods. One such high point was the twentieth century, when language, the power of the word, the chain of signifiers and the symbolic order were enthroned in order to enclose the unutterable and nondiscursive in this language—as its "obscene underside" (Slavoj Žižek) and as the "real" defined by Jacques Lacan as constitutive of the symbolic order. At the same time, however, there were always attempts to claim a balance, a mutual support of language and matter, or to couch this balance in theoretical and conceptual terms, in particular in the philosophy of Gilles Deleuze.

Likewise, a look at the art of the second half of the twentieth century shows the extent to which language as a system of representation took centre stage, providing subject matter for conceptual art and groups like Art and Language. Language became a powerful structure that not only conveyed reality but actually generated it. Long before the affect-laden attack on the system of representation, however, philosophical positions like that of Deleuze were already criticizing this primacy of language. In his book on Foucault, published twenty years after *The Order of Things* in 1986, Deleuze drew attention to a possible error on the part of Foucault, who had linked the disappearance of (modern) man, his reformation, and the emergence of new power relations to language, writing that the "dispersion of language" could be reversed, that "to discover the vast play of language contained once more within a single space might be [a] decisive [. . .] leap towards a wholly new form of thought."[13] Deleuze underlines the fact that Foucault assigns this power to neither life nor labour—the other two terms in the Foucauldian triad besides *language*—attributing it exclusively to language and above all to literature (disconnected from linguistics). As Foucault wrote, language responded to its "demotion" as an object of academic study in nineteenth-century linguistics by generating a countertendency, regrouping to "emphasize a 'being of language' beyond whatever it designates and signifies, beyond even the sounds."[14] But what Foucault did not see, Deleuze continues, is that biology and work also had to regroup in order to be accorded a new existence in the "genetic code" (of molecular biology) and in "cybernetics and information technology" (third-generation machines).[15]

Although he noted the signs of the times (rise of biology and molecular biology, dawn of the cyber age), it is uncertain, as Paul Rabinow writes in his *Essays on the Anthropology of Reason,*[16] whether Deleuze was able to properly gauge the importance of these new practices. For today, as Rabinow stresses, one's assumptions must be based on a fragmenting of language, life and labour, calling for an engagement with the question of *anthropos*. And whatever one's position on this question, any project seeking to grasp these developments can be described as follows: "What if we took up recent changes in the logoi of life, labor, and language not as indicating an epochal shift with a totalizing coherence but rather as fragmented and sectorial changes?" Changes that are currently seeking their form—thus necessarily taking the figure of the *anthropos* with them. Today, "anthropos is that being who suffers from too many logoi."[17] We, then, are witnesses to a reformulation of *anthropos*.

In his account of the twentieth century,[18] Alain Badiou has identified its second half—the golden age of (post-) structuralist theory—as a moment marked by a conflict between "life" and "concept", a conflict in which two philosophical currents that had crossed paths again and again, always trying to throw the other off balance, joined forces for one instant in history. Badiou calls them "philosophy of concept" and "philosophy of life". The latter runs from Henri Bergson to Gilles Deleuze, the former from mathematical formalism (as elaborated by Léon Brunschvicg) to Louis Althusser and Jacques Lacan. For the brief moment when they meet and intertwine, these two movements outline a dispute over the concept of the subject. From this moment in the late 1960s, Badiou claims, the subject can no longer be based on Cartesian rationality nor on self-reflexivity. Instead, it must be something experienced more in terms of life and the body, something more comprehensive than the conscious subject, something that is more comparable with a production or creation and that unites more far-reaching forces within itself.

Psychoanalysis plays an ambivalent role here. On the one hand, during this period it became *the* institution in which the theory of the subject took on a radical form. On the other, as Foucault and Deleuze/Guattari never tired or repeating, it trusted too little in its own radicality. These thinkers, as Badiou explains, thus developed a concept of the subject along psychoanalytical lines with a different understanding of the unconscious and its explosive power within society, a concept first presented by Deleuze and Guattari in their "schizoanalysis" in *Anti-Oedipus*. As these exciting years slowly neared their end (the era of adventure, in Badiou's account, being followed by a period of re-ordering), the French voices were joined by others, who mounted attacks on the philosophy of concept and who pushed that of life in a direction that no longer pursued the philosophy of Deleuze and Guattari.

Analytic philosophers of language like John Searle were also actively involved in the debate against the dominance of language. Searle, who with John L. Austin cofounded speech act theory (which has made a comeback within discussions of performance), had declared years previously that the twentieth century was the century of the unconscious and thus the century of psychoanalysis; now, he argued, the time of consciousness has come and hence the time of neurology, biology and the digital regulation of networks and feedback. Today, this appears increasingly prescient: The brain as the seat of consciousness is now being analysed using methods of cognitive psychology and neurophysiology, as well as new recording and visualization technologies, to find out how and where human feelings and affects originate and take effect. Cognition is now portrayed only in connection with emotion and affect, and there is a consensus, following the American neurologist Antonio Damasio, that feeling is the basis of our being: "I feel therefore I am".[19]

In 2004, Hans Ulrich Gumbrecht published *Production of Presence: What Meaning Cannot Convey*, in which he sets himself vehemently apart from the recent trend toward proclamations of a "beyond", "after" or "post". With this gesture, he draws attention to a materiality, a physicality and a sensuality that have been radically lost, to the point where we no longer know we ever had them:

> But would we also have to say—to admit?—that today we are experiencing a stage beyond that point of—seemingly—absolute loss, a stage where, paradoxically, the desire for what we had absolutely lost is coming back? A stage where, strangely enough, this lost desire is even being imposed 'back' upon us? For contemporary communication technologies have doubtlessly come close to fulfilling the dream of omnipresence, which is the dream of making lived experience independent of the locations that our bodies occupy in space (and in this sense, it is a 'Cartesian' dream).[20]

Gumbrecht states clearly why we are now being reminded of this original loss: With their promise of immediacy and ubiquity, he says, digital media give us something like a premonition that there could be something else, something more.

And indeed, the first cyber wave did cause quite a stir. With its promise of tactility, immediacy, and the dissolution of time and space, there seemed to be a new paradise in the making, a paradise where language—as the founding, existential category of the human—would be dislodged from its dominant position.

Derrick de Kerckhove, who worked with Marshall McLuhan and directed the Program in Culture and Technology at Toronto University until 2008, went so far as to confer on new media the task of compensating for the collateral damage caused by the alphabet. Today, he argues, the computer and the brain are defined as parallel facilities that have entered into a now inescapable synthesis with far-reaching consequences, as the human body with all its senses becomes integrated into the new devices. Its sensory and preconscious reactions in particular play an increasingly important role here since the forms of communication in digital media simply omit the stage of articulation in words, entering into a gradual symbiosis with the physical body. The extent to which new media machines have already conquered the body can be seen in the computer games boom. In Kerckhove's view, immersing oneself and being drawn in like this is a fascinating new phenomena, heralding an "end of theory" (and of the associated distance) as well as an "end to the dominance of the visual". In their place, the senses of smell, touch and hearing are being "cyberculturally" adapted.[21]

In the next section, we see how strongly such comments are driving talk of new turns ("somatic turn", "emotional turn") in film and art theory.

FROM VIEWING PLEASURE TO EMOTION MACHINE[22]

From 1970 until the mid-1980s, film theory was dominated by apparatus theory with its founding in post-Marxist ideology and psychoanalysis. According to Jean-Louis Baudry, one of its main proponents, cinema is an ideological state apparatus (in the sense of Louis Althusser[23]) that constitutes visitors in a specific way as viewers, comparable to the way the church treats believers, schools treat pupils, families treat their members, and armed forces treat soldiers. The specific quality of cinema is that it possesses a setting that couches the viewers—like small children—in the mirror stage of screen, camera and gaze (the model of the mirror stage was developed by Jacques Lacan to define the psychosexual development of the child as a visual idealization of its self). During this period, the cinema appeared as *the* place to illustrate the ideological construction of the subject. Everything that takes place between viewer and screen is analysed (from the viewpoint of the Other) as an imaginary production between mother-child-mirror or screen-camera-gaze.[24] Rather than inquiring into the impact of cinema, apparatus theory asks why films are able to exert such a powerful libidinous attraction. The answer it gives is that sexuality and desire, as the driving forces of the subject, are always already inscribed in the field of the visible (visual), as well as forming the basis for a dynamic that extends beyond the visible.

In the meantime, however, apparatus theory has been displaced by cognitive film theory, which now largely shapes the discussion on emotion and affect in the cinema, drawing on psychology and its repertoire of empirical theories of emotion. The techniques of film are discussed in relation to the cognitive makeup of the viewer in order to explain why cinema can make an emotional impact. The question posed by the two main proponents of cognitive film psychology, David Bordwell and Kristin Thompson,[25] can be summed up as follows: How do depicted, staged emotions produce the emotions felt by the viewers? One reason for the rise of cognitive film theory is certainly the recent tendency within neuroscience to try to grasp feelings and affects via digital computing and recording techniques. In her contribution to the *Mediale Emotionen* anthology, Sigrid Weigel offers a good analysis of this notion of feeling, which is not strictly speaking emotion, but brain activity that has been localized and recorded, and then interpreted as emotion: "The current concept of feelings (emotions) represents [. . .] the return of a pathos formula from the age of sensibility".[26] As early as the eighteenth century, she explains, emotion was conceived of as a medium between a *sensibilité morale* and a *sensibilité physique*, bridging the gap between mind and body. In the same anthology, Andreas Keil and Jens Eder summarize the relationship between audiovisual media and emotional networks today, showing the wide range of phenomena now understood to be "affective": brief, intense emotions on a romantic happy end; diffuse, subliminal moods at the opening of a horror film; and reflex-like reactions to explosions in a spectacular action scene; but also empathy, sympathy and desire, as well as aesthetic enjoyment and political or ideological concern.[27] At the beginning of their essay, the authors stress that a shift in film theory can be observed in the early 1990s, pushing out "psychoanalytical affect theories" like those of Laura Mulvey and Louis Baudry because they were viewed as undifferentiated and unempirical.[28] It must be stressed, however, that affect was not an explicit theme in the structural film theory of the 1970s and 1980s nor in apparatus theory, with the focus instead on unconscious identification and the ideological production of the subject.

In the course of an unmistakable focusing on affect in media and cultural theories, psychoanalysis (and the film theory long based on it) was now accused of having criminally neglected the emotions. In *Moral Spectatorship,*[29] Lisa Cartwright summarizes the dispute over representation versus affect that shaped debate in the 1970s, accusing psychoanalysis and especially the feminist film theory of this time of having ignored affect on political grounds. Not so much conviction as political considerations, she argued, had motivated feminist scholars to support Lacanian psychoanalysis. But now, she claimed, an affective turn was necessary, calling for a new orientation toward such models as the object relations theory of Donald Winnicott and Melanie Klein and the affect theory of Silvan Tomkins.

ON THE RETURN OF THE CINEMATOGRAPHICALLY REPRESSED

Shifts in the premises of film theory began much earlier, however. With Deleuze's *L'Image-mouvement* and *L'Image-temps*,[30] if not before, a new way of talking about the cinema was introduced and with it a new theoretical angle. The focus was on cinema, the body and the brain, the cinematographic creation of the body, and brain research, which, according to Deleuze, not only created a break but actually enforced "new orientations" with regard to the classical image.[31] In the wake of these books, numerous other essays and books expressed a more or less explicit opposition to psychoanalytical film theory, criticizing it as too rigid and not suited to the moving image.[32]

In the 1990s, film and media theory began to address the bodies of film viewers in terms of motion. Of course, this was due not only to theoretical shifts but also to the development of specific media conditions and environments, such as computer games and their deployment of the body.[33] This appearance of the body within the media setting was briefly accompanied by a return of older positions in film theory, including Vivian Sobchak's phenomenological film analysis that had heroically defended cinema against the new digital images in the 1980s. According to Sobchak, the experiencing body of the viewer is awakened to life by the cinema screen, because the film is experienced not as a thing but as a representation portraying an objective world, the viewer is able to partake of this embodied experience. While film gives access to experience, then, photography mummifies and electronic media establishes a meta-world where everything is about "representation per se". Digital media, she argues, produce a system of nonreferential simulation, referentiality having become intertextuality, so that representations refer only to each other, forfeiting any link to the real outside world. Sobchak relates this to a process of disembodiment, as the space of experience offered by film had, in her view, been completely lost.[34] Unlike today's talk of the affective pull of film images, this involvement of the body in film is not direct, still being seen in a symbolic and phantasmal dimension.

In this context, one can also mention two movements within cinema itself that focused on the material language of film: the "Cinema of the Body", founded by Maria Klonaris and Katharina Thomadaki, and the "Expanded Cinema" of the 1960s and '70s, with Gene Youngblood, VALIE EXPORT, Peter Weibel and Birgit and Wilhelm Hein. Both positions illustrate the struggle for a subject between life and concept described by Badiou, between the material and the symbolic—between the materiality of the cinematic apparatus and the language of the cinematographic.[35]

However, these parallel developments and countermovements also clearly reflect the extent to which the philosophies of "concept" and "life" are interwoven in the media sphere. Today, the tendency toward letting the material speak for itself has become more important, corresponding on the side of the viewer with the right to be drawn in by the film or media artwork, to be touched and overwhelmed. But for a brief moment—roughly from the mid-1980s to the mid-1990s—when cyber theory unfurled its first banners and science fiction produced a succession of beings that lost their bodies or experienced them as nothing more than a meaningless fleshy burden, the philosophy of life collapsed. The jubilant embrace of the new digital potential was repeatedly interrupted by an abrupt sense of uncertainty over whether the bodiless state toward which everything seemed to be striving would actually be so desirable, and above all, would it be livable? *Neuromancer* philosophy.[36]

Today, this ambivalence has been swept aside by an emphatic focus on the body. The complaints about the "obsolete body" have long since fallen silently away, and the body has been reinstalled with unflagging passion at the centre of (new) media, film and art theory and the corresponding practices.

In *The Skin of the Film,* Laura Marks speaks about a "haptic visuality" that allows the film to be seen through the skin as a multisensory experience.[37] In her next book, video, multimedia, and even television are praised for giving an experience of haptic realities. Among other things, she describes the tendency toward "analogue nostalgia" that makes the immaculate digital image appear dirty again:

> Paradoxically, the age of so-called virtual media has hastened the desire for indexicality. In popular culture, now that so many spectacular images are known to be computer simulations, television viewers are tuning in to 'reality' programming, and Internet surfers are fixing on live webcam transmissions in a hunt for unmediated reality. Among digital videomakers, one of the manifestations of the desire for indexicality is what I call analogue nostalgia, a retrospective fondness for the 'problems' of decay and generational loss that analogue video posed.[38]

In *Performing Live,*[39] Richard Shusterman argues similarly when he stresses—in an allusion to Judith Butler's *Bodies That Matter*[40] — that, today, bodies (as material and indexical traces) matter even more. In his view, the media society with its simulacra, virtual worlds and second realities support this concentration on the body, which has become the sole guarantor of identity (however *identity* is defined). The more one becomes lost in these images, the more important the body becomes as a sensitive, intuitive medium of differentiation that fixes the place and time of the individual. This concern with the body is not as new as is sometimes claimed, but its current intensity completely upends Butler's theory of matter as necessarily signified. In response to criticism of her theory of "doing gender",[41] Butler tried to make it clear that matter (i.e., the body) does not appear or act as a body per se but that it has to enter the chain of signifiers in order to be readable, to be perceivable as a female or male body. In view of today's talk of a body that feels, acts, and intuitively knows, however, Butler's "doing" seems to have been superseded. Instead, great emphasis is placed on the body moving itself, a body that feels above all, that is affected by other bodies, and that anchors and guides the individual in the world.

The descriptions by Marks and Shusterman outlined here can be seen as components in a development that is increasingly concentrating on the body. What Marks describes for the "dirtied" digital image and Shusterman for the body in a media society also applies to the body of the visitor (to museums, galleries, video installations). For although visitors do still find themselves in front of pictures, increasingly they are also "in the picture", and, echoing Shusterman's theory, it is claimed that these digital images and media installations demand the active involvement of the body in new ways. The more all-encompassing and total the audiovisual environment, the argument goes, the more urgently the body is called upon to reinstall the lost orientation by means of affective selection.

FRAMER FRAMED

When Trinh T. Minh-Ha published *Framer Framed*[42] in 1992, the book marked a high point in postcolonial criticism. The observer and colonialist, the white man whose gaze (with or without a camera) framed its object, was himself subjected to scrutiny. At the time, there was an interest in deconstructing the ways that film and video, as viewing and recording technologies, structure and frame their subject matter. In 2004, Mark Hansen published *New Philosophy for New Media,* naming one of his chapters after Trinh's book.[43] The focus here was on digital images, their production, their framing and their impact on the viewer, making Hansen another prominent voice arguing that the specific essense of the digital image necessitates a new philosophy of the image and a new ontology of perception. Like so many others, Hansen's reading of Deleuze led him to Henri Bergson's philosophy of perception. He uses Bergson's concepts of the affective body and the world as image to analyse various examples of net and video art, showing that the framelessness of the digital image calls for a framer, bringing into play the affective body that not only perceives and feels but also selects the visual universe of the viewer in the world. Later, we will return in more detail to Bergson's theory of perception with its emphasis on the affective body. But first we must proceed step by step to understand the central position now occupied by the body in the universe of digital imagery.

In an interview with the *Journal of Visual Culture*, Hal Foster explains that the earliest signs of a trend in contemporary art that he describes ironically as the "trouble of walking into art" can be traced back to minimalism.[44] In minimalist art, the body and space emerged as significant vectors. In the meantime, Foster continues, more and more artists have begun making site-specific work, preferring the synchronous over the diachronic. Today, these developments converge strikingly in the work of the Danish artist Olafur Eliasson. In 2003, he realized his installation *The Weather Project* at Tate Modern, designing a sun that lit the whole of the Turbine Hall, turning it into a sacred place where visitors lay on the floor to soak up the atmosphere. Although at first Foster makes fun of the sun-worshipping visitors, at the end of the interview he highlights a positive aspect of the project: It shows the immersive vortex created by the artist to play with the visitor's desire to be overwhelmed. The work, he claims, can be seen as prototypical for the artist's aim to involve all of the visitor's senses and to bypass thought: "Lie down and be quiet!"[45]

As well as representing a new kind of immersive art, however, Eliasson's "sun" has also been compared with Turner's sunset paintings, thus positioning it within a history of perception and its techniques. Jonathan Crary, whose *Techniques of the Observer* discusses the discovery of the body as the subjective basis for human perception, explicitly relates his analysis to Eliasson's projects. But unlike the visual experiments of the nineteenth century, Crary writes, Eliasson destabilizes basic parameters and repeatedly uses technical means to call into question the distinction between object and viewing subject.[46] In the catalogue for *The Weather Project*, Bruno Latour, too, speaks of Eliasson's transgression of traditional dichotomies: "What Sloterdijk does in philosophy, Olafur Eliasson does in art." Both, he argues, have thrown overboard the tired old dichotomies of wild versus domesticated, private versus public, and, ultimately, science versus general knowledge. The artist becomes a member of a laboratory researching the conditions of our life—"simply to explore the nature of the atmospheres in which we are all collectively attempting to survive".[47]

For Foster, space and time became progressively differentiated in Minimalist art at the same time as helping to produce the first signs of what he calls a "faux-phenomenological art". This "false" art, he writes, articulates itself in the focus on a media space—a space that uses technical equipment to overwhelm the viewer rather than fostering a contemplative attitude by means of "natural" conditions. Such an art space overpowers the viewer's body and creates a kind of "techno-sublime":

> Today this seems to be the desired effect of much art—digital pictorial photography, say, as well as projected image installations—so much so that this secondary line of art after Minimalism now appears to be the dominant one. And people love it, of course, in large part because it aestheticizes, or rather artifies, an 'experience' already familiar to them, the intensities produced by media culture at large. For the most part, such art is happily involved with an image space that goes beyond the distractive to the immersive.[48]

Much as I share Foster's assessment of the overall tendency within society and of this specific artistic trend, his critique of immersive art purely in terms of technical equipment is hard to accept. It reflects a view of art that still (or once more) distinguishes between technological/media art and art made by hand. In this view, media art (to use the term without further discussion) is an inferior art because it is executed by technology. Clearly, the old debate on the technical reproducibility of the artwork and the loss of aura (Walter Benjamin) is still running here.

After Eliasson's installation-based works, I want to take a brief look at Bill Viola's video works that not only mark the development of immersive art at an earlier point in time but that have also influenced the debate on the essence of the digital. Viola himself has often spoken about the specific dramaturgy of his digital image spaces, describing them as media art that envelops the viewer (thus prefiguring discussions on the affect image). Viola is interested in a linking of the senses, a relating of body and mind, that facilitates a holistic bodily experience with the help of new technologies. On the one hand, there is photography, the photographic moment that, for the first time in history, created an image without human intervention, an image created by the touch of light without artistic input. And on the other there is television, which introduced seeing at a distance, anywhere, at (almost) the same time, making it possible to literally extend what we understand by presence.[49] This aspect is something that reappears in discussions of the digital image.

When Viola speaks of the photographic moment in terms of touch, then this touching has a double connotation for us here: first, in the literal sense, pointing to the promise or alleged potential of digital images to enhance tactility, privileging the haptic over the visual; and second, this touching by light is also well established in the theory of photography and film as a metaphor for the affectedness of the subject. In *Camera Lucida,* Roland Barthes uses the term *punctum* to refer to a detail that speaks to the viewer, catching her somewhere in her unconscious memories.[50] And film theory has often used Lacan's "sardine example" to reassure itself that the gaze is the bright light in which the viewing subject is mirrored without being seen by the Other, instead being merely a spot in the tableau.[51] Although this aspect of being touched, of being drawn in by (digitally produced) immersive content, is often attributed to (media) art in general, the interesting point here is how this supposedly special link between digital images and affective response takes effect and how it is produced.

Many years ago, Lev Manovich was already trying to calm the euphoria surrounding digital images, pointing out that there have been no dramatic changes to the picture surface, even if the basis of its production has changed a great deal:

> Since its beginnings 50 years ago, computerization of photography (and cinematography) has by now completely changed the internal structure of a photographic image; yet its 'skin', i.e. the way the image looks, still largely remains the same. It is therefore possible that at some point in the future the 'skin' of an image would also become completely different, but this did not happen yet. So we can say at present our visual culture is characterized by a new computer 'base' and old photographic 'superstructure'. [. . .] What remains to be seen is how the 'superstructure' of a photographic image—what it represents and how—will change to accommodate this 'base'.[52]

Brian Massumi, too, considers the widespread talk of a digital age and the end of the analogue image as misleading.[53] But what, then, does digitization bring about? Why does it prompt such speculations about a new quality of the image? In her essay "Morphing: Profiles of the Digital", Ulrike Bergermann examines the inconsistencies in the "analogue versus digital" debate, defining their relationship as one that is not "productive",[54] as one that is only used to generate added value by means of difference. In her survey of the various approaches to the debate, she highlights the ever-decreasing difference (between analogue and digital), concluding with the following summary by Wolfgang Coy: "The difference between analogue and digital storage may be a large and infinitely scaleable leap in terms of quantity, but they are not wholly alien to each other in essence."[55] This argument is based on the modus operandi of structural linguistics, according to which every sign, in order to be a sign, must set itself apart from another sign. But if digital and analogue images are so closely related in essence, why all the excitement about these new images? Which takes us back to the fundamental issue of how language and image become entangled in one another, always already passing through the matrix of the code.

VIRTUALLY UNCONSCIOUS—UNCONSCIOUSLY VIRTUAL

From the outset, the computer as a universal machine was associated with the promise and expectation of being able to go beyond the human into a virtuality where the opposition of man and machine was miraculously transcended. For Friedrich Kittler, digital code achieves this by allowing computers to operate on a level not accessible to the sensomotorically embedded individual.[56] Consequently, Kittler continues, the question of the essence of the human fails to take current developments into account. New dimensions are now at stake, where the human brain merges with digital technology. Talk of "unconscious code" should thus come as no great surprise. Psychoanalytical vocabulary has long since become inscribed in media theory relating to computers, leading to many and varied translations and attributions: Slavoj Žižek compares the interface relationship with a regression to preoedipal times; Henning Schmidgen has explored the unconscious of machines in Lacan and Deleuze and Guattari; and Sherry Turkle sees the cyberworld as an implementation of poststructuralist theories of the subject.[57] Schmidgen analyses concepts of the machine and the sign in the philosophy of Deleuze and Guattari and in Lacanian psychoanalysis, scanning them for references to the mechanical quality of the mind and the psychological machinations of individual and society. Nevertheless, the many attempts to hypostatize Deleuze as a philosopher of the net, to equate his concept of the virtual with virtual reality, and to turn his nomadic subjects into cybernerds must be viewed as dead ends. A technically generated virtuality is virtual in neither a philosophical, psychoanalytical nor anthropological sense. As Stefan Rieger shows in his *Kybernetische Anthropologie*, the concept of the virtual brings together various definitions related by a common constitutive moment; virtual and digital cannot be equated—their genealogies are quite different.[58] Instead, it is important to highlight the difference between human virtuality, which has gone by different names in the history of western philosophy, and the virtuality of the digital: "Human" virtuality consists in the ability of human beings, unlike animals or machines, to transcend their own existence via language and symbols, enabling them to imagine a potentially different being. This brings us back to the difference between philosophy of concept and philosophy of life. Descartes, Kant, Heidegger and Lacan base their assumptions on this ability (or, one might say, inability), by which the subject is catapulted out of the immanence of existence. But it is also possible to situate this transcendental break and its imaginative potential in human "nature", and then it is the potential forces within this very nature that drive the human subject: According to the definitions of Spinoza,

Bergson and Deleuze, virtuality is something embedded in this material corporeality.

Cybernetic research focuses on still another kind of virtuality. Here, attempts are made to map the programme of the human brain onto the programme of intelligent machines. Each of these three virtualities has its own history, their definitions varying in important ways, sometimes to the point of being mutually exclusive. The capacity for transcendence, whether it is conceived of as an attribute of the mind or of the body, is interwoven in various ways with technical apparatuses (written media, visual media, digital media). "Seeing oneself seeing" and "making oneself seen", as Lacan describes the principle fault line running through the consciousness, point to the image as the fundamental basis of the subject. Not for nothing did film theory make sustained use of Lacan's mirror phase and his theory of the gaze to explain the transmission between viewer and screen.[59] But in the cinema, this making oneself seen is played out over a duration that is also significant for the mental function. Only in and through this duration does the mind come to itself—in the form of memory, as Deleuze has described: "According to Kant, time was the form in which the mind affected itself, just as space was the form in which the mind was affected by something else: Time was therefore 'auto-affection' and made up the essential structure of subjectivity. But time as subject, or rather subjectivization, is called memory."[60] Film is unparalleled in deploying and staging these two aspects of "seeing oneself seeing" and "being affected by time": even from very different theoretical viewpoints (Lacan and Deleuze), they define the very character of the medium. Perception of movement and perception in motion are what the cinematographic impulse hinges on—an impulse that not only links cinema to cybernetic research[61] but also on which both focus attention.

Digital spaces detach the "seeing oneself see" from the viewer's body differently again, stylizing the moving body into a centre of experience—or at least according to theorists of the digital image who claim that unlike the cinematic space, digital images set the viewers in motion so that they see themselves move, either matching or contrasting with their actual mobility.

As Stefan Rieger writes, seeing movement provides a prototype of "what escapes control [. . .] allowing it to become one of the showpieces of cybernetic theory in the broadest sense."[62] In other words, human perception can only be technically grasped and replicated to a certain degree, with part always remaining in the unconscious. Like neurobiology today, nineteenth-century physics credited this unconscious with the highest levels of efficiency. It was viewed as a capacity for transcendence, virtuality, and phantasm, which is particular to human perception and which can be neither measured nor grasped in any other way. It is this unconscious "auto-movement" of human existence, so to speak, that goes beyond the data of the body.

Whereas traditional cinema keeps viewers still and casts its spell by means of camera, editing, montage, and sound, digital data spaces (audiovisual installations and environments) force viewers to move. Physically enthralled, they risk losing control of their corporeality. The identification-based reception of traditional cinema is replaced by immersion that overrides self-control, addressing the affective body more than it does conscious perception.

UNFRAMED

> Digitization explodes the frame, extending the image without limit not only in every spatial dimension but into a time freed from its presentation as variant series of (virtual) images. In this sense, the digital image poses an aesthetic challenge to the cinema, one that calls for a new 'will to art' and one whose call is answered by the neo-Bergsonist embodied aesthetic of new media art.[63]

Before Mark Hansen, Lev Manovich in particular identified framing as one of the major changes in digital image production, but although the mode of production has completely changed, we still refer to what we see on the real-time screen as "images". What has changed, then, is the base of production, while the superstructure—the surface of the images that we see and read—remains intact. In his *New Philosophy*, Hansen refers extensively to Manovich's approach, which fails to meet his expectations. Manovich, Hansen argues, adopts a humanist position from which images are only ever relevant in relation to a viewer (consumer), added to which they are always perceived and interpreted as film images. Hansen insists that Manovich fails to get a theoretical grip on his promising distinction between new and old images, reducing the new to a mere amplification of the old.[64] As a result, he continues, Manovich completely fails to recognize the specific quality of digital images because he clings to the primacy of the cinematographic. But unlike conventional cinema, he writes, even before cinema there were already technical options combining perception and tactility: In the case of the stereoscope, the panorama, and the mutoscope, viewers had to use their hands, move around, or adopt a specific pose in order to see the images in question, making a physical effort to manoeuvre themselves into the required receptive position. This, Hansen claims, is comparable with today's virtual realities like computer games and simulated environments, calling for a new philosophy that connects the body with its senses as active agents. Hansen proposes the philosophy of Henri Bergson, who conceives of the various image registers always and exclusively in connection with the affective body.[65] In *New Philosophy*, as well as relating Bergson's theory of the affective body to digital media, Hansen also subjects Deleuze's cinema theory to a severe critique. Unlike Bergson, he argues, Deleuze detached affect from the body and entrusted it to the technical proceedings. In Hansen's view, Deleuze interpreted affect very differently from Bergson, conceiving of it as a mode of perception and not as an autonomous modality of the body. Deleuze, then, separates affect from the body and links it with the movement-image, thus situating it outside the subject, where it becomes a question of technology. Hansen counters this by citing new developments in neuroscience, suggesting—as Bergson already claimed—that the body frames information. According to Bergson, there is no perception without affect if one takes into account the

> fact that our body is not a mathematical point in space, that its virtual actions are complicated by and impregnated with real actions, or, in other words, that there is no perception without affection. Affection is, then, that part or aspect of the inside of our body which we mix with the image of external bodies; it is what we must first of all subtract from perception to get the image in its purity.[66]

For Hansen, then, the body of the viewer acquires a centrality regarding the reception of digital images that is not only new but also exclusive: "In a very material sense the body is the 'coprocessor' of digital information."[67]

In her analysis of video installations, Ursula Frohne, too, has identified the question of framing and reframing as significant for a new form of viewer behaviour.[68] The dissolution of the picture frame leads to the question of "framing the viewer" and to a description of a different, new way of looking or viewing. As she explains,

> The observer's position, which, to this point, had had a defined frame of reference in a museum, loses its certainty regarding the object of reception, because the observer's ability to synthesize information when viewing images is challenged by the time factor. This paradigmatic change is primarily characterized by the fundamental instability of the viewer—which is, by the way, increased by the freedom of the viewer to move around in front of and inside the video installation. In a museum setting, the concentration is upon the viewer's optical reception of the work. Under such changed circumstances as these, however, concentration is shifted with a focus upon the responsibility of the observer.[69]

But where Frohne speaks of a responsibility that is delegated to the viewer so that video works are not actually complete until they have been synthesized by their audience, Hansen has a succinct answer: The production of framing takes place "in and through our own bodies."[70]

For Hansen, the works of media artist Char Davies play a very special role. *Osmose*[71] and *Ephémère*[72] are typical examples of immersive art. The viewers are taken in, enveloped and presented with an overwhelming natural spectacle, during which their bodies are experienced as a transitional portal. Through these works, Hansen demonstrates how the structure of perception is tactile through and through. In his view, Davies's installations represent the radical shift from an initially misunderstood visually dominated interface to a "bodily or affective interface".[73]

He is not alone in this view. At the Ars Electronica Festival in 2005, Char Davies's work was celebrated as a manifestation of queer hybrids, not as an affective embodiment, but as a *reembodiment*: "In virtual space, it is irregular mirrorings, spiralings, floatings and the surprising cultural freedom of bodies set loose to breathe, drift, crawl, fly and freefall in elemental spaces".[74]

As the selection of exhibition titles at the beginning of this chapter makes clear, emotions and affects are not only being staged in virtual, electronic spaces, but there is also a wide range of approaches to affective, tactile media art. Examples include projects by the Fur collective (*PainStation* and *LegShocker*[75]), *The Emotion Vending Machine*[76] and *Emotion's Defibrillator*.[77] These are machines and programs that inflict pain when players make mistakes, calculate mechanisms and distributions of global emotions, or reduce the digital apparatus to its physiological basis in order to demonstrate its effectiveness even more starkly. It is striking, however, that the auditory dimension still receives too little attention, although it seems obvious that affect and hearing are profoundly connected.[78] One of the rare studies to focus on this aspect is *Digital Aesthetics*[79] by Sean Cubitt, who highlights the importance of sound technologies. For Cubitt, the acoustically monopolized space of contemporary cinema competes with the medium's two-sided claim to reality. As sound technologies are perfected and auditory data organized within the space, this new quality of sound emerges as a rival to the image. In his study, Cubitt accords digital sound technology the status of a spatial art that intervenes between the old alliance of the film apparatus and its production of reality. The watching and listening space of cinema forms an interface between the media virtuality of the action on screen and the reality of the viewer's body completely absorbed by what is happening on the soundtrack. What Cubitt describes here can be heard and experienced especially well in the works of Janet Cardiff and George Bures Miller. In *The Paradise Institute* (2001),[80] the *Berlin Files* (2003), and the audio and video walks (since 1991), image and soundtrack go separate ways, each producing its own rhythm. This leads to disorientation or to heightened perception of one's own physical position in the space, as Cardiff has often emphasized. According to Jörg Heiser, Cardiff and Miller "translate the classical philosophical and religious body-and-soul-dualism debate into a contemporary art chiasmus: [. . .] of physical presence and absence on the one hand and media-psychological making-present and making-distant on the other."[81] Rather than the mere simulations found in many media art projects, Heiser continues, the audience gains physical access to the original experience of cinema. Here we have yet another version of the kind of haptic cinema described by Laura Marks—"seeing the film through the skin"—in this case hearing through the skin or being touched by sound.

This brings us to the definition of *affect* as an intermediary zone, relay, or skin contact—a definition associated in particular with Deleuze's books on cinema in which he presents his adaptation of Bergson to the film medium. In Bergson's concept of the image, the auditory is not separated from the visual but included within it. Bergson understood the world as an image in which we—ourselves a special kind of image—move: "There is no perception which is not prolonged into movement."[82] But precisely this moment of not-yet movement—the interval placed by Bergson between one movement and the other—is described by Deleuze as the moment of affect, which points to a movement that is not yet action:

> Affection is what occupies the interval, what occupies it without filling it in or filling it up. It surges in the centre of indetermination, that is to say in the subject, between a perception which is troubling in certain respects and a hesitant action. It is a coincidence of subject and object, or the way in which the subject perceives itself, or rather experiences itself or feels itself 'from the inside'.[83]

But unlike Bergson, who sees every perception prolonged into movement, Deleuze stresses that in the moment of affection, movement "ceases to be that of translation in order to become movement of expression."[84]

We will encounter this definition again, though with important modifications, in Brian Massumi's cultural theory approach to affect as an asocial zone of time too full to be grasped. In Deleuze, affect is still firmly inscribed within the relationship between viewer and image; it is the bracket through which a space opens up, an emptied, separated space, neither geometrical nor geographical nor social in the strict sense. This "any-space-whatever"[85] is marked by optical or sound situations, referred to by Deleuze as "opsigns and sonsigns", which point to a "crisis of the action-image".[86] In chapter 3, we see how Mark Hansen chooses precisely this "any-space-whatever", locating it within digital art practices and linking it (now without any cinematographic framing) with autonomous affect. This brings an important difference into play, for the autonomy of affect in Deleuze is one that goes beyond the subject, to catch up with it again from outside. In Hansen's work, on the other hand, affect joins with a neurobiological view that not only reontologizes the body but also moves away more generally from the question of the subject and its language.

EMOTIONAL NAVAL GAZING

Rather than pointing to a general revival of sensual pleasures, the signs of a new focus on affect described here should be interpreted as a conquering of the affective body. This may sound banal, but in the general frenzy of emotion that also seems to have seized the theorists of affect, it should not be swept under the carpet. In his essay "Zu spät, zu früh?"[87] Thomas Elsaesser draws attention to this, speaking of the emotion of key players in the film theory business. He, too, sees cinema now being merely celebrated as event, while psychoanalysis, especially in its Lacanian form, has been radically abandoned. But in his view, this unease with theories of spectatorship is in itself an emotion that is shared by various factions, even if they use completely different terminologies. For him, the key concept in this discussion is that of "experience", which by definition cannot give access to immediacy and presence. But besides this focus on the temporality of experience, special emphasis has also been placed on the related issue of trauma.[88] Just as Walter Benjamin defined the *choc* with regard to the photographic instant as something that escapes consciousness but that nonetheless (or precisely for this reason) is inscribed on the body as a trace of memory, Elsaesser describes our current situation as an "experience without experience",[89] a mode of experience whose only remaining recourse is a bodily reaction (trauma) since conscious processing can no longer function due to the ceaseless flow of incoming impressions. By inundating us with images and sounds, he claims, the media are not innocent, producing a

> somatic context for perception that is so saturated with media experiences that its modes of reception, reaction and action would require various kinds of detachment and disconnection of the sensomotoric apparatus in order to function. 'Successful' immersion in this context would correlate to a 'traumatic' mode of viewership, by which I mean flexible attentiveness and selective

> affective blunting to absorb the periodic emotional intensity, the flatness of memory, the tedium of repetition, and the lack of physical traces of violence that accompany constant contact with the media world. Here, trauma would be the solution.[90]

Rather than a new intensive relationship between the viewer's body and the film screen, Elsaesser understands this somatic turn as a sign of an injury, as the expression of a *new malady of the soul*.[91]

Approaching from a slightly different angle but with a similarly critical voice, the American historian of science Ruth Leys has analysed the affective turn (in which trauma now occupies a prominent position), noting a significant shift from guilt to shame.[92] Chapter 3 deals in more detail with the renaissance of shame, as the affect theory of Silvan Tomkins in particular has triggered a veritable boom in shame-related work in cultural studies. At this point, I only want to note that Leys sees this turn toward affect (and the accompanying turn toward shame) as part of a general tendency to degrade cognition as a whole, a tendency she says began in the second half of the twentieth century. Since the mid-1990s, she argues, we have been faced with an overall reorientation that supports noncognitive models, focusing attention on affect, the body, and materiality. In her opinion, however, this shift is based on numerous misunderstandings (especially with regard to the Tomkins-Ekman paradigm[93]) that have been overlooked or ignored when paradigms from the natural sciences have been adopted by cultural studies.

In art and media theory in particular (but also in other disciplines), affect, emotion and feeling are now considered not only as categories to be taken seriously but also in many cases to be taken for granted. Instead of grasping the naturalization of affects as a new form of normativity, instead of understanding affects as "affective troubles" and dealing with them accordingly, they are very often used to close something off from intruders such as meaning and representation.

NOTES

1. Oliver Grau and Andreas Keil (eds.), *Mediale Emotionen. Zur Lenkung von Gefühlen durch Bild und Sound* (Frankfurt, Germany: Fischer, 2005).
2. Matthias Brütsch, Vinzenz Hediger, Ursula von Keitz, Alexandra Schneider, and Margrit Tröhler (eds.), *Kinogefühle. Emotionalität und Film* (Marburg, Germany: Schüren Verlag, 2005).
3. Sara Ahmed, *The Cultural Politics of Emotions* (Edinburgh, UK: Edinburgh University Press, 2004).
4. Nancy J. Chodorow, *The Power of Feelings* (New Haven, CT: Yale University Press , 1999).
5. Daniel Heller-Roazen, *The Inner Touch: Archaeology of a Sensation* (New York: Zone Books, 2009).

6. Margaret Wetherell, *Affect and Emotion: A New Social Science Understanding* (London: Sage, 2012).
7. Melissa Gregg and Gregory J. Seigworth (eds.), *The Affect Theory Reader* (Durham, NC: Duke University Press, 2010).
8. A joint exhibition by Geementemuseum Helmond (NL) and Cultuurcentrum Mechelen (BE).
9. Symposium at the Jan van Eyck Akademie, Maastricht, September 2006, organized by Ils Huygens.
10. *Timing of Affect*, international symposium, Academy of Media Arts Cologne, 31 May–1 June 2013.
11. Margit Tröhler and Vinzenz Hediger, "Ohne Gefühl ist das Auge der Vernunft blind," in Matthias Brütsch, Vinzenz Hediger, Ursula von Keitz, Alexandra Schneider, and Margrit Tröhler (eds.), *Kinogefühle. Emotionalität und Film* (Marburg, Germany: Schüren Verlag, 2005), 7–22, here 17.
12. Jonathan Crary, *Techniques of the Observer: On Vision and Modernity in the Nineteenth Century* (Cambridge, MA: MIT Press, 1992).
13. Michel Foucault, *The Order of Things: An Archaeology of the Human Sciences* (New York: Routledge, 2005), 334.
14. Gilles Deleuze, *Foucault* (London: Continuum, 1999), 108.
15. Ibid., 109.
16. Paul Rabinow, *Essays on the Anthropology of Reason* (Princeton, NJ: Princeton University Press, 1996), 92.
17. Paul Rabinow, *Anthropos Today: Reflections on Modern Equipment* (Princeton, NJ: Princeton University Press, 2003), 14, 6.
18. See Alain Badiou, *The Century* (New York: Polity, 2007); and Alain Badiou, *The Adventure of French Philosophy* (New York: Verso, 2012).
19. Antonio R. Damasio, *The Feeling of What Happens: Body and Emotion in the Making of Consciousness* (New York: Harcourt Brace, 1999).
20. Hans Ulrich Gumbrecht, *Production of Presence: What Meaning Cannot Convey* (Stanford, CA: Stanford University Press, 2004), 138f.
21. See Simone Mahrenholz, "Derrick de Kerckhove—Medien als Psychotechnologien," in Alice Lagaay and David Lauer (eds.), *Medien-Theorien. Eine philosophische Einführung* (Frankfurt, Germany: Campus, 2004), 69–95, here 86f.
22. Ed S. Tan, *Emotion and the Structure of Narrative Film: Film as an Emotion Machine* (Mahwah, NJ: Lawrence Erlbaum Associates, 1996).
23. Louis Althusser, "Ideology and Ideological State Apparatuses," in Louis Althusser, *On Ideology* (London: Verso, 2008).
24. The founding texts of apparatus theory are two pieces by Jean-Louis Baudry: "Ideological Effects of the Basic Cinematographic Apparatus," in *Film Quarterly*, 28.2 (1974), 39–47; and "The Apparatus: Metapsychological Approaches to the Impression of Reality in Cinema," in *Camera Obscura*, 1 (1976), 104–26. See also Christian Metz, "The Imaginary Signifier," in *Screen*, 16.2 (1975), 14–76; and Laura Mulvey, "Visual Pleasure and Narrative Cinema," in *Screen*, 16.3 (1975), 6–18 .
25. David Bordwell and Kristin Thompson, *Film History: An Introduction* (New York: Columbia University Press, 1994).
26. Sigrid Weigel, "Phantombilder," in Oliver Grau and Andreas Keil (eds.), *Mediale Emotionen. Zur Lenkung von Gefühlen durch Bild und Sound* (Frankfurt, Germany: Fischer, 2005), 242–76, here 244.
27. See Andreas Keil and Jens Eder, "Audiovisuelle Medien und neuronale Netzwerke," in Oliver Grau and Andreas Keil (eds.), *Mediale Emotionen. Zur Lenkung von Gefühlen durch Bild und Sound* (Frankfurt, Germany: Fischer, 2005), 224–41, here 224.
28. See ibid., 238.
29. Lisa Cartwright, *Moral Spectatorship: Technologies of Voice and Affect in Postwar Representations of the Child* (Durham, NC: Duke University Press, 2008).
30. Gilles Deleuze, *Cinema 1: The Movement-Image* (Minneapolis: University of Minnesota Press, 1986); and Gilles Deleuze, *Cinema 2: The Time-Image* (Minneapolis: University of Minnesota Press, 1989).
31. Deleuze, *Cinema 2*, 211.
32. See, among others, Steven Shaviro, *Cinematic Body* (Minneapolis: University of Minnesota Press, 1993); and Steven Shaviro, *Post-Cinematic Affect* (New Alresford, UK: John Hunt Publishing, 2010).

33. See Britta Neitzel, Matthias Bopp, and Rolf F. Nohr (eds.), *'See? I'm real . . .' Multidisziplinäre Zugänge zum Computerspiel am Beispiel von 'Silent Hill'* (Münster, Germany: LIT, 2005). From the outset, computer games focused on the involvement of the body. Today, there is more emphasis on creating affective bonds with the player, exemplifying a new synchronization of man and machine. See my comments on the new addictive computer design as analysed by Natasha D. Schüll in chapter 6.

34. See Vivian Sobchak, "The Scene of the Screen: Envisioning Cinematic and Electronic Presence," in Hans Ulrich Gumbrecht and K. Ludwig Pfeiffer (eds.), *Materialities of Communication* (Stanford, CA: Stanford University Press, 1994), 83–106.

35. Mathias Michalka (ed.), *X-SCREEN* (Vienna: Museum Moderner Kunst, 2004); on Maria Klonaris and Katharina Thomadaki, see http://www.klonaris-thomadaki.net/artsite.htm (retrieved 22 May 2014).

36. William Gibson, *Neuromancer* (New York: Ace, 1984).

37. "Haptic cinema appeals to a viewer who perceives with all the senses. It involves thinking with your skin, or giving as much significance to the physical presence of an other as to the mental operations of symbolization. This is not a call to wilful regression but to recognizing the intelligence of the perceiving body. Haptic cinema, by appearing to us as an object with which we interact rather than an illusion into which we enter, calls on this sort of embodied intelligence. In the dynamic movement between optical and haptic ways of seeing, it is possible to compare different ways of knowing and interacting with others." [Laura U. Marks, *The Skin of the Film: Intercultural Cinema, Embodiment, and the Senses* (Durham, NC: Duke University Press, 2000), 18].

38. Laura U. Marks, *Touch: Sensuous Theory and Multisensory Media* (Minneapolis: University of Minnesota Press, 2002), 152.

39. Richard Shusterman, *Performing Live: Aesthetic Alternatives for the Ends of Art* (Ithaca, NY: Cornell University Press, 2000), 137.

40. Judith Butler, *Bodies That Matter: On the Discursive Limits of "Sex"* (New York: Routledge, 1993).

41. Judith Butler, *Gender Trouble: Feminism and the Subversion of Identity* (New York: Routledge, 1999).

42. Trinh T. Minh-Ha, *Framer Framed: Film Scripts and Interviews* (New York: Routledge, 1992).

43. Mark B. N. Hansen, *New Philosophy for New Media* (Cambridge, MA: MIT Press, 2004), 85f.

44. See Hal Foster, "Polemics, Postmodernism, Immersion, Militarized Space," in *Journal of Visual Culture* 3.3 (2004), 320–35.

45. Stefan Kaufer, "Leg dich hin und sei still. Olafur Eliasson hat in der Galerie Tate Modern in London ein überwältigendes Szenario installiert," *Frankfurter Rundschau* online, 4 January 2004.

46. See Jonathan Crary, "Your Colour Memory: Illuminations of the Unforeseen," in Olafur Eliasson and Gitte Ørskou (eds.), *Olafur Eliasson: Minding the World* (Aarhus, Denmark: ARoS Aarhus Kunstmuseum, 2004), 209–25 (exhibition catalog), http://www.olafureliasson.net/publications/download_texts/Your_colour_memory.pdf (retrieved 3 July 2014).

47. Bruno Latour, "Atmosphère, Atmosphère," in Susan May (ed.), *The Weather Project* (London: Tate, 2004), 30 (exhibition catalog, The Unilever Series, Tate Modern, 16 October 2003–21 March 2004).

48. Foster, "Polemics, Postmodernism," 327.

49. See "Viola on How Technology Has Influenced Our Perception of the World," from a conversation with Bill Viola, Peter Sellers, and David Ross, San Francisco Museum of Modern Art, 26 June 1999, www.sfmoma.org/media/features/viola/inter04.html (retrieved 22 May 2014).

50. See Roland Barthes, *Camera Lucida—Reflections on Photography* (New York: Hill and Wang, 1981).

51. As a young man, Lacan went out with some fishermen. During the trip, when they saw a sardine can floating on the waves and catching the sun, one of the crew said to Lacan, "See that can? Do you see it? Well, it doesn't see you!" [Jacques Lacan, *The Four Fundamental Concepts of Psychoanalysis: The Seminar XI* (New York: Norton, 1998), 95].

52. Lev Manovich, "image_future" (spring 2004), www.manovich.net/index.php/projects/image-future (retrieved 4 July 2014).

53. See Brian Massumi, *Parables for the Virtual: Movement, Affect, Sensation* (Durham, NC: Duke University Press, 2002), 143.

54. Ulrike Bergermann, "Morphing. Profile des Digitalen," in Petra Löffler and Leander Scholz (eds.), *Das Gesicht ist eine starke Organisation* (Cologne, Germany: DuMont, 2004), 250–74, here 264.

55. Quoted in Bergermann, "Morphing," 264. Wolfgang Hagen, too, has assessed the development of digital photography and highlighted its negative impact especially "in terms of cultural history and with regard to the epistemes of knowledge" [Wolfgang Hagen, "Die Entropie der Fotografie. Skizzen einer Genealogie der digital-elektronischen Bildaufzeichnung," in Herta Wolf (ed.), *Paradigma Fotografie. Fotokritik am Ende des fotografischen Zeitalters, vol. 1* (Frankfurt, Germany: Suhrkamp, 2002), 195–238, here 195f].

56. See Friedrich Kittler, *Short Cuts* (Frankfurt, Germany: Zweitausendeins, 2002).

57. See Marie-Luise Angerer, *Body Options: Körper.Spuren.Medien.Bilder* (Vienna: Turia & Kant, 1999), 33–55; Henning Schmidgen, *Das Unbewusste der Maschinen, Konzeptionen des Psychischen bei Guattari, Deleuze und Lacan* (Munich, Germany: Fink, 1997); Slavoj Žižek, "Lacan with Quantum Physics," in George Robertson, Melinda Mash, Lisa Tickner, Jon Bird, Barry Curtis, and Tim Putnam (eds.), *FutureNatural: Nature/Science/Culture* (New York: Routledge, 1996), 270–92; and Sherry Turkle, *Life on the Screen: Identity in the Age of the Internet* (New York: Simon & Schuster, 1995).

58. See Stefan Rieger, *Kybernetische Anthropologie* (Frankfurt, Germany: Suhrkamp, 2003), 191.

59. Jacques Lacan, "The Mirror Stage as Formative of the I Function," in *Écrits: The First Complete Edition in English* (New York: Norton 2006), 75–81; and Lacan, *Four Fundamental Concepts*, 67–79.

60. Deleuze, *Foucault*, 88.

61. See Ute Holl, *Kino, Trance & Kybernetik* (Berlin: Brinkmann & Bose, 2002) on attempts by Maya Deren and others to stage the cinema as a cybernetic machine.

62. Rieger, *Kybernetische Anthropologie*, 100.

63. Hansen, *New Philosophy*, 35.

64. Ibid., 32f.

65. For more detail on this, see chapter 3.

66. Henri Bergson, *Matter and Memory* (New York: Cosimo, 2007), 60.

67. Tim Lenoir, foreword, in Mark B. N. Hansen, *New Philosophy for New Media* (Cambridge, MA: MIT Press, 2004), xiii–xxvii, here xxvi.

68. Ursula Frohne, "That's the only now I get—Immersion and Participation in Video-Installations by Dan Graham, Steve McQueen, Douglas Gordon, Doug Aitken, Eija-Liisa Ahtila, Sam Taylor-Wood," www.medienkunstnetz.de (retrieved 4 July 2014).

69. Ibid.

70. Hansen, *New Philosophy*, 76.

71. *Osmose* (1995) is an immersive, interactive virtual reality installation with 3D computer graphics and 3D sound; users wear a head-mounted display with real-time motion tracking that reacts to breathing and balance.

72. The iconography of *Ephémère* is based on nature as a metaphor. Archetypal elements, such as rocks and rivers, combine with body organs, bones, and blood vessels, pointing to a subterranean relationship, an exchange, between the interior of the body, its materiality, and the interior of the earth. The project is divided vertically into three levels: Landscape, Earth, and Body. More on both projects at Char Davies, "Immersence," www.immersence.com (retrieved 22 May 2014).

73. Hansen, *New Philosophy*, 76.

74. Carolin Guertin, "Queer Hybrids: Cosmopolism and Embodied Arts," in Gerfried Stocker and Christine Schöpf (eds.), *Hybrid: Living in Paradox: Ars Electronica 2005* (Ostfildern-Ruit, Germany: Hatje Cantz, 2005), 166–69, here 169. The artist's understanding of herself further underlines this interpretation: "As an artist, I [. . .] have two choices: I can either unplug and never go near a computer again or I can choose to remain engaged, seeking to subvert the tech-

nology from within, using it to communicate an alternative worldview. My strategy has been to explore how the medium/technology can be used to 'deautomatize' perception [. . .] in order that participants may begin to question their own habitual perceptions and assumptions about being in the world, thus facilitating a mental state whereby Cartesian boundaries between mind and body, self and world begin to slip." [Mark B. N. Hansen, "Embodying Virtual Reality: Touch and Self-Movement in the Work of Char Davies," in *Critical Matrix: The Princeton Journal of Women, Gender and Culture*, 12 (2004), 112–47].

75. *PainStation* and *LegShocker* are projects by the artists' collective //////////fur/ /// (Tilman Reiff, Volker Morawe and Robert Kirschner), who developed the work at the Academy of Media Arts (KHM) Cologne, http://www.painstation.de (retrieved 23 May 2014).

76. Maurice Benayoun in Transmediale, *Smile Machines. Humor Kunst Technologie* (exhibition catalog, transmediale 06, Berlin, 2006), 100.

77. *Emotion's Defibrillator* (Tobias Grewenig, 2005), a project also developed at KHM, http://www.tobiasgrewenig.com/emotions_defibrillator/index.html (retrieved 23 May 2014).

78. One of the few examples is Holger Schulze, "Klang Erzählungen. Zur Klanganthropologie als einer neuen, empfindungsbezogenen Disziplin," in Oliver Grau and Andreas Keil (eds.), *Mediale Emotionen. Zur Lenkung von Gefühlen durch Bild und Sound* (Frankfurt, Germany: Fischer, 2005), 215–23, and more recently the work of Chris Salter, who develops multisensory installations within which visitors must rely solely on their sensory perceptions. See Chris Salter, "Atmospheres of Affect," in Marie-Luise Angerer, Bernd Bösel, and Michaela Ott (eds.), *Timing of Affect: Epistemologies, Politics, Aesthetics* (Zurich, Switzerland: diaphanes and University of Chicago Press, forthcoming).

79. Sean Cubitt, *Digital Aesthetics* (London: Sage, 1998).

80. Canadian Pavilion, Forty-ninth Venice Biennial, 2001.

81. Jörg Heiser, "Imagination: The Making Of," in *The Secret Hotel* (Bregenz, Austria: Kunsthaus Bregenz, 2005), exhibition catalog, 30.

82. Bergson, *Matter and Memory*, 111.

83. Deleuze, *Cinema 1*, 65.

84. Ibid., 66.

85. Deleuze, *Cinema 2*, 5.

86. Ibid.

87. Thomas Elsaesser, "Zu spät, zu früh? Körper, Zeit und Aktionsraum in der Kinoerfahrung," in Matthias Brütsch, Vinzenz Hediger, Ursula von Keitz, Alexandra Schneider, and Margrit Tröhler (eds.), *Kinogefühle. Emotionalität und Film* (Marburg, Germany: Schüren Verlag, 2005), 415–39, here 416.

88. See Jill Bennett, *Empathic Vision: Affect, Trauma and Contemporary Art* (Stanford, CA: Stanford University Press, 2005); Wolfgang Ernst, "Temporalizing Presence and 'Re-Presencing' the Past: The Techno-Traumatic Affect," in Marie-Luise Angerer, Bernd Bösel, and Michaela Ott (eds.), *Timing of Affect: Epistemologies, Politics, Aesthetics* (Zurich, Switzerland: diaphanes and University of Chicago Press, forthcoming).

89. Elsaesser, "Zu spät, zu früh?" 438.

90. Ibid., 438f.

91. See Julia Kristeva, *New Maladies of the Soul* (New York: Columbia University Press, 2005).

92. Ruth Leys, *From Guilt to Shame: Auschwitz and After* (Princeton, NJ: Princeton University Press, 2007).

93. The Tomkins-Ekman paradigm posits the existence of innate movements of the facial muscles by which the affects are always already and universally expressed. This now plays a major role in data recognition by computers. See Leys, *From Guilt to Shame*, 137f.

TWO

Human | Posthuman | Transhuman

> The Age of Postbiological Man would reveal the human condition for what it actually is, which is to say, *a condition to be gotten out of*. Friedrich Nietzsche, the philosopher, had already seen the truth of this back in the nineteenth century: 'Man is something that should be overcome', he had written in 1883. 'What have you done to overcome him?' Back then, of course, the question was only rhetorical, but now in *fin-de-siècle* twentieth century, we had all the necessary means in front of us [. . .] for turning ourselves into the most advanced transhumans imaginable.[1]

The affective turn described in chapter 1 has been taking place alongside a transition from human to posthuman/transhuman, into which it is in fact inscribed. What does this transition mean for a subject conceived of in political, ethical, biological, and psychological terms? What is shifting in its theoretical and philosophical formulation? What is the significance of the phase of antihumanist thought that first arose at the end of the nineteenth century and that was unmistakably over by the end of the twentieth? Why is this phase now dismissed not only as outdated but in some cases also as positively harmful for politics, society, and theory? Which new subject, or rather agency, is now emerging?

In recent years, there has been much discussion of "governmentality",[2] which, based on Foucault's analysis of power, has emerged as a new paradigm, focusing attention on the interplay of forces between power and subject, techniques of the self, knowledge and transmission, life and technology. These relational functions (the so-called government of mankind) work on and against the concept of the human, thus operating within the matrix first established in the eighteenth century. Today, this version of the human is opposed by a range of forces. In addition to posthuman cyborg fantasies advocating the obsolescence and electronic enhancement of the body, there is a more widespread celebration of our departure from the human (*anthropos*). For a long time, the human was defined in terms of a key difference based on the ontological divide between the phenomenon in its appearance and the world as such. Today, we can observe an implosion of this difference, potentially causing the human subject, who opened up this difference through language, to disappear.

THE HOMELESS SUBJECT

At the end of *The Order of Things*, Michel Foucault describes man as "neither the oldest nor the most constant problem that has been posed for human knowledge".[3] Indeed, he writes, one can wager "that man would be erased, like a face drawn in the sand at the edge of the sea."[4]

When Foucault was writing these lines, research into genetic engineering, and the political processes that facilitate it, had, from today's point of view, only just begun to reveal their true scale. But against the backdrop of his description of the gradual emergence of a specific "concept of the human", it was certainly legitimate to imagine that it could one day be replaced by a different mode of thinking, knowing, and acting. "It is no longer possible to think in our day", Foucault writes, "other than in the void left by man's disappearance. For this void does not create a deficiency; it does not constitute a lacuna that must be filled. It is nothing more, and nothing less, than the unfolding of a space in which it is once more possible to think."[5]

But what is the meaning of this *concept of the human*, whose establishment Foucault traced and whose future transformations (which for him were clearly coming) he attempted to anticipate and understand? First and foremost, it means forming a vision of this man, rendering him susceptible to description and analysis, and finally deciding on a truth about him. Foucault noted a change that took place in the course of the seventeenth century concerning the relation of signs to the world, the significance of language to the empirical reality it signifies. As a related or parallel phenomenon, new knowledge complexes were emerging that divided up the world (as an object of knowledge) in new ways. This new model differed from previous approaches in important respects. Whereas in former systems of thought, such as that of the Renaissance, things derived their significance and position from similarity, now meanings arose from differences, in turn producing identities. Inscribed within this new way of thinking was a new question concerning the human. At the end of the eighteenth century, Kant asks, What are we today, here and now? What are we at present? A departure, then, from such questions as, What can we know? What is truth? What is man? This Kantian focus on the here and now, on the finite existence of man, rewrote the relationship between human thought and action. Metaphysics gave way to a critique—the critique of a constitutive nonfiniteness in which man is construed as being posited by a boundless divinity. With Kant, the Cartesian cogito is defined as something finite, no longer a divine-boundless "I think" but a secularized "I that thinks" and, via this thinking, explores its borders (the finitude of both its existence and its cognitive faculties). A century later, this "I" will have to accept that it is not its own master, governed instead by forces largely beyond its control. The Freudian formula "Where Id was, there Ego shall be"[6] culminates in the mid-twentieth century in Lacan's radical claim that Being (in the sense of the Real) and thinking are mutually exclusive.

On its way from Descartes to Kant, then, the meaning of the formula "cogito, ergo sum" changed completely. The infinite ceded its dominant position to the finite, launching what Gilles Deleuze has described as the "irreducible heterogeneity" of the mind. From now on, receptivity and spontaneity are the two modes in which the subject exists (thinks and acts): "Receptivity of space-time, spontaneity of 'I think'. Finally, man becomes deformed, in the etymological sense, i.e. dis-formed. He limps on two forms that are heterogeneous and not symmetrical: receptivity of intuition and spontaneity of 'I think'."[7] For Kant, Deleuze continues, the cogito has become broken, no longer "fully intact like an egg" (*plein comme un oeuf*). With the arrival of constituent finitude, God, by whom it was previously surrounded and permeated, departed, leaving behind a cracked cogito:

> The 'I think'—spontaneity—determines my existence, but my existence is only determinable as that of a receptive being. Thus, I, as a receptive being, conceive of my spontaneity as the operation of another on me, and this other is 'I'. What does Kant do? Where Descartes saw two terms and one form, he sees three terms and two forms. Three terms: determination, the undetermined, and the determinable. Two forms: the form of the determinable and the form of determination, i.e. intuition, space-time, and the 'I think'.[8]

"Language", as Foucault writes, "did not return into the field of thought directly and in its own right until the end of the nineteenth century."[9] And with this new status, Foucault argues, it left the classical age behind it for good and entered the modern age. Against this background, language (as a finite open system) launches the first decisive turn, the linguistic turn, via Ferdinand de

Saussure's structural linguists and via the analytical language philosophy of Wittgenstein and others. In the 1960s, this manifested itself in Structuralism and later in poststructural theories.

Exactly two decades before Foucault, in 1946, Martin Heidegger wrote his "Letter on Humanism", in which he states that the human has always been underestimated by humanism and its metaphysics. For the human to be properly conceived of or understood, he argues, it should be thought about not in terms of *animalitas* but with regard to its *humanitas*.[10] In his "Response to the Letter on Humanism", Peter Sloterdijk formulates his "Rules for the Human Zoo",[11] pointing to a gap in Heidegger's critique of classical humanism. Heidegger, he says, postulated an "ontological primitive"—the famous "clearing for Being" (*Lichtung des Seins*[12]) as man's dwelling place—which he subjected to no further questioning. Sloterdijk, on the other hand, wishes to shake up this primitive relationship in order to render visible the "social history of the openness of man to the *Seinsfrage*, and a historical progression in the nature of the ontological divide"[13] that are inscribed within it. This also prompts him to expose Lacan's similar error with regard to this ontological difference. For, like Heidegger, he says, Lacan, too, postulated a primal relationship: the infant in front of the mirror that hallucinates its body as intact and whose truth and reality is, from the outset and unavoidably, psychosis.[14] But from antiquity to the present, Sloterdijk says, something has remained unthinkable: the "domestication of man".[15] And today, we are more radically subjected to this than ever before, as witness genetic engineering, stem-cell research, artificial/synthetic life, and postprosthetic bodies.

Initially, Heidegger's critique of metaphysics takes a similar direction: European metaphysics persistently defined man as the "rational animal" who acquires culture via training and education (the "civilizing" process), thus learning to set himself apart from animals. But, he argues, an intrinsic difference between man and animal must be assumed because man "has world" and is in the world, whereas plants and animals just live in their respective surroundings. This "having the world" (*Welt-haben*) and "being-in-the-world" is organized via language, which is not simply used by man as a means of communication but is a mode of being in which man exists.

From here, it is clearly just a small step to Lacan's linguistic-structural rewriting of Freudian psychoanalysis.[16] For Lacan, too, the subject is a subject of language, an effect of the flows of signifiers. Whereas Heidegger calls for an "analytic of man" in terms of *humanitas* and asserts an intrinsic difference, Giorgio Agamben's *Homo Sacer*[17] presents the history of the always already double life of man as a being consisting of *zoe* and *bios*: simply partaking of natural life (just as animals do) and at the same time belonging to a specific group of beings that define, regulate and monitor this life. What for Heidegger was a philosophical break (the need to conceive of being and its specific particularities), Agamben cast as a historical arc, showing how the *zoe-bios* duality runs right through western history. In the twentieth century, this culminates in the concentration camps, where "bare life" was faced with a "sovereign power" that judged it. For his analysis, Agamben refers to Foucault's three-volume *History of Sexuality* focusing on power and its manifestations. In the first volume, *The Will to Knowledge*,[18] Foucault shows how, from the second half of the eighteenth century, state power and its institutions (family, religion, school, military, etc.) intervened more and more forcefully into the individual and physical sphere, the biosphere, thus transforming the public and private terrains of power. To understand how an individual is made into (or makes itself into) a subject, besides the concept of technologies of the self, Foucault also introduced the notion of a bio-power, a political power that measures, regulates and domesticates life (both individual and collective) not by banning or punishing certain actions, but (in a Žižekian twist) via a hedonistic imperative to enjoy.[19]

Agamben criticizes Foucault for not having been radical enough in reframing his concept of power for the twentieth century, failing to make the connection between the paradigm of this century—the concentration camp—and his biopolitics. "Bare life", which is also "sacred life", is the concept introduced by Agamben to grasp the radicalized or totalitarian biopolitics of National Socialism. Using court records from the Nuremberg Trials relating to medical experiments, Agamben demonstrates the cynical fusing of bio- and thanatopolitics. In an approach similar to Slavoj Žižek's argument that democracy's inherent "obscene underside"[20] is also one of its constitutive elements, Agamben shows the degree to which "bare life" is inscribed in politics, with politics and life always interlocked. Today, this interlocking is reflected in the debates on genetic engineering and euthanasia and in discussions about assisted dying and embryo research. What is at stake here, however, is not just seeing the degree to which politics interferes in life but understanding the degree to which this life is the constitutive core of any politics. (A fact, I would stress here, that Foucault was always aware of, as his writings on neo-liberalism made abundantly clear.)

This brings us back to Heidegger and his discussion of the essence of the human. For Agamben, politics

> appears as the truly fundamental structure of Western metaphysics insofar as it occupies the threshold on which the relation between the living being and the logos is realized. In the 'politicization' of bare life—the metaphysical task par excellence—the hu-

> manity of living man is decided. In assuming this task, modernity does nothing other than declare its own faithfulness to the essential structure of the metaphysical tradition. The fundamental categorical pair of Western politics is not that of friend/enemy but that of bare life/political existence, zoē/bios, exclusion/inclusion. There is politics because man is the living being who, in language, separates and opposes himself to his own bare life and, at the same time, maintains himself in relation to that bare life in an inclusive exclusion.[21]

Heidegger's version of the human, that man is not a civilized animal but a being in and through language, thus forms the core of a biopolitics that divides people into bare and political life and that both assures and denies existence. But when this version of the human becomes brittle, when an altered view of life is supported and favoured by other definitions and scientific objectifications (such as genetic information theory, which is beginning to alter the position of man as a bio-being on the scale of life), then the question of the essence of the human is posed anew, calling for a close examination of the desire that is pushing for such a reformulation.

At the end of *The Order of Things*, as well as saying that man as a problem may disappear, Foucault also issues a warning that concerns the specific nature of those disciplines that deal with this problem, the human sciences. As Foucault sees it, they possess a drive toward ever-greater transparency and unveiling: "On the horizon of any human science", he writes, "there is the project of bringing man's consciousness back to its real conditions, of restoring it to the contents and forms that brought it into being, and elude us within it."[22] The problem of the unconscious is thus not merely a problem within the human sciences but a "problem that is ultimately coextensive with their very existence. A transcendental raising of level (that is, on the other side, an unveiling of the non-conscious) is constitutive of all the sciences of man."[23]

It is a good thirty years since the figure of the cyborg first came along to trouble the world of these sciences. It was introduced by Donna Haraway, among others, with the aim of breaking down the divide between the natural and human sciences and demonstrating the nonfunctionality of this divide in the face of recent political and technological developments. The figure of the cyborg was meant not only as the outline of a possible posthuman development but also as an attack on the status of the human in general. Today, the emphasis is less on the fear of a mechanization of the human (as it was at the beginning of the debate on cyborgs and other replicants) and more on the position of the human subject within the field of "life" more generally.

"Rimbaud's premonition", writes Paul Rabinow, "of future men 'filled with animals' can be made to seem perfectly sound."[24] Today, he continues, we are facing a reformulation of nature and culture in which the category of the social may fall by the wayside. This future scenario is not meant to sound forbidding; instead, Rabinow matter-of-factly underpins it using his own studies on postmodern social structures and formations: "In the future, the new genetics will cease to be a biological metaphor for modern society and will become instead a circulation network of identity terms and restriction loci, around which and through which a truly new type of autoproduction will emerge, which I call 'biosociality'."[25] Unlike Haraway, whose "Cyborg Manifesto"[26] makes a categorical distinction between the modern discipline-based societies of yesterday and Deleuze's postmodern "society of control" of today, Rabinow appeals for an analysis of the current shifts and the ways they overlap.

LEAVING THE HOUSE OF LANGUAGE—CYBERNETICS, CULTURAL STUDIES, CYBERSPACE

> We usually think of language as corresponding to the essence of the human being represented as *animal rationale,* that is, as the unity of body-soul-spirit. But just as ek-sistence [*sic*]—and through it the relation of the truth of being to the human being—remains veiled in the *humanitas* of *homo animalis,* so does the metaphysical-animal explanation of language cover up the essence of language in the history of being. According to this essence, language is the house of being, which is propriated by being and pervaded by being. And so it is proper to think the essence of language from its correspondence to being and indeed as this correspondence, that is, as the home of the human being's essence.[27]

Language (or, as Lacan was to call it, the symbolic order) is the true house of man, at the same time as being the famous "prison" described by Nietzsche. Into his language-based "house of Being", Heidegger built an insurmountable alienation or cleaving of the subject. Whereas in his *Course in General Linguistics,*[28] Saussure still admitted a natural link between words and their users, the relationship between the speaking subject and language itself as a semantic-performative system would subsequently undergo further differentiation in three directions. First, it gave rise to the speech act theory of John Austin and John Searle (that has made a comeback in Judith Butler's "doing gender"[29] and in the "performative turn" of the early 1990s). Second, cybernetics developed a view of language as information transmission (language as code). And finally, at the same time as cybernetics, Lacan's rewriting of psychoanalysis reasserted the Heideggerian variant that grasps language as that which always precedes the subject and which therefore always necessarily eludes it.

In this light, the homelessness of man can be understood in a twofold sense, as homelessness within the structure of thought and politics and as placelessness, or at most as an intermediate place of being with regard to the primacy of language. The invention of man, as described by Foucault, brings new problems, raising the question of how to think this man, where he is assumed to reside, and how to conceive of his truth? For Žižek, "modern subjectivity emerges when the subject perceives himself as 'out of joint', as *excluded* from the 'order of things', from the positive order of identities."[30] This could be said to stand at the beginning of a history that comes to a close in the mid-twentieth century. When Foucault spoke of the void being the only place from which the human can be thought, he was not the only one bidding farewell to the human in this way, but the valedictory choir was predominantly French. Jean-François Lyotard[31] was another voice proclaiming the end of the grand narratives. These swan songs had something new in mind, however, which becomes clear as soon as one recalls the accompanying sociopolitical conditions: student and feminist movements, the Vietnam War, oil crisis, peace activism.

With man's dwelling in language as formulated by Heidegger, a school of thought emerged that recognizes the human as a category in its own right while simultaneously expropriating it. Man does not possess this language in the same way he is not his body. The dispute about this informed the second half of the twentieth century in particular: Who speaks when id speaks? Until the late 1990s, answers to this question were pushed back and forth, deferred. Judith Butler's claim that "doing gender" is a doing not preceded by an intentioned subject exemplifies this. In the early 1990s, her attempt to interrelate psychoanalysis and speech act theory in order to obtain yet another concept of construction that is supposed to also do justice to the material side of action caused quite a stir among feminist theorists. But this excitement was very soon swept away by the digital (and slightly later the performative) hype. From then on, everyone and everything acts/does.

But the digital hype, too, had a long prehistory dating back to the beginnings of information theory and cybernetics in the United States in the 1940s. At the same time as Heidegger's "Letter" and Lacan's linguistic-structural "return to Freud", the first steps were taken toward not sectioning off the linguistic side of the human but integrating it into a network of rules obeyed by man and machine alike.[32] Norbert Wiener's cybernetics was of course highly attractive to disciplines in the social and human sciences because its declared aim was to become a universal theory of man, technology and society. It comes as no surprise, then, that psychologists and therapists adopted a systems-based approach, as they came into very early contact—via Gregory Bateson, Margaret Mead, and others—with cybernetics and its basic concepts of feedback, metacommunication and autopoiesis.[33] In the next chapter, I show how cybernetic self-regulation found its way into the affect theory of Silvan Tomkins (who is very highly regarded in current Anglo-American cultural and media studies) to install a systemic concept of affect against the Freudian model of the drives.

But let us return to the question of how the relationship between the speaking subject and the system of language has been discussed and which concepts have been introduced in order to privilege either the unconscious or the intentional dimension of speech. Derrida and Searle, for example, used the concepts of iteration and articulation to explain their respective positions. Articulation here refers to the spatialization of the temporal structures of language and the temporalization of the realm of language, covering the various differences that characterize language/speech (pauses, stuttering, giggling, etc.). Iteration, on the other hand, denotes the moment of repetition, of coming-to-oneself (*venir à soi*) and of being-at-home (*être chez soi*). But while repetition for Derrida is never identical, as every repetition also involves a modification, for Searle it is precisely this moment that marks or permits an identity—he sees repetition as the actual moment of linguistic meaning that leads to the intentionality of the speaker.[34] This was never accepted by Derrida, who insisted that language consists primarily in its repeated and iterable utterance, resulting in a constant displacement of the self-articulating subject, which is thus always already an articulated subject.[35] John Austin always based his distinction between various linguistic categories on the "normal use" of language, thus excluding all that is theatrical and playful as parasitic. But for Derrida, as for Freud and Lacan, this is precisely the essence of language.

Transferred into political and media theory, these two concepts took on still other specific meanings. In a sense, iteration and articulation are combined here because articulation denotes only a moment of closure, a temporary semantic fixing of meaning. The concept has its roots both in linguistics and in neo-Marxist cultural theories of the 1970s.[36] *Articulation* refers to an identity that builds on differences that are also (necessarily) ignored in order to uphold this identity—at least temporarily. With this concept, introduced into the field of the political by Ernesto Laclau in particular, the moment of dwelling is extended, with language cast as a symbolic order and its structure as universal. Laclau follows Derrida in grasping the entirety of social conditions as a necessarily open system in which meanings flow and erode. In this view, identities always function along the axes of antagonism and exclusion. Only the continual fixing of discursive nodes allows differential reality to come to rest, making it possible to partially fix it as unambiguous.[37]

Within cultural studies, a central position is occupied by the question of the production of meaning in open symbolic/media systems. Stuart Hall introduced the concept of articulation as practice to explain the construction of nodes that enable people to understand their historical situation and experience it as meaningful. Hall thus understands articulation as the "form of the connection that can make a unity of two different elements, under certain conditions".[38] In articulation, then, contingent elements combine to "make sense" at the moment of closure. This recalls Laclau's use of contingency to denote what is symptomatic about the combination of social forces and ideological manifestations. Laclau makes clear that the arbitrary, random, nonimperative is not only always included in this combination but also that it is constitutive of it. In order for a political and mental system to be maintained, however, it must be repressed, replaced, masked or fetishized. This aspect has never really been brought to bear in cultural studies, instead being increasingly ignored (just as the discipline's interest in psychoanalysis as a whole has steadily waned). With this focus on the production of meaning, cultural studies has lost sight of an aspect that is of fundamental importance to both Lacan and Laclau, that is, understanding images, narratives, discourses in their function as facades that mask the meaninglessness of the subject. But precisely this notion that the subject cannot be completely grasped has in recent years been voiced increasingly loudly as an accusation against postmodern/poststructuralist theories. These theories, the argument goes, have paved the way for posthuman thinking by always defining the core of the subject as hollowed out, resulting in the loss of the entire frame of the human. Stanley Aronowitz, for example, accuses Lacan, Althusser and Foucault of having anticipated Haraway's figure of the cyborg by propagating a subject whose soul was only ever a fiction; this in turn has opened the door to a way of thinking now culminating in the concept of a "terminal identity"; man has been reduced to a mere shell for a computer-controlled system.[39] Far more numerous, however, are those who euphorically welcome the demise of this unloved subject, and their voices are louder. In *The Second Self*,[40] and especially in *Life on the Screen*, Sherry Turkle tells us how lucky we are to be free of this theoretical baggage at last, thanks to the digital communications revolution. "Thus", she writes, "more than twenty years after meeting the ideas of Lacan, Foucault, Deleuze, and Guattari, I am meeting them again in my new life on the screen. But this time, the Gallic abstractions are more concrete. In my computer-mediated worlds, the self is multiple, fluid and constituted in interaction with machine connections."[41] According to this view, language materializes itself in the ocean of digital data. The fragmented subject posited by psychoanalysis has become a play of figures, a matter of buttons that generate the respective modes of being online. In Turkle's analysis, the equivalences are simple: theory and online practice, communication and experience, role play and *doing gender*, consciousness and the unconscious.[42] According to a comparison made by Lacan, the unconscious is structured like a language, and the way it works can be understood in terms of the functioning of language. But being and subject are radically separated by language. As Lacan states,

> If we choose being, the subject disappears, it eludes us, it falls into non-meaning. If we choose meaning, the meaning survives only deprived of that part of non-meaning that is, strictly speaking, that which constitutes in the realization of the subject, the unconscious. In other words, it is of the nature of this meaning, as it emerges in the field of the Other, to be in a large part of this field, eclipsed by the disappearance of being, induced by the very function of the signifier.[43]

There is another form of overlap between cybernetic machines and a "machinic" subject. Deleuze's philosophy of becoming or immanence, in particular, proposed a specific concept of the machinic. In *Anti-Oedipus*[44] and *A Thousand Plateaus,*[45] together with Félix Guattari, Deleuze writes against a version of the subject only framed by reason, meaning and consciousness. They also argue against a psychoanalytical version of the subject understood as oedipal and of desire as rooted in lack-in-being (*manque à l'être*). Instead, they campaign for a body without organs or rather organization[46] that is traversed by different modes of subjection and intense lines of desire. In this context, they speak of machines of subjection and subjectivization that produce their respective subjects using different strategies. Whereas in archaic states, machinic subjection made people into parts of the machine, people today, in capitalism, are subjected to machines in order to be made into subjects with regard to a state, a nation, a corporation. In this process, technical machines played a key part in the development toward ever-greater subjection. The modern state, Deleuze and Guattari claim, used technical machines and replaced machinic subjection with social subjection; "capitalism arises as a worldwide enterprise of subjectivization."[47] With the new machines of cybernetics and information technology, however, the tables are turned again. In the view of Deleuze and Guattari, the old regime of subjection is reestablished: "recurrent and reversible 'humans-machines systems' replace the old nonrecurrent and nonreversible relations between the two elements."[48] This old-new subjugation functions via norms, modelling and information, and it functions via "language, perception, desire, movement".[49] In late capitalism, Deleuze and Guattari tell us, subjectivization and enslavement are two extreme forms of subject production whose links with technical machines have reached a kind of ergonomic intensity.[50] But the authors never conceived of subjection and enslavement as static and total, instead following the vanishing lines that escape them, thus repeatedly tipping the subject out of its molar state, becoming "other" via molecular compositions. Language, too, plays a double role here: On the one hand, it organizes commands and code words; on the other, it is minoritarian and breaks the axes of usage and meaning. Here, the authors also state clearly that the structure of language cannot be adequately described in terms of representation, information, and communication alone.[51]

In view of the across-the-board enthusiasm for Deleuze, Spinoza and Bergson in the various disciplines, Foucault's hunch that the twenty-first century might be a Deleuzian century is not entirely unjustified. But as I show, this enthusiasm also often leads to borrowings and interpretations that are based on misunderstandings.

DO MACHINES THINK?

> When we say: 'The machine thinks', we are tempted to believe that we know how we ourselves think—just because we know how the machine 'thinks'. In syntactic terms, however, the difference is plain to see, for when the machine 'thinks' it does so in inverted commas: quote think unquote. Besides the name, the functions 'think' and 'think' have nothing in common![52]

Artificial intelligence, constructivism, and cognitive science are currents that developed out of and alongside cybernetics. In the following, I present specific aspects of these developments that postulate posthuman thinking and the posthuman condition as desirable, as a liberation, and as a definitive rejection of modern man.

In Stanisław Lem's *Golem XIV*,[53] the protagonist explains to his audience that he does not have something that humans have, namely emotions. But, he says, far from being a lack, his life without emotion and passion is better than the endless ups and downs to which humans are subjected throughout their life. Emotions are understood here as something deeply human, which corresponds closely to the current trend toward defining *affects* and *emotions* as qualities for tuning bodies to their environment. In Marge Piercy's novel *He, She and It*,[54] the cyborg Yod, too, loses his mechanical-electronic credibility the moment he is overpowered by feelings. In other words, machines become more like humans when they begin to feel, when they experience hate, anger, and desire. A speaking machine like ELIZA (the first therapeutic computer programme, developed by Joseph Weizenbaum) was not especially convincing because the language it possessed drew exclusively on information theory: repetition, reduction of redundancy, elimination of noise. Today, computers have not only come to look more human, but their interaction is also being more and more closely adjusted to human gestures and facial expressions.[55]

When Deleuze and Guattari referred to the machines of cybernetics as new machines of subjection, they did so in part because they integrate the human organism into the technical assemblage in a new way, which also explains the interest of cybernetics in studying the human organism as a whole, focusing attention not only on language and body movement but above all on the functioning of perception. The question here is how the eye as an instrument, tool and machine perceives reality and translates it into a meaningful image. Performance, introduced by speech act theory as the third dimension of language, was long ignored by cybernetic research. The phenomenon of "attention" was studied but without actually taking into account the subjective dimension of communication partners (how does someone perceive someone else, what effect does this have on his situation, which actions result and where do they lead?).

A prominent role in the history of cybernetics—including the aspects of language, information, subjectivity and the unconscious under discussion here—is played by the Macy Conferences Group, whose members included Bateson, Mead, Kubie, McCulloch, von Foerster and Shannon. The British cyberneticist Donald MacKay, for example, proposed a model that introduced subjectivity as a variable: "Subjectivity, far from being a morass to be avoided, is precisely what enables information and meaning to be connected."[56] In his *New Philosophy for New Media*, Mark Hansen also refers to this, stressing that the group's development could have taken a different turn if other members had been more influential. Finally, it was Shannon with his mathematical theory of communication who prevailed. Information now became a quantifiable, measurable variable that was to be asserted against the noise of the communication channels. Today, Hansen writes, the other side, the repressed body, is being rediscovered and privileged.[57] At the time of the Macy Conferences, Donald MacKay was working on two sides of the communication process: the production of representation and the function of this representation, for which he used the terms *selection* and *construction*. *Selection* corresponds to the formal understanding of Shannon's concept of information, while *construction* refers to the context in which this selection takes place. In other words, "whereas Shannon and Wiener define information in terms of what it *is*, MacKay defines it in terms of what it *does*."[58] The "Shannon-Weaver model" equates meaning with altered behaviour, Hansen writes, whereas the MacKay model preserves the autonomy of the nontechnical.[59] This nontechnical context that defines the selection and meaning of information now leads directly to the body of the viewer. With the help of Bergson's "subtraction theory of perception", this results in an embodied individual as the central site for information processing:

> Here are the external images, then my body, and, lastly, the changes brought about by my body in the surrounding images. I see plainly how external images influence the image that I call my body: they transmit movement to it. And I also see how this body influences external images: it gives back movement to them. My body is, then, in the aggregate of the material world, an image which acts like other images, receiving and giving back movement, with, perhaps, this difference only, that my body appears to choose, with certain limits, the manner in which it shall restore what it receives.[60]

But the Macy Group also discussed the role of emotions as a feedback force. Lawrence S. Kubie demonstrated the vital function of the emotions by describing them as a "governor on a machine"[61] that add a psychological quality to every experience. This means that, consciously or unconsciously, experiences are either negatively or positively amplified. Whereas joyful excitement and enthusiasm are normally experienced consciously, anger and vexation operate more subconsciously. The same distinction also applies to depression and fear: the former is experienced more consciously, the latter more unconsciously. Fear and depression cause prompt avoidance of the experiences associated with them, whereas enthusiasm and anger stimulate repetition. This resonates with the affect theory of Silvan Tomkins, which, as mentioned above, has recently triggered a new boom in affect-related research in cultural studies, with a particular focus on shame. In the 1960s, Tomkins referred to cybernetics when describing affects as (positive and negative) amplifiers, thus setting his approach apart from Freud's drive-based model.

Within the Macy Group, the role of the emotions was discussed in the context of language and neuroses, raising the question of the unconscious and whether such a thing can even exist. Kubie affirms the existence of an unconscious on the grounds that there are things that escape the knowledge of the individual. Today, some neurobiologists refer to the unconscious as a matter of course and claim that Freud's model was correct. For psychoanalysis, the unconscious is only born with language: the symbolic order produces an unconscious, another scene to which no empirical reality can be attributed. Today, on the other hand, attempts are being made to localize the unconscious as a biological reality at various sites in the brain.[62] Fifty years ago, Gregory Bateson raised an interesting question in this debate, asking whether there might be a link between the conscious/unconscious distinction and the double coding of language, noting an unconscious dimension inherent in language itself: "Language is a double coding: both a statement about the outside and a statement about the inside: It is that doubleness which gives this conscious-unconscious quality to it." In response to the further question of whether a process of symbolization could take place without conscious control by the speaker, Kubie said, "Yes, it is of the essence of neurosis that the process is symbolic and that the subject does not know what it is symbolizing." Teuber then asked, "To whom?" and Heinz von Foerster answered, "To himself."[63]

This question is interesting, not only because those asking it still assume language to have an unconscious dimension, but also with regard to the further development of Bateson's communication theory. This double quality of language prompted him to posit a "content aspect" and a "relational aspect" in all communication.[64] If the two diverge (double-bind), then communication is no longer possible as the individual is confronted with an impossible task and breaks down—into psychosis. I mention this here for the following reason: today, with increasing focus on emotion and affect as basic body language, this relational aspect may be being discretely revived in order to underline the emotional dimension and affective underside of the semantic content of communication. In Bateson's theory, the relational aspect already played this unconscious role (as a bodily, not entirely controllable dimension of the speaker), but today we see its place being taken over by affect.

Humberto Maturana and Francisco Varela, who later joined the Macy Group, pushed the divorce between language and mind to new lengths. In their definition of *perception* as a flow of information and as a biological system of adaptation, both the context (of selection) and the double dimension of language lose their influence. Using the example of a frog's eye, Maturana demonstrated that, instead of representing reality, the eye models reality according to its own structure. Here, then, perception is defined in biological terms and as an "autopoietic" system. In *Autopoiesis and Cognition,*[65] Maturana and Varela present this biological apparatus of perception that functions as a quasi-closed system, only obeying its own rules and barely subject to influence or control from the outside world. The outside reaches perception by interaction alone: "Living systems operate within the boundaries of an organization that closes in on itself and leaves the world on the outside."[66] Today, consciousness is routinely defined in biological terms, its primary function being to guarantee inner presence, the organism's knowledge about itself. As Antti Revonsuo writes, "Consciousness matters. [. . .] You exist only insofar as your subjective psychological reality exists. When it is wiped out for good, the world-for-you will be gone, and so will you."[67] Revonsuo advocates a "biological realism" that understands subjective consciousness as a real phenomenon instead of dismissing it as an illusion or intellectual error. Biological realism views consciousness as a natural phenomenon that can be explained in natural terms without reference to mystical, supernatural dimensions. In today's philosophical approaches, however, he notes a surprising antibiological position due simply to the fact that these philosophers are not aware of biological realism.[68] The sole exception, he writes, is John Searle, who focused his attention on studying consciousness. Searle, who once argued with Derrida about the intentionality of language, is now a vociferous advocate of brain research with regard to the analysis of consciousness.[69] His prediction that consciousness would be the main theme of the twenty-first century has long since come true. Neurobiology and psychology have both produced manifestos declaring that the bitterly fought battles of the last two centuries are over.

As I show, the dimension of the unconscious has a long and ambivalent tradition. (Even Freud was obliged to introduce a "system within a system", his "tip of the iceberg".) When neurobiology and cognitive psychology fight over the domain of the brain, accusing philosophy of never having solved the body-mind problem, it is only fair to add that this problem still has not been solved today.

This debate is conducted in particular around the theme of free will, with neurobiology positing the brain as an agent, while the other side posits consciousness. In my view, however, the terms of this debate are badly chosen, as both sides ignore or misconceive what Freud described as the strongest dimension of the human: the unconscious. In his "Project for a Scientific Psychology",[70] the unconscious was already more than a mere repertoire of neuronal tensions, it was already a domain of translations and displacements. And this is precisely where the discussion is taking place today, around the question of how the biology of the brain gives rise to the conscious experience of an individual, how a reality emerges from perception, why people react to something or someone in a specific way. Or, in a question already discussed within the Macy Group: Why does a baby smile? Is it because neuronal processes instruct its facial muscles to perform this action or because the baby wishes to articulate something? In this debate, Jürgen Habermas is among the opponents of brain research, holding on to free will and the possibility of conscious decision by the individual, thus merely reaffirming once again what he has long since elaborated in his approach based on communicative action, for example in *Knowledge and Human Interests*.[71] According to Habermas, the Ego or consciousness regains the status of "master in its own house" by repetition, working through, and acceptance of the repressed content. Alfred Lorenzer argues in a similar way, seeing the power of psychoanalysis in its ability to make the individual freer through the recognition of repressed content.[72] This misconception is characteristic of the second generation of the Frankfurt School. A key role here is played by the levelling of language, which Apel, Habermas and Lorenzer define as communication and not as the articulation of a demand or desire that is always directed at or uttered by an Other. The whole of communication studies in the German-speaking world has never really managed to move beyond Habermas, and it has completely ignored the whole French phase of the post-structural debate.

Since the beginning of the nineteenth century, the history of the analysis of the apparatus of human perception, which has always included the question of the origins and function of consciousness, has developed in two directions: one follows a biological foundation, while the other attempts to define *perception* and *consciousness* as symbolic. In the early decades of the nineteenth century, the German physiologist Johannes Müller proved that perception is completely subjective because it is grounded in the body. He also described the relationship between signal (stimulus) and reaction (sensation) as arbitrary, as a not necessarily causal chain.[73] At the end of the century, Freud was to present his "psychical apparatus", describing it initially in terms of optical instruments. He soon abandoned this optical metaphor and concentrated on "memory traces". At the same time, Bergson was developing his theory of *Matter and Memory*, in which the affective body forms the centre of the processes of perception and memory. Today, following its rediscovery by Deleuze, Bergson's theory has made a comeback, especially in discussions of digital art and media philosophy.

TRAVERSING THE SUBJECT

At the beginning of the 1980s, the figure of the cyborg[74] was introduced into academic discourse by Donna Haraway as a deliberate break with a school of thought in which, as she saw it, the subject (even if conceived of as being structured by symbolic orders) still possessed a "quasi-transcendental" dimension.[75] This quasi-transcendental aspect, based on the self-referentiality of the human being while describing this self as nonidentical, is cast off by Haraway and others, primarily with reference to Deleuze.[76] Having revived Spinoza's concept of immanence, Deleuze rejects the transcendental as metaphysical in an attempt to eschew the dichotomy of mind and matter. But the Deleuzian nomadic subject, too, features an a-human aspect as a constitutive moment. It is not a posthuman but a machinic moment that is separated from the subject, as the vanishing lines developed by Deleuze and Guattari always already exceed the limitation of the individual, referring explicitly to an a-personal flux. Ignoring this, Haraway discarded it as a last remnant of metaphysics. Haraway's cyborg coincides entirely with the surface of the body, lacking any depth, spiritual or otherwise.

Besides Haraway, it was above all N. Katherine Hayles who undertook a comparison between a psychoanalytical version of the subject, corresponding to the medium of the book as belonging profoundly to modernism/modernity, and its posthuman counterpart. Hayles borrows Haraway's modern/postmodern distinction, replacing *postmodern* with *posthuman*. Lacan, she writes, still speaks of "floating signifiers", but in the digital world these have long since been superseded by "flickering signifiers". Whereas the former derive their value from their different relations (in the Saussurian sense), making them comparable with Freud's "fort-da game",[77] the "flickering signifiers" play with "pattern/randomness" and are subject to the movement of mutation. What castration was to modernity, mutation is to the posthuman age, whose basis is "computation". Consequently, she continues, to perceive the radical difference between a modern yesterday and the posthuman today, it is necessary to compare Freud's "fort-da game" with David Cronenberg's film *The Fly* (1976). At the moment when, during his process of transformation, the main character's penis falls off, he experiences this not as a castration but as becoming posthuman.[78] But might this description by Hayles not be read as a Freudian slip by the author? That the loss of his penis, of all things, signals his transition to a posthuman existence? Does that mean that the posthuman age, too, begins with castration as a symbolic cut, as a prerequisite for the emergence of a new subject?

The tale of *Robinson Crusoe* as retold by Michel Tournier offers a striking illustration of this transformation. Returning to Daniel Defoe's story from 1719, Tournier gives it an entirely different character; in spite of the parallels between *Friday or The Other Island*[79] and the original, there are crucial differences. Tournier attempts to describe Robinson's humanity, portraying its gradual breakdown as a process of decomposition, as a metamorphosis in the course of which the erasure of the difference between man and nature is accompanied by the erasure of sexual difference. After Robinson fails in an attempt to have sexual intercourse with a tree trunk, and after the arrival of Friday, who comes too late for Robinson, he becomes the "bride of heaven", the bride of his island Esperanza:

> He felt as never before that he was lying on Esperanza as on a living being, that the island's body was beneath him. Never before had he felt this with so much intensity. [. . .] The almost carnal pressure of the island against his flesh warmed and excited him. She was naked, this earth that enveloped him, and he stripped off his own clothes. Lying with arms outstretched and a stirring in his loins, he embraced that great body burned all day by the sun. [. . .] How closely and how wisely were life and death intermingled at this elemental level! His sex burrowed like a ploughshare into the earth and overflowed in immense compassion for all created things. [. . .] He lay exhausted, the man who had married the earth.[80]

Over time, Robinson stops feeling like a man, he becomes a women and then, as a further step, he becomes like the animals and plants of the island. Tournier's *Friday* paints a striking picture of what Deleuze and Guattari describe as a process of deterritorialization, becoming-animal, the body without organs, and overcoming the difference between nature and culture.

Haraway and Hayles have long since bid farewell to the subject, banishing it to the modern age. All of this signals a breaking open of the old Logoi, and new ones are already emerging from this upheaval. The focus is now on the question of the separation of human and nonhuman, even at the risk of losing specific segregations within the human itself.

Slavoj Žižek has named three levels on which this inner segregation shows itself as an ontological difference constituting the human: First, in the nonaccessible, excessive gap between nature and culture that marks the "zero-level of humanity" as a "vanishing mediator"; then, in the real of antagonism, the moment that precedes the difference that it introduces; and finally, in a minimal difference that consists of the fact that the subject is never full, never capable of completely filling the gap (with himself); "man is a lack which, in order to fill itself in, recognizes itself as something."[81]

Language, sexuality and the unconscious are the three dimensions that articulate themselves in this ontological difference. Their interaction, the way they constitute each other, is attacked, rejected and, ultimately, wiped out by the *desire for affect*.

The "sex sells" culture of the online world and television may appear to champion a hedonistic society, but this superficial impression is soon dispelled. Instead, cybersex must be read as a sign of a collapsing subject. Many years ago, Žižek warned of the "information anorexia"[82] that develops as a reaction when, rather than receiving answers to its demands, the subject is stuffed with food. The only way to uphold the difference between need and demand consists in closing one's mouth.[83] Anyone logging on in search of erotic content and sex is offered thousands of similar images of men and women, inevitably annulling desire or rendering it ironic. Freud's concept of the sexual as a drive, perpetuated in Lacan's concept of desire, has now been replaced by the evidence of neurons, genes and hormones. These, too, function via the exchange of information, but the added value of the linguistic dimension of the sexual, and with it that of desire, has fallen by the wayside.

NOTES

1. Edward Regis, *Great Mambo Chicken and the Transhuman Condition: Science Slightly over the Edge* (Harmondsworth, UK: Penguin, 1992), 175.
2. Michel Foucault, *On the Government of the Living: Lectures at the Collège de France, 1979–1980* (Basingstoke, UK: Palgrave Macmillan, 2014); and Ulrich Bröckling, Susanne Krasmann, and Thomas Lemke (eds.), *Governmentality: Current Issues and Future Challenges* (London: Routledge, 2011).
3. Michel Foucault, *The Order of Things: An Archaeology of the Human Sciences* (New York: Routledge, 2005), 421–22.
4. Ibid.
5. Ibid., 373.
6. Sigmund Freud, "The Dissection of the Psychical Personality" (1933), in Sigmund Freud, *New Introductory Lectures on Psycho-Analysis* (New York: Norton, 1989), 71–100, here 100.
7. "Réceptivité de l'espace-temps, spontanéité du 'Je pense'. Enfin l'homme devient difforme; difforme au sens étymologique du mot, c'est-à-dire dis-forme, il claudique sur deux formes hétérogènes et non symétriques: réceptivité de l'intuition et spontanéité du 'je pense.'" [Gilles Deleuze, "Les cours de Gilles Deleuze": Cours Vincennes—St Denis: Leibniz (Foucault—Blanchot—Cinéma) 01/00/1982." (trans. NG), http://www.webdeleuze.com/php/texte.php?cle=77&groupe=Image%20Mouvement%20Image%20Temps&langue=1 (retrieved 22 May 2014)].
8. "Le 'je pense'—spontanéité—détermine mon existence, mais mon existence n'est déterminable que comme celle d'un être réceptif. Dés lors, moi, être réceptif, je me représente ma spontanéité comme l'opération d'un autre sur moi, et cet autre c'est 'Je.' Qu'est ce que fait Kant? Là où Descartes voyait deux termes et une forme, lui il voit trois termes et deux formes. Trois termes: la détermination, l'indéterminé et le déterminable. Deux formes: la forme du déterminable et la forme de la détermination, c'est-à-dire l'intuition, l'espace-temps, et le: 'je pense.' La réceptivité et la spontanéité." [(trans. NG), ibid].
9. Foucault, *Order of Things*, 305.
10. See Martin Heidegger, "Letter on 'Humanism'" (1949), in William McNeill (ed.), *Martin Heidegger: Pathmarks* (Cambridge, MA: Cambridge University Press, 1998), 239–76, here 246.
11. Peter Sloterdijk, "Rules for the Human Zoo: A Response to the Letter on Humanism", *Society and Space*, 27 (2009), 12–28.
12. In chapter 6 I return to this clearing, where, according to Bruno Latour, the existence of humankind is transformed into a question of design.
13. Sloterdijk, "Rules for the Human Zoo", 20 (translation modified).
14. See Peter Sloterdijk, *Bubbles: Spheres Vol. 1: Microspherology* (Los Angeles: Semiotext(e), 2011), 533.
15. Sloterdijk, "Rules for the Human Zoo", 23.
16. From this point on, not before, Sloterdijk chose a different path. Although he, too, points to neoteny and the human infant's long dependency as the central fact defining the specific essence of the human, he locates the beginning of this neoteny and the beginning of audiovisual life in the womb. He thus criticizes Lacan's theory of the mirror phase for completely misjudging the image

and overrating the mother-child dyad. The image cannot give the infant its "self-image", Sloterdijk argues; instead, this image must have already been defined by tactile and sensory input. See Sloterdijk, *Bubbles*, 533f.

17. Giorgio Agamben, *Homo Sacer: Sovereign Power and Bare Life* (Stanford, CA: Stanford University Press, 1998).

18. Michel Foucault, *The History of Sexuality, Vol. 1: The Will to Knowledge* (1976) (London: Penguin, 1998).

19. On the imperative to enjoy, see Slavoj Žižek, *Enjoy Your Symptom! Jacques Lacan in Hollywood and Out* (New York: Routledge, 2001); and Paul Verhaeghe, *Love in a Time of Loneliness: Three Essays on Drive and Desire* (New York: Other Press, 1999).

20. This "obscene" underside, the excluded but always constitutive element of a democracy, a universality, a state, a theory, and so on, is a theme found in many works by Slavoj Žižek. See especially Slavoj Žižek, "Class Struggle or Postmodernism? Yes, Please!" in Judith Butler, Ernesto Laclau, and Slavoj Žižek, *Contingency, Hegemony, Universality* (London: Verso, 2000), 90–135.

21. Agamben, *Homo Sacer*, 8.

22. Foucault, *Order of Things*, 397.

23. Ibid.

24. Paul Rabinow, *Essays on the Anthropology of Reason* (Princeton, NJ: Princeton University Press, 1996), 98.

25. Ibid., 99. This "biosociality" corresponds with the "biomediated body" discussed in chapter 6.

26. Donna J. Haraway, "A Cyborg Manifesto: Science, Technology, and Socialist-Feminism in the Late Twentieth Century" (1983) in Donna J. Haraway, *Simians, Cyborgs, and Women: The Reinvention of Nature* (New York: Routledge, 1991), 149–81.

27. Heidegger, "Letter on 'Humanism,'" 254.

28. Ferdinand de Saussure, *Course in General Linguistics* (1916) (Glasgow,UK: Fontana/Collins, 1977).

29. According to Judith Butler, rather than being innate features, gender identities are produced via the constant repetition of norms and sets of norms. Rather than gender being expressed or displayed by gestures, behaviour, or language, then, the performativity of gender retrospectively produces the illusion of a core of gender identity. See Judith Butler, *Gender Trouble: Feminism and the Subversion of Identity* (New York: Routledge, 1999); and Judith Butler, *The Psychic Life of Power: Theories in Subjection* (Stanford, CA: Stanford University Press, 1997).

30. Slavoj Žižek, *The Ticklish Subject* (London: Verso, 2000), 157.

31. Jean-François Lyotard, *The Postmodern Condition: A Report on Knowledge* (Minneapolis: University of Minnesota Press, 1984).

32. An allusion to Samuel Weber's *Return to Freud: Jacques Lacan's Dislocation of Psychoanalysis* (Cambridge, UK: Cambridge University Press, 1991) and to Lacan's own title, "The Freudian Thing, or the Meaning of the Return to Freud in Psychoanalysis" (1955) in Jacques Lacan, *Écrits: The First Complete Edition in English* (New York: Norton, 2006), 334–63.

33. See Heinz von Foerster, *Short Cuts 5* (Frankfurt, Germany: Zweitausendeins, 2001), 114f.

34. See John Searle, *Intentionality: An Essay in the Philosophy of Mind* (Cambridge, UK: Cambridge University Press, 1983).

35. See Jacques Derrida, "Signature Event Context", in Jacques Derrida, *Limited Inc.* (Evanston, IL: Northwestern University Press, 1977), 1–21; and Uwe Wirth (ed.), *Performanz* (Frankfurt, Germany: Suhrkamp, 2002), 17f.

36. The concept of articulation is used by Marx in *Capital* and is adopted in the 1960s by Althusser (and later Balibar, Macherey, Rancière, etc.). In the late 1970s, Ernesto Laclau introduced it into his theoretical concept for the discussion of a new Marxist understanding of politics. Via this route, the concept also found its way into cultural studies, especially in the work of Stuart Hall, who deployed it against a reductionist understanding of class in Marxist debate. See Marie-Luise Angerer, *Body Options: Körper.Spuren.Medien.Bilder* (Vienna: Turia & Kant, 1999), 106–9.

37. See Ernesto Laclau, "Subject of Politics, Politics of the Subject", in Ernesto Laclau, *Emancipation(s)* (London: Verso, 1996), 47–65, here 52–53.

38. Stuart Hall, "On Postmodernism and Articulation: An Interview with Stuart Hall", in David Morley and Kuan-Hsing Chen (eds.), *Stuart Hall* (London: Routledge, 1996), 131–50, here 141.
39. See Stanley Aronowitz, "Technology and the Future of Work", in Gretchen Bender and Timothy Druckrey (eds.), *Culture on the Brink: Ideologies of Technology* (Seattle: New Press, 1998), 15–30.
40. Sherry Turkle, *The Second Self: Computers and the Human Spirit* (Cambridge, MA: MIT Press, 1984).
41. Sherry Turkle, *Life on the Screen: Identity in the Age of the Internet* (New York: Simon & Schuster, 1995), 15.
42. Turkle equates Butler's "doing gender" with gender swapping. Today, Turkle has changed her mind about the freedom of the Internet dramatically. In *Alone Together* she no longer speaks about freedom of choice but of the cruelty of alienated communication. See Sherry Turkle, *Alone Together: Why We Expect More from Technology and Less from Each Other* (New York: Basic Books, 2011).
43. Jacques Lacan, *The Four Fundamental Concepts of Psychoanalysis: The Seminar XI* (New York: Norton, 1998), 211.
44. Gilles Deleuze and Félix Guattari, *Anti-Oedipus: Capitalism and Schizophrenia* (1972) (Minneapolis: University of Minnesota Press, 1983).
45. Gilles Deleuze and Félix Guattari, *A Thousand Plateaus: Capitalism and Schizophrenia* (1980) (Minneapolis: University of Minnesota Press, 1987).
46. This alludes to the concept of the "body without organs" that stands in the philosophy of Deleuze and Guattari for a subversion of the organized, coopted, classified body. See Deleuze and Guattari, *Thousand Plateaus,* 149f.
47. Ibid., 547.
48. Ibid., 458.
49. Ibid.
50. See ibid.
51. See ibid., 89.
52. von Foerster, *Short Cuts 5*, 116.
53. Stanisław Lem, "Golem IV", in Stanisław Lem, *Imaginary Magnitude* (San Diego: Harvest, 1985).
54. Marge Piercy, *He, She and It* (New York: Random House, 1991).
55. As Frank Pasemann explained to me (in 2006, as director of the Intelligent Dynamics research group at the Fraunhofer Institute for Autonomous Intelligent Systems), such motivation in machines can only be achieved via a "lack": If a machine is constantly updated about its energy supply status, and if this level sinks, creating hunger, the machine sets itself in motion in order to overcome this imbalance. First, then, machines must be informed about "themselves."
56. Quoted in N. Katherine Hayles, *How We Became Posthuman: Virtual Bodies in Cybernetics, Literature, and Informatics* (Chicago: University of Chicago Press, 1999), 56.
57. See Mark B. N. Hansen, *New Philosophy for New Media* (Cambridge, MA: MIT Press, 2004), 78.
58. Hayles, *How We Became Posthuman*, 56.
59. Hansen, *New Philosophy*, 78f.
60. Henri Bergson, *Matter and Memory* (New York: Cosimo, 2007), 4f.
61. Claus Pias (ed.), *Cybernetics/Kybernetik, The Macy Conferences 1946–1953, Essays & Dokumente, Vol. 1* (Zurich, Switzerland: diaphanes, 2003), 312.
62. In chapter 6, we see how the "unconscious" turns into an "affective nonconscious."
63. Pias (ed.), *Cybernetics/Kybernetik*, 316.
64. This view was extremely popular in the 1970s and '80s in applied communications theory and in Ronald D. Laing's studies of schizophrenia.
65. Humberto Maturana and Francisco Varela, *Autopoiesis and Cognition: The Realization of the Living* (Dordrecht, Netherlands: Reidel, 1980).
66. Quoted from Hayles, *How We Became Posthuman*, 136.
67. Antti Revonsuo, *Inner Presence: Consciousness as a Biological Phenomenon* (Cambridge, MA: MIT Press, 2006), xvi.
68. See ibid., xvii.
69. See John R. Searle, *The Rediscovery of the Mind* (Boston: MIT Press, 1992); and John R. Searle, *Freedom and Neurobiology* (New York: Columbia University Press, 2007).

70. Sigmund Freud, "Project for a Scientific Psychology" (1895), in *The Standard Edition of the Complete Psychological Works of Sigmund Freud, Vol. 1* (London: Hogarth Press, 1950), 281–391.

71. Jürgen Habermas, *Knowledge and Human Interests* (London: Polity, 1987).

72. Alfred Lorenzer, *Die Wahrheit der psychoanalytischen Erkenntnis. Ein historisch-materialistischer Entwurf* (Frankfurt, Germany: Suhrkamp, 1976).

73. See Jonathan Crary, *Techniques of the Observer: On Vision and Modernity in the Nineteenth Century* (Cambridge, MA: MIT Press, 1992), 93–96; and Bernd Stiegler, *Theoriegeschichte der Photographie* (Munich,Germany: Wilhelm Fink, 2006), 72–86.

74. Haraway's cyborg is female, a girl who rejects all forms of traditional femininity.

75. The *quasi-transcendental,* a term Derrida borrowed from Rodolphe Gasché, names the "conditions of the possibility of a phenomenon", which are always simultaneously the "conditions of the impossibility of its purity." The specific I is transcended only by the ideality of the sign "I" by which it is spoken. See Geoffrey Bennington and Jacques Derrida, *Jacques Derrida* (Chicago: University of Chicago Press, 1993), 276–77.

76. In her "Cyborg Manifesto", Haraway draws a clear distinction between modern and postmodern. In her view, the unconscious belongs to the modern age, a period during which subjects were subdued by means of control, punishment, and confession. In the postmodern age, conformity and subjugation work in more subtle ways. The old methods have been replaced by strategies of normalization and naturalization, rendering an institution like psychoanalysis superfluous, for psychoanalysis constantly forces subjects back into an old corset, leaving them inadequately equipped for the postmodern age. See Haraway, "Cyborg Manifesto", 48f. Hayles also touches on this when she describes the posthuman age as one where control and subjugation are no longer necessary, an age when a positive approach to oneself and one's body is in fashion. In her view, anorexia and other pathological eating disorders are typical modern ailments that can now be viewed as anachronistic. See Hayles, *How We Became Posthuman*, 5. See also Marie-Luise Angerer, "Cybertroubles: The Question of the Subject in Cyberfeminism", in Claudia Reiche and Verena Kuni (eds.), *Cyberfeminism: Next Protocols* (New York: Autonomedia, 2002), 18–31.

77. Freud observed his grandson, who, once his mother was out of the room, threw a wooden reel with a piece of string attached out of his cot and then—with a different sound—pulled it back and made it reappear. Using this game, Freud tries to explain how the infant learns to "symbolically" compensate for his mother's absence and integrates this experience into his own world (of linguistic differences). See Sigmund Freud, "Beyond the Pleasure Principle" (1920) in *The Standard Edition of the Complete Psychological Works of Sigmund Freud, Vol. 18* (London: Hogarth Press, 1955), 7–66, here 14–16.

78. See Hayles, *How We Became Posthuman*, 30–34.

79. Michel Tournier, *Friday or The Other Island* (1967) (London: Penguin, 1984).

80. Ibid., 103f.

81. See Slavoj Žižek, *The Parallax View* (Cambridge, MA: MIT Press, 2006), 44.

82. See Slavoj Žižek, *The Plague of Fantasies* (London: Verso, 1997).

83. Charles Shepherdson, "The Gift of Love and the Debt of Desire", *Differences* 10 (1998), 66.

THREE

Affect Versus Drive, or the Battle over Representation

So far we have examined the developing shifts in thinking the human in order to broadly outline the current focus on affect, but without actually analysing affect itself. Situating today's resurgence of affect and emotion within a theoretical arc, allowing us to look both backward and forward, this chapter explores the main fields involved in the discussion. Psychoanalysis in particular is now being accused of having ignored the affects in favour of language and the symbolic order. Rather than shedding new light on historical facts, however, these accusations seem to be aimed more at discrediting the "psychoanalytical subject" as such, as there is now a clear preference for a version of the human that makes no mention of ontological difference. Instead, today's affect theory posits an unclouded, unbroken relationship between the human being and its environment.

THE BODY AS INTERFACE

> The perceiving subject stands with his body in a torrent of external images that envelop him in a network of solidarity, at whose centre he finds himself.[1]

Henri Bergson is an essential part of any discussion of the difference or nondifference between external and inner reality and of reality as image. Although they were contemporaries, Bergson and Freud never met, but their theories on humor, jokes, laughter and dreams display many similarities and affinities. Both began in the last third of the nineteenth century to address the question of how reality is grasped by the individual, what impact it makes, what happens to it over time and how it becomes inscribed in memory via repetition and forgetting. One year after Freud's *Project for a Scientific Psychology* (1895), Bergson presented his theory of the relation between mind and body in *Matter and Memory*.

As Bergson states, "*My body* is that which stands out as the centre of these perceptions; *my personality* is the being to which these actions must be referred."[2] According to Bergson, it is this body that processes perception like a filter, sorting the relevant aspects out of any given totality of potential perceptions; "my body, then, acts like an image which reflects others, and which, in so doing, analyses them along lines corresponding to the different actions which it can exercise upon them. [. . .] Conscious perception signifies choice, and consciousness mainly consists in this practical discernment."[3]

But on the question of consciousness, Freud and Bergson went in totally different directions. Freud felt obliged to introduce a consciousness as a "system within a system", whereas Bergson centered his thinking on a theory of the affective body as mediator. Both men, the future psychoanalyst and the philosopher, assume the existence of sensations, stimuli that travel via nerve paths to the brain, where they trigger responses. In his *Interpretation of Dreams*,[4] a continuation of the "Project", Freud defines *perception* and *memory* as differences of facilitations and engrams. Bergson names the affective body as the center of the universe of images, an affective body that, as Mark Hansen writes, not so much sees as feels, producing an affective response that connects the body to its environment.

In the 1950s, when Jacques Lacan began focusing on the question of the ego's relation to the object world, the "Project" provided a key basis and point of orientation for his rewriting of Freud. "Following the path of the eighteenth-century philosophers", Lacan writes, "and like every one else at the time, Freud reconstructs everything, memory, judgement etc., starting off from sensation, and only stopping for one moment in the quest for the object in itself." But, he continues, "he finds himself returning to the primary process in so far as it concerns sleep and dreams. And this is how even this mechanical reconstruction of reality leads to the dream."[5] However, as Lacan further explains, Freud's conception of memory "as a succession of engrams, as the sum of a series of facilitations" proves inadequate

> if we don't introduce the notion of the image into it. If one assumes that a series of facilitations, a succession of experiences, brings into existence an image in a psychic apparatus conceived of as a simple sensitive sheet, it goes without saying that as soon

> as the same series is reactivated by a new excitation, pressure or need, the same image is reproduced. In other words, all stimuli tend to produce hallucinations.[6]

As Lacan explains, this has to do with the precarious status of the system of consciousness, introduced by Freud as a buffer system, a system within the system, to balance out reality and ego. For a long time, Freud's system of perception does perfectly well without consciousness. But then he introduces it in a paradoxical form, as a system possessing very unusual rules. Again and again in Freud's work, Lacan claims, the same difficulty arises: "One doesn't know what to do with the system of consciousness." Moreover, its introduction takes an interesting turn, as "any kind of construction of the object world is always an attempt to rediscover the object, *Wiederzufinden*".[7] Freud, then, posits an individual that finds itself confronted with a reality that constantly makes demands or that constantly puts it in states that upset its balance. The key thing, however—and this sets Freud apart from all other theories of affect—is that this relation always already presupposes a "narcissistic relation of the ego to the other". This, as Lacan explains, is in fact the "primary condition for any objectification of the external world—of naive, spontaneous objectification no less than that of scientific objectification".[8]

Even if Freud does not associate this consciousness with language, he does (beginning with *The Interpretation of Dreams*) define language in its relationship to the unconscious. In language, the id condenses, transposes, represses and negates itself. It is through language that the subject experiences its Other as the Real.

Bergson, on the other hand, repeatedly criticized language, accusing it of distorting reality and of not being able to do justice to the processual quality of experience. What Wittgenstein simply took as a given, that language cannot say everything,[9] Bergson interpreted as detrimental, concentrating instead on affect and the image.[10] The image in Bergson is not an image in the ordinary sense, not a representation, but more a presentation between imagination and object. This image is distinct both from representation and from a feeling that comes from within.[11]

This should be compared with Freud's distinction between word- and thing-presentation that plays a major role with regard to repression (of affect). Whereas for Bergson, feelings and ideas coincide in an image, Freud distinguishes clearly between soma and its representation, defining the drive as something that can only be grasped via representatives, not in and of itself. The concept of the ideational representative is introduced by Freud in order to position the "ideational as opposed to the affective".[12] According to Freud, repression can only apply to a representative but not to affect. I will return to this in more detail later in my remarks on the dispute between psychoanalysis and theories of affect.

Freud places the drive as a transitional concept at the threshold between soma and psyche. Bergson casts the body as the site where inner sensations and external images meet. This body is not passively receptive but a "centre of action" that selects those images that are relevant for possible actions.[13] In this model, the body acts as a body memory produced via repeated movements. This means that the body not only selects the images of reality but also simplifies this selection procedure by means of patterns of action inscribed in body memory.[14] Bergson himself speaks of the image as a "photographic plate", a comparison that recalls Freud's equation of the psychical apparatus with the medium of photography. According to Bergson, an image is the result of contrast, selection and simplification.[15] Freud, on the other hand, soon abandoned the image-making metaphor of photography, switching to the concept of traces, which he understood not as affective grooves but as inscriptions in the sense of an engraved mark. In this way, he began to frame the essence of memory as difference. Jacques Derrida summed up this shift as follows: "It is the difference between breaches [facilitations] which is the true origin of memory, and thus of psyche."[16] The work of breaching (facilitation) concerns "not only forces but also locations".[17]

In the mid-1990s, Brian Massumi, one of today's most prominent theorists of affect, stressed the need for a cultural theory of affect. Perhaps anticipating the extent to which affect would become anchored in neurobiology in the years to come, his first attempts at defining *affect* drew on various sources. He speaks of traces engraved in the body—affect traces. They lie dormant, so to speak, ready to be actualized by the body at any time. This also reflects the legacy of Bergson (patterns of body memory), but when Massumi speaks of traces, he does not mean Freud's memory traces, arriving instead, with the help of Spinoza, at a definition of *traces* as unfolding contexts: "The *trace* of past actions *including a trace of their contexts* [is] conserved in the brain and in the flesh, but out of mind and out of the body understood as qualifiable interiorities, [. . .] past actions and contexts [are] conserved and repeated, autonomically reactivated, but not accomplished; begun, but not completed."[18] According to this definition, affect is pure intensity belonging to a different order: "Intensity is embodied in purely autonomic reactions most directly manifested in the skin—at the surface of the body, at its interface with things."[19] This also shows the first difference between the approaches of Massumi and Hansen, that is, the difference between a Bergsonian analysis of memory and subjectivity and a conception (indebted to Spinoza and Deleuze) of affect as an autonomous, a-human zone of the body in which the body appears "without image".[20]

When Deleuze describes perception and memory as intrinsically different, he cuts Bergson's theory in two. While perception on the side of matter unfolds a-personally, memory marks the terrain of the mind, creating a subjectivity in which affectivity, pure memory (*mémoire souvenir*), and habitual memory (*mémoire habitude*) coexist. Perception and memory constantly intermingle before meeting at a virtual point.[21] Affectivity, then, is always also subjectivized because memory is always already intervening in perception. Hansen, too, notes that this may not do justice to digital experience, prompting him to turn to Massumi and his "autonomy of affect", as a hole in time, pointing to the specific "timing of affect". In spite of the new aspects that Massumi introduces into the discussion, the line of his argument can be traced back historically to the theories of perception whose common denominator consists in noting a specific time delay in perception.[22]

In the 1970s, a research team led by Hertha Sturm discovered a measurable delay in the reactions of television viewers (especially children), which they called the "missing half-second".[23] At the time, Sturm's work remained unknown to a broader audience, with only the emerging discipline of media education (rather conservative in orientation) briefly using her results. From the missing half-second, Sturm and her colleagues concluded that television footage needed to slow down and that news programs should take great care in selecting image material for each item in order to be properly understood by viewers. As their empirical studies showed, there is a time lapse between perception and consciousness, and television must close this divide if it is to be understood.

In a Deleuzian twist, Massumi defines this "divide" as a positive event, seeing not a lack but a superabundance in which too much takes place: "Pastnesses opening onto a future, but with no present to speak of. For the present is lost with the missing half-second, passing too quickly to be perceived, too quickly, actually, to have happened."[24] In his version of affect, Spinoza and Bergson meet. For Spinoza, body and mind are different orders of the same extent; rather than being opposites, they are different arrangements of motion and rest, each thing defines itself by its length and breadth, by its longitude and latitude. The length of a body here refers to ratios of rapidity and slowness, of rest and motion between its particles, and its width comprises the sum of its affects, all of its intensive states.[25] Bergson's theory of virtuality and movement corresponds to this. According to Bergson, the whole of reality is continuity in motion (which language is unable to grasp), and each instance of perception means stasis. Even if the two positions approach action and the activity of perception from different angles, both focus on the body's own movement—in time. For Bergson, a view of the world emerges from the movements of the body, and according to Spinoza, there is an activity in the sense of a potentiality (*conatus*) that can be understood as an agent. While for Bergson the body selects the visual universe by contracting and simplifying it, for Spinoza varying degrees of intensity are responsible for the different affections of *potentia*. This potentiality is a force that fundamentally affirms existence. A death drive of the kind introduced by Freud would be inconceivable and unacceptable for Spinoza's philosophy and for Bergson (and hence also for Deleuze).

In these definitions of the body and affect, the focus is on time and duration and on their momentary suspension. Besides time, movement (of the body) is the key to affectivity. External stimuli and proprioception act upon the skin to prompt various levels of motor response. Whereas Deleuze defines "man's non-human becomings"[26] as affect, Massumi defines affect as asocial, causing it to become both a kind of untouchable zone and something that builds the basis for the entire universe, for without this elusiveness, the universe would be pure entropy; it would, Massumi stresses, be dead because living forms exist only via that which escapes: "Their autonomy is the autonomy of affect."[27] This means that affect as an autonomous zone forms the basis for the whole. It is, so to speak, the "outside" that renders the entire system possible. Transposed onto media, this "outside zone" of affect gives rise to a new way of reading digital space.

In his writings on cinema, Deleuze detaches affect from the viewer, depersonalizing it and assigning it to the movement-image, rendering the viewer's body into an image in the Bergsonian sense. What Deleuze developed for the "any-space-whatever"[28] of the cinema, Mark Hansen transfers to digital art spaces, claiming that they are no longer in any way connected to any kind of human activity. Their singularity and their potential are autonomous, neither comprehensible to nor occupiable by humans. Whereas in the cinema, affect appears as a formal correlate, in digital space affect means a "bodily *supplement,* a response to a digital stimulus that remains fundamentally heterogeneous to human perceptual (visual) capacities. In sum, affection becomes affectivity."[29] Tactility (haptic, tactile space), thus, has entirely different meanings in the cinema and in digitally generated space. As Hansen makes clear from the outset, this is due to the new status of the affective body. Digital space is only tactile "because it catalyzes a nonvisual mode of experience that *takes place* in the body of the spectator, and indeed, as the production of place within the body".[30] For Massumi, whom Hansen quotes on this point, the fascination of affect consists in its radical openness: rather than restricting itself to the limitations of a given body, affect inscribes itself into the body as an autonomous zone in order to go beyond the body. Several criticisms of Massumi and Hansen can be raised here, but first I would like to introduce a second group of affect theories that refer to psychology and cybernetic systems theory and that are currently popular, especially in Anglo-American media and cultural studies.

AFFECT VERSUS DRIVE

In her essay "Invoking Affect",[31] Clare Hemmings expresses her unease concerning the affective self-embrace of cultural and media studies. She lays most of the blame on Brian Massumi and Eve Kosofsky Sedgwick for what she calls an "ontological turn" that totally calls into question the legitimacy of the theoretical developments of recent decades. In Hemmings's view, Massumi's declaration of "autonomous affect" is more than disconcerting, and Eve Kosofsky Sedgwick, a theorist of the political repression of forms of sexuality,[32] produces precisely the thing she formerly criticized: in her call to adopt the affect theory of Silvan Tomkins, those who do not (or cannot) follow her are excluded from the community of theorists of affect.

With her discovery of Tomkins's theory of affect, Kosofsky Sedgwick chose an entirely new theoretical direction, a psychology of affects from the 1960s that flirts with the cybernetic notion of self-regulation. To make Hemmings's accusations understandable, however, a brief description of Tomkins's affect theory is needed. In their reader titled *Shame and Its Sisters*[33] Kosofsky Sedgwick and Adam Frank present the work of Silvan Tomkins to a broader audience for the first time. In 2003, this was followed by *Touching Feeling: Affect, Pedagogy, Performativity*,[34] in which Kosofsky Sedgwick also includes a section on Tomkins's key ideas.

Tomkins's model is based on a system of pairs: The positive affects are interest/excitement and joy/enjoyment; the neutral affects are surprise/startle; and the negative affects are distress/anguish, fear/terror, anger/rage, disgust/dismell and above all shame/humiliation.[35] The latter is understood by Tomkins as the central affect.[36] What Tomkins lists here as *affect* is referred to elsewhere as *emotion* or *feeling*. This must be stressed, as these terms are used carelessly in the literature and the various schools of cognitive emotional psychology and neurobiology propose very diverse categorizations and models for affect, emotion and feeling.

Tomkins developed his work in the 1950s and '60s at Princeton. He broke off his own psychoanalytical treatment and was familiar with the ideas of Jacques Lacan. Subsequently, Tomkins developed his affect theory as explicitly distinct from psychoanalysis because he considered (a) that the system of drives it worked with was too small to act as an all-encompassing model[37] and (b) that it had ignored shame as the key affect. Within his model, the affects constitute the human's primary system of motivation, with the Freudian system of drives as a smaller subsystem.[38] The central affect within the basic group is shame, which structures the entire psychophysical organism and develops as a fundamental component by the repression of interest. Tomkins defined his affects on the basis of systems theory, which was very popular at the time. In his model, the affects stand in a dichotomous relationship to one another: Depending on its intensity, neural stimulation causes the affective situation to swing into plus or minus. Shame is closely linked to visibility, especially the face (and its powers of expression). As Tomkins writes, "Man is, of all animals, the most voyeuristic. He is more dependent on his visual sense than most animals, and his visual sense contributes more information than any of his senses."[39] At the same time, however, he notes a taboo on looking into each other's eyes: "The universal taboo on mutual looking is based not only on shame but on the entire spectrum of affects."[40] If we compare this with Freud's remarks on scopophilia and exhibitionism, there are major similarities, as Freud also takes the profoundly cultural dimension of these drives for granted. According to the Freudian model, the childish pleasure in looking and showing changes in the course of the individual's development due to the obstacle presented by feelings of shame.[41] But Tomkins is unable to convincingly explain why shame should occupy such a central position: "Insofar as any human being is excited by or enjoys his work, other human beings, his body, his self and the intimate world around him, he is vulnerable to the variety of vicissitudes in the form of barriers, lacks, losses and accidents, which will impoverish, attenuate, impair or otherwise prevent total pursuit and enjoyment."[42]

Tomkins accuses Freud of having defined the human instinct of self-preservation in purely biological terms. He, on the other hand, links food intake from the outset with the affects of joy and excitement. One need hardly mention that both Freud and Lacan repeatedly and unequivocally stated that the oral drive can only be understood as a biological need in part and that demand and desire are at play from the outset. Freud set his concept of libido apart from other psychical energies, precisely in order to make clear that sexual drive and hunger do not operate on the same level.[43]

Tomkins and his followers also feel obliged to introduce their own theory of sexuality. Donald Nathanson, founding director of the Tomkins Institute, explains this move by referring to the mutual influence of drive and affect that characterizes any psychobiological system. Affects act as amplifiers—good moods get better, bad ones worse. Nathanson illustrates this using the example of the increase in sexual arousal to orgasm:

> The more we are excited by this arousal, the more we become aroused. The addition of positive affect makes the thrilling irritation of arousal into something even more pleasant; the increase in arousal produced by further stimulation of the affected areas triggers even more excitement, leading to even more arousal until the arousal is terminated by orgasm, its genetically programmed terminal analogic amplification. Orgasm is cherished all the more because it triggers the affect enjoyment/joy, which is pleasant in direct proportion to the amount of stimulus it reduces and the rapidity with which that stimulus is decreased.[44]

Nathanson must admit, however, that certain things are more complicated in humans than in animals. With the development of a memory that allows affects to form complex "ideo-affective linkages", the ongoing evolution of man has led the "nature of sexual emotionality" to make the human species shy with regard to "generative play".[45] Even if Freud's explanations are more differentiated in cultural and historical terms, his version of the amplification of drives is quite similar. His basic drives, the life drive and the death drive, also attract or repulse each other, constantly forming aggregates. In this way, with the addition of sexual aggression, a lover can become a rapist and a killer.[46]

In their introduction to Tomkins's work, Kosofsky Sedgwick and Frank stress the narrowness of Freud's concept of the drives and the potential benefits of Tomkins's system of affects for the humanities, for the affects are viewed by Tomkins in terms of freedom, and he uses the cybernetic metaphor of a complex system to show the different levels with their specific degrees of freedom. According to this model, the computer is freer than the calculator, which can only perform specific calculations, whereas the computer as a universal machine can process everything (image, sound, language):

> Affect, unlike the drives, has a degree of competency and complexity that affords it the relative ability to motivate the human to greater degrees of freedom. For freedom is measured quantitatively, in degrees of cognitive competency and complexity. Tomkins even proposes a principle for freedom, suggesting Freud's pleasure principle as the model. He calls it the information complexity, or 'degrees-of-freedom principle'.[47]

Where Tomkins criticizes psychoanalysis from the perspective of systems psychology, faulting it on a supposed pansexuality and narrow conception of the drives, André Green criticized Lacan in the 1970s for having ignored affect in favour of representation. Green himself based his clinical work above all on the study of narcissistic-affective disorders, defining *affect* as follows: "It is through affect that the ego gives an unrepresentable representation of itself."[48] Green's attacks on Lacan arose from the recurring dispute between different dogmas and schools of psychoanalysis over the question of how to treat psychotic patients and schizophrenia. Freud and Lacan were both very reserved on this issue, seeing psychoanalysis primarily as a therapy for neuroses, whereas others (especially R. D. Laing's schizophrenia studies in Britain and the object relation theories of Donald W. Winnicott and Melanie Klein) included other groups of patients, such as children and psychotics. Green also criticizes analysts as a profession for the way they have built a position of supremacy via language and the silence of the analyst, as well as viewing the affective dimension as too dangerous, excluding it from the process of transference and returning it to language.[49]

But the charge that language won out over other systems and methods for political reasons alone falls short. Instead, one must trace the triumphal progress of the signifier throughout the twentieth century and acknowledge the implementation of linguistic structures into thinking in general.

Lacan defended himself on several occasions against accusations of ignoring affect, explaining why he did not consider it a possible object of analysis:

> What is anxiety? [. . .] To introduce it, I'll say it's an affect. Those who follow the movements of affinity or aversion in my disquisition [. . .] no doubt think that I'm less interested in affects than anything else. That's absurd. [. . .] I've tried on occasion to say what affect is not. It is not Being in its immediacy, nor is it the subject in a raw form either. It is in no respect protopathic. [. . .] It isn't repressed. [. . .] It's unfastened [*désarrimé*], it drifts about. It can be found displaced, maddened, inverted or metabolized, but it isn't repressed. What are repressed are the signifiers that moor it.[50]

Here, Lacan follows the definition offered by Freud in *Inhibitions, Symptoms and Anxiety*: "We call it an affective state, although we are also ignorant of what an affect is."[51]

Green's charge that Freud doesn't even mention affect in connection with anxiety is thus not true,[52] and in his seminars on *The Ethics of Psychoanalysis*, Lacan makes a detailed statement on affect, mainly concerning the success of analysis: "I don't need to do more than remind you of the confused nature of the recourse [by psychology] to affectivity; it reaches a point where, even when the reference is made within analysis, it always leads us toward an impasse, toward something that we feel is not the direction in which our research can really make progress."[53]

REPRESS, REPEAT, WORK THROUGH

If this discussion gives the impression of having very little to do with art and media, then Lisa Cartwright's *Moral Spectatorship* is proof to the contrary.[54] As mentioned earlier, Cartwright used the dispute between Lacan and Green to show how feminist film theory had sided with the dominant ideology for reasons of power politics. In the 1970s, this meant siding with Lacan. Without going into great detail, I would like to outline the debate in feminist media and art theory of the 1970s and '80s in order to cast a slightly more positive light on individual figures than Cartwright does. It may be helpful at this point to restate the difference in theory reception between America and Europe that should now be viewed more critically on both sides. Many interpretations (regardless of whether they are correct, distorted or erroneous) can only be meaningfully understood in the context of a specific academic culture. The reception of psychoanalysis is a perfect example that shows how many projections and misunderstandings are involved in establishing hegemonic theories.

In the 1970s, the feminist discussion in Europe had a strong focus on France, with Luce Irigaray, Héléne Cixous and Monique Wittig as important representatives of a "feminine language and aesthetic", while in England at the same time Laura Mulvey and Mary Kelly were working on questions of the representation of femininity. Artists and theorists spoke of women in opposition to men. In the foreword to the exhibition *MAGNA—Feminismus: Kunst und Kreativität* curated by VALIE EXPORT, Lucy Lippard writes: "Art has no gender, naturally, but artists do. Which is why separate rooms for women are necessary in order to bestow public attention and thus recognition upon the invisible sex."[55] For as VALIE EXPORT herself had written three years earlier, "THE HISTORY OF WOMAN IS THE HISTORY OF MAN because man has shaped the image of woman for man and woman alike."[56]

In 1975, Laura Mulvey's essay "Visual Pleasure and Narrative Cinema"[57] explored the gaze and the image and their linking of the male and the female. At the same time, Irigaray published *Speculum of the Other Woman.*[58] Using Freud and Lacan, Mulvey analyses a cinema-specific coding of female and male via the gaze and being-in-the-image. Irigaray's critique is directed at the patriarchal order as a whole, and in her view, psychoanalysis is part of this order. She reads Freud against the grain and holds up a mirror to women, showing them their own history, a history of erasures and the eradication of traces, a history that must first be reexcavated before it can be passed on to future generations: "Woman's only relation to origin is one dictated by man's. She is crazy, disoriented, lost, if she fails to join in this *first* male desire. This is shown, specifically, in the way she is forced to renounce the marks of her ancestry and inscribe herself on man's pedigree. She leaves her family, her 'house', her name."[59] In this critique, woman is excluded from the patriarchal economy of language; strictly speaking she has no gender, and any mention of woman or feminine is embedded in a phallogocentric gesture that defines woman as derived from a masculine universal. She, the woman, cannot be articulated in and by the language of patriarchy.[60] From this symbolic nonexistence of woman, it follows that there are no images of her. Whenever images of women circulate, they are pictures by men for men. If, as an artist, a woman wants a different representation of the feminine, then she must not produce images; instead, as a first step, she must develop her own visual language. Armed with a mix of psycho-Marxism and feminist critique, the key project of these years involved sounding out the terrain of a "feminine aesthetics": one's own body, one's own voice, one's own gaze, one own camerawork, one's own visual language.[61]

Against this backdrop, it may be easier to understand the struggles over the politics of representation conducted by women academics and artists at the time and their fear of essentialist attributions. The female body, especially the body of the mother, was thus the site where the battle of language versus affect was fought. Irigaray's position, her exclusive focus on the female body, came under attack. The distance between Irigaray and (post-) structuralist feminism increased from the mid-1980s, when she declared the existence of a "goddess" (of transcendence). At the same time, projects like Judy Chicago's *Dinner Party* were realized, stirring up public opinion and causing art by women to be dismissed and stigmatized as body art. Because women had always been defined via their bodies, which were always defined as more natural than the male body, it is perfectly understandable that this amalgamation (woman-body-nature) needed to be dealt with analytically. Psychoanalysis, especially the Lacanian version, proved particularly well suited to this task because it formulates the radical nonexistence of *woman*, tying her neither to physicality nor to a female or male mentality. Instead, the female and male positions are grasped as specific failures with regard to the symbolic order.[62]

Let's return to Lisa Cartwright's interpretation, which attempts to view the rejection of affect in the context of the irresolvable problem of the representation of the feminine. After the period of French-dominated feminist theory, with the emergence of the concept of "gender" in the mid-1980s, the debate (on issues of feminine sexuality, the female spectator and female strategies of identification) was largely dominated by Anglo-American theory. Cartwright refers, among others, to Jacqueline Rose's *Sexuality in the Field of Vision*, which proposes a more complex reworking of Lacan's interpretation of "femininity and representation". She mentions André Green but always in connection with Lacan, whose reading she ultimately prefers. Cartwright shows that Green was not unknown to women film theorists but that his approach (in part due to his closeness to Irigaray) was too body- and affect-centric. In her section on psychoanalytical readings of Hamlet, Rose mocks Green accordingly:

> As if completing the circuit, André Green turns to D. W. Winnicott's concept of the maternal functions as the basis for his recent book on *Hamlet*. Femininity now appears as the very principle of the aesthetic process. Shakespeare's Hamlet forecloses the femininity in himself, but by projecting onto the stage the degraded and violent image of a femininity repudiated by his character, Shakespeare manages to preserve in himself that other femininity which is the source of his creative art: [. . .] Creativity *per se* [. . .] arises for Winnicott out of a femininity which is that primordial space of being which is created by the mother alone. It is a state of being which is not yet a relationship to the object because there is as yet no self, and it is, as Green defines it, "au-delà de la représentation", before the coming of the sign. [. . .] But it is worth noting how the woman appears at the point either where language and aesthetic form start to crumble or else where they have not yet come to be. "Masculinity does, femininity is", is Winnicott's definition.[63]

This lengthy quotation clearly shows the kind of images of the feminine that dominated these years of intense feminist debate. Today, however, these images are no longer the sole focus of attention, as there are now also images in circulation of the male body which has clearly lost its safe, unquestionable, invisible status. In fact, thanks to the postmodern tendency toward the breaking-down of dichotomies, coupled with the spread of digital networks, there are now images in circulation of everyone and everything. Images have acquired a new quality of self-evidence, allowing cultural and media theorists to return to the body as affective body.

In the 1960s, after the great schism within the French school of psychoanalysis, Green played his theory of affect against Lacan's supposed hegemony of representation. In *Le discours vivant*[64] published in 1973, he goes back to Freud as a point of departure for a reworking of affect. This book formed the basis for Green's contestation (with Otto Kernberg and others) of Lacan and his school. But Green's work is also linked with that of another French thinker who plays a key role within the feminist discussion—Julia Kristeva. Her *Revolution in Poetic Language*[65] in particular offered an unparalleled demonstration of the semiotic analysis of psychical processes in literature, showing how the two sides of language, the symbolic and the semiotic, cannot be separated, but instead, the semiotic constantly erupts into and speaks through the symbolic order. Two decades later, she wrote about today's harried men and women having no time to represent psychical experience.[66] But in the early 1960s, she, too, sided with Green against Lacan, whom she accused of eroding drive and affect as the irreducible variables of Freudian psychoanalysis. "There is no doubt", writes Jacqueline Rose on this subject, "that the push here is against language itself, even though Kristeva herself is again the best analyst of the dangers this might imply".[67] Rose quotes Kristeva from an interview in 1977 where she describes the nonverbal aspects of American culture as signs of resistance that are more radical than any possible verbal critique.[68] Writing ten years after the interview took place, it is no surprise that Rose views this development on the part of Kristeva as worrying—worrying because the semiotic runs the risk of becoming a safe haven for motherly, ahistorical, meaningless existential certainties.

What this brief look at the situation in the 1970s through to the mid-1980s also shows is that the dispute over language versus affect not only has a long tradition but that it also periodically comes to a head and that we are currently seeing a new phase of such heightened contestation.

In the case of Silvan Tomkins, I have tried to show how extremely close his concept of affect comes to Freud's concept of the drive and how desperately he attempts to escape from the net of the sexual that Freud allegedly stretched over man by force. I have also expressed my astonishment at the way Kosofsky Sedgwick deals with Tomkins's attack on what he saw as the "biologism" of psychoanalysis. Although she has to admit that the assumption of innate affects is not easy to accept, she calls on her readers to try nonetheless. With their reception of Tomkins, both Kosofsky Sedgwick and Cartwright are pursuing a fight against the dominance of a cognitive psychology of emotion that is gaining strength especially in media and film theory and whose attraction, in combination with neurological research, is growing. It is doubtful, however, whether Tomkins's affect theory is the right weapon for this fight.

Within media and cultural theory, attempts are now being made to forge alliances with neurobiology or at least to consider such an alliance desirable, and the psychoanalytical movement itself is at pains to establish a biological base for its teachings, declaring neurobiology and psychoanalysis as two sides of the same coin.

In his book *The Chains of Eros*,[69] André Green speaks of a "metabiology" that is more meaningful than the "meta-psychology" pursued by Freud. But Green is also critical of developments within his own camp, noting a gradual displacement or even dismissal of the sexual from psychoanalytical concepts themselves, in particular under the influence of object relations theory. This is already evident in the work of Winnicott and Klein, Green writes, although the former moved back closer to Freud in his later work.[70] In Winnicott's model, the primary position is occupied by the child's emotional anchoring in reality—ahead of any libidinous, autoerotic factor. Evidently this orientation toward reality converges with many other interests. But using the work of Antonio Damasio, I would like to show the degree to which psychoanalysis is realigning itself, in order to regain some ground via a neurobiological revision. With his theory of innate affects as a strategy for survival, Damasio has now influenced many psychoanalysts (although his readers also include many in the humanities and cultural studies). And as I show in chapter 6, his work is widely accepted and forms the basis for new approaches within philosophy and other disciplines, such as the plasticity of the brain as developed by Catherine Malabou.

FROM THE SOUL OF THE BRAIN TO FEELINGS AS SELF-CARE OF THE ORGANISM

Freud was right!

Slogans in this vein are used by brain research to promote its greatest endeavor: decoding the functions of the brain and demonstrating how somatic actions and reactions are transposed into mental translations, revealing the development of human physical and mental reactions by using the latest recording techniques to observe them in situ.

Antonio Damasio defines affect and emotion as the phylo- and ontogenetic basis of human existence. In *Looking for Spinoza: Joy, Sorrow, and the Feeling Brain,*[71] he goes in search of Baruch Spinoza to show that his philosophy of immanence was just waiting for neurobiology to come along. In Damasio's view, Spinoza's refusal to consider body and mind as separate entities, grasping them instead as a question of different intensities, is the first step toward a biological definition of consciousness.[72] Not unlike Tomkins's system of innate affect, Damasio defines affect as the primary body-environment system responsible for man's survival. For him, affect is the general term covering emotion and feeling: "Primary or universal emotions: happiness, sadness, fear, anger, surprise, disgust. Secondary or social emotions: embarrassment, jealousy, guilt, pride. Background emotions: wellbeing, malaise, calm, tension."[73] Emotions unfold on the stage of the body, Damasio explains, whereas feelings take possession of the mind. Emotions are the unconscious (bodily) aspect; feelings are what can be symbolized and discussed. Surprisingly, the two central concepts chosen by Damasio to connect consciousness, feelings, and emotions are "patterns" and "images": images are mental and not only visual, conscious images are only accessible to the individual, whereas images as neuronal patterns only reveal themselves to an observer using imaging technologies, while thoughts are a flow of images.[74] On first reading, this talk of the flow of images recalls Bergson and his universe of images within which the body emerges as a special kind of image. It soon becomes clear, however, that Damasio is operating with a different concept of the image entirely, and his concept of affect, influenced by Spinoza, comes surprisingly close to Tomkins. Spinoza writes: "By affect I understand affections of the body by which the body's power of acting is increased or diminished, aided or restrained, and at the same time, the ideas of these affections."[75] Concerning the body as the object of these ideas, which he calls mind, Damasio also follows Spinoza. The body, then, is present in the mind as feeling, represented in the form of a "pattern". But for Damasio there is a barrier that he simply cannot ignore: consciousness. As he stresses, however, he was clever enough not to follow the widely held view that consciousness can only be approached via language, understanding it instead without language:

> Consciousness begins when brains acquire the power [. . .] of telling a story without words, the story that there is life ticking away in an organism, and that the states of the living organism, within body bounds, are continuously being altered by encounters with objects or events in its environment, or [. . .] by thoughts and by internal adjustments of the life process. Consciousness emerges when this primordial story—the story of an object causally changing the state of the body—can be told using the universal nonverbal vocabulary of body signals. The apparent self emerges as the feeling of a feeling. When the story is first told [. . .] without it ever having been requested, and forevermore after that when the story is repeated, knowledge about what the organism is living through automatically emerges as the answer to a question never asked. From that moment on we begin to know.[76]

Rather than originating in language, then, consciousness comes into being when feelings produce images of the body, thus facilitating thoughts, which are then translated into language. Today, various psychologists have accused Damasio of resurrecting the old "James-Lange theory of feelings". According to William James, we are sad because we feel tears, we are angry because we strike out, we are shocked because we tremble, and so on. At the same time (in the last quarter of the nineteenth century) and independently of James, Carl Lange, too, arrived at the same view that feelings are corollaries of physical reactions. This approach barely distinguishes between instinct-based actions and emotional reactions. Aesthetic, moral and ethical feelings are not taken seriously by James because they can also take place without bodily reactions.[77]

Translations of biological entities into neural, mental or symbolic-psychical phenomena are currently enjoying great popularity, with one prominent example being the neurophysiological translation or reinterpretation of psychoanalysis. This trend within popular science, willingly cited by the media, is well illustrated by François Ansermet and Pierre Magistretti's book *Biology of Freedom*: Here, psychoanalysis is combined in an easily understandable way with neurobiological commonplaces that create a familiar atmosphere in which the consumer gains insights into the nature of his or her mental problems. Like all of their colleagues, Ansermet and Magistretti use everyday examples in their attempts to illustrate the complex activity of the brain.[78] A mental image of sea, sun and sand, for example, produces physical reactions that are responsible for a somatic state. Why, the authors ask, is this the case? Because, they answer, the body plays a greater role than we might first imagine. Damasio's approach is then used to support their entire chapter on "Perceptions and Emotions". Not a single reference to psychoanalysis, from which the authors borrow only the concept of an "unconscious inner reality"[79] but without ever explaining it. What do *unconscious, somatic, autonomic nervous system,* and *immediate* mean here? The reader can only guess, as Ansermet and Magistretti merely repeat Damasio's theory of a merging of external perception and inner emotions, the so-called somatic markers. In their section on "Milk and the Sound of the Door: Psychic Traces and Somatic States",[80] they quote a key example from psychoanalysis and Lacan's "thing", but the highly complex repertoire of need, demand, and desire is reduced to a model of unpleasure that can be summarized as follows: The somatic state of the infant generates a vital drive that is resolved in screaming; this screaming is a biological screaming that is not yet capable of possessing any mental intentionality; in spite of this, it triggers an action in another person—the mother gives the infant her breast; this breast is at first real (the Lacanian "thing", as the authors write)—but then, over time, it becomes increasingly mixed with other associations, via so-called mechanisms of plasticity[81] (that create memory traces), thus becoming increasingly abstract. In this model, an experience of satisfaction might equally be marked by the sound of a door or a pink blouse.[82] These examples only serve to emphasize once again the naivety and superficiality of the theoretical explanations offered here, and one cannot seriously speak of an alliance between neurobiology and psychoanalysis. But it is typical of the current shift, even within the ranks of psychoanalysis itself, that simple readings are more attractive, making it easier to believe in a purely neurobiological basis to human existence. At the end of *Looking for Spinoza,* Damasio poses the key question: Why do we need the mind or consciousness at all if the organism and the brain that constantly interacts with it are responsible for man's survival? Why are "neural maps" not enough? By way of an answer, he refers to the "sense of self" that is necessary if one is to orient oneself in the world:

> The sense of self introduces, within the mental level of processing, the notion that all the current activities represented in brain and mind pertain to a single organism whose auto-preservation needs are the basic cause of most events currently represented. The sense of self orients the mental planning process toward the satisfaction of those needs. That orientation is only possible because feelings are integral to the cluster of operations that constitutes the sense of self, and because feelings are continuously generating, within the mind, a *concern* for the organism.[83]

As we see in chapter 6, Catherine Malabou also quotes Ansermet and Magistretti when introducing her theory of the plasticity of the brain and in a second step, in cooperation with Adrian Johnston, a theory of the "emotional self" that builds the new center of a libidinal economy, where plasticity and self-healing movements play a major role.

NOTES

1. Mirjana Vrhunc, *Bild und Wirklichkeit. Zur Philosophie Henri Bergsons* (Munich, Germany: Fink, 2002), 167.
2. Henri Bergson, *Matter and Memory* (New York: Cosimo, 2007), 44.
3. Ibid., 46.
4. Sigmund Freud, *The Interpretation of Dreams* (1900) (New York: Basic Books, 1955).
5. Jacques Lacan, *The Seminar of Jacques Lacan: Book II: The Ego in Freud's Theory and in the Technique of Psychoanalysis* (Cambridge: Cambridge University Press, 1988), 101.
6. Ibid., 108.
7. Ibid., 99–100.
8. Ibid., 94.
9. "115: A picture held us captive. And we could not get outside it, for it lay in our language, and language seemed only to repeat it to us inexorably." [Ludwig Wittgenstein, *Philosophical Investigations*, revised 4th ed. (Chichester, UK: Blackwell, 2009), 98.]
10. See Vrhunc, *Bild und Wirklichkeit*, 191.
11. Bergson, *Matter and Memory*, 310–12.
12. Jean Laplanche and Jean-Bertrand Pontalis, *The Language of Psychoanalysis* (London: Karnac, 1988), 204.
13. See Vrhunc, *Bild und Wirklichkeit*, 168, 171.
14. See ibid., 172.
15. Bergson, *Matter and Memory*, 208f.
16. Jacques Derrida, "Freud and the Scene of Writing", in Jacques Derrida, *Writing and Difference* (Chicago: University of Chicago Press, 1978), 196–231, here 201.
17. Ibid., 204.

18. Brian Massumi, "The Autonomy of Affect", in Paul Patton (ed.), *Deleuze: A Critical Reader* (Cambridge, MA: Blackwell, 1996), 217–39, here 223f.
19. Ibid., 218f.
20. On the concept of the "body without image", see Marie-Luise Angerer, *Body Options . Körper.Spuren.Medien.Bilder* (Vienna: Turia & Kant, 1999), 174f.
21. See Gilles Deleuze, *Bergsonism* (New York: Zone, 1988), 51–72.
22. Jakob von Uexküll assumes a gap of 1/18 second: Eighteen beats per second are experienced as a constant pressure, eighteen oscillations per second as a uniform tone, and so on, a fact that will be exploited by film as the technical medium that operates on the basis of motion as infinitesimal calculus. See Stefan Rieger, *Kybernetische Anthropologie* (Frankfurt, Germany: Suhrkamp, 2003), 175–86.
23. Hertha Sturm and J. Ray Brown (eds.), *Wie Kinder mit dem Fernsehen umgehen. Nutzen und Wirkung eines Mediums* (Stuttgart, Germany: Klett-Cotta, 1979); Hertha Sturm, Christine Altstötter-Gleich, Jo Groebel, and Marianne Grewe-Partsch, *Fernsehdiktate: Die Veränderung von Gedanken und Gefühlen. Ergebnisse und Folgerungen für eine rezipientenorientierte Mediendramaturgie* (Gütersloh, Germany: Bertelsmann, 1991). Since then, as discussed in chapter 6, the missing half-second has reached the laboratories of brain research (Benjamin Libet) and has stimulated studies on the history of the missing time zone going back to Hermann von Helmholtz and his contemporaries in the mid-nineteenth century.
24. Massumi, "The Autonomy of Affect", 224.
25. See Gilles Deleuze, *Spinoza: Practical Philosophy* (San Francisco: City Lights, 1988), 127.
26. Gilles Deleuze and Félix Guattari, *What Is Philosophy?* (London: Verso, 1994), 183.
27. Massumi, "The Autonomy of Affect", 229.
28. Gilles Deleuze, *Cinema 2: The Time-Image* (Minneapolis: University of Minnesota Press, 1989), 5–6.
29. Mark B. N. Hansen, *New Philosophy for New Media* (Cambridge, MA: MIT Press, 2004), 209.
30. Ibid., 211.
31. Clare Hemmings, "Invoking Affect", in *Cultural Studies*, 19.5 (2005), 548–67.
32. Eve Kosofsky Sedgwick, *Epistemology of the Closet* (Berkeley: University of California Press, 1990).
33. Eve Kosofsky Sedgwick and Adam Frank (eds.), *Shame and Its Sisters: A Silvan Tomkins Reader* (Durham, NC: Duke University Press, 1995).
34. Eve Kosofsky Sedgwick, *Touching Feeling: Affect, Pedagogy, Performativity* (Durham, NC: Duke University Press, 2003).
35. Silvan Tomkins, *Affect, Imagery, Consciousness*, 2 vols. (New York: Springer, 1962/1963).
36. A look at the current literature in the field of cultural studies confirms the influence of Tomkins's reception, especially his enthronement of shame. Within a short period, many books on shame have been published, and theoretical models are shifting under the new dominance of shame. See, for example, Elspeth Probyn, *Blush: Faces of Shame* (Minnesota: University of Minnesota Press, 2005).
37. See also Martin Dornes, who levels a similar charge at psychoanalysis against a different theoretical background: By clinging to the theory of the drives, he argues. Psychoanalysis was unable to develop a satisfactory theory of affect. See Martin Dornes, "Wahrnehmen, Fühlen, Phantasieren", in Gertrud Koch (ed.), *Auge und Affekt. Wahrnehmung und Interaktion* (Frankfurt, Germany: Fischer, 1995), 15–38, here 23f.
38. In contrast to this, Teresa Brennan developed a model of affect-controlled drives: affects consist of drive material, and drives are wrapped up in affects. With this conception of affect, Brennan appeals for a language that reestablishes a closer link with the codes of the body. See Teresa Brennan, *The Transmission of Affect* (Ithaca, NY: Cornell University Press, 2004). For more detail on this, see also chapter 5.
39. Silvan Tomkins, quoted in Kosofsky Sedgwick and Frank, *Shame and Its Sisters*, 144.

40. Ibid., 148.
41. See Sigmund Freud, "Civilization and Its Discontents" (1930) (New York: Norton, 1989).
42. Silvan Tomkins, quoted in Kosofsky Sedgwick and Frank, *Shame and Its Sisters*, 150.
43. In *Three Essays on the Theory of Sexuality*, Freud writes, "In thus distinguishing between libidinal and other forms of psychical energy we are giving expression to the presumption that the sexual processes occurring in the organism are distinguished from the nutritive processes by a special chemistry. The analysis of the perversions and psychoneuroses has shown us that this sexual excitation is derived not from the so-called sexual parts alone, but from all the bodily organs. We thus reach the idea of a quantity of libido, the mental representation of which we give the name 'ego-libido,' and whose production, increase or diminution, distribution and displacement should afford us possibilities for explaining the psychosexual phenomena observed." Sigmund Freud, *Three Essays on the Theory of Sexuality* (1905) (New York: Basic Books, 2000), 83.
44. Donald L. Nathanson, *Shame and Pride: Affect, Sex, and the Birth of the Self* (New York: Norton, 1992), 290f.
45. In Nathanson's view, this is proved by the fact that humans normally have sex in the dark of night, whereas animals usually do it during the day. See ibid., 292.
46. See Sigmund Freud, *An Outline of Psycho-Analysis* (1938) (New York: Norton, 1989).
47. Kosofsky Sedgwick and Frank, *Shame and Its Sisters*, 35.
48. André Green, *Life Narcissism and Death Narcissism* (London: Free Association Books, 2001), 96.
49. See André Green, "Against Lacanism: A Conversation with Sergio Benvenuto", in *Journal of European Psychoanalysis*, 2 (Fall 1995–Winter 1996).
50. Jacques Lacan, *Anxiety: The Seminar of Jacques Lacan, Book X* (Cambridge, UK: Polity, 2014), 14.
51. Sigmund Freud, *Inhibitions, Symptoms and Anxiety* (1926) (New York: Norton, 1989), 60. Lacan assessed Freud's affect-as-signal as follows: "As far as the psychology of affects is concerned, Freud always manages to give in passing significant and suggestive hints. He always insists on their conventional and artificial character, on their character not as signifiers but as signals, to which in the last analysis they may be reduced. This character also explains their displaceable significance, and, from the economic point of view, presents a certain number of necessities, such as irreducibility. But affects do not throw light on the economic or even dynamic essence which is sought at the horizon or limit from an analytical perspective. That is something more opaque, more obscure, namely, analytical metaphysics's notions concerning energy." Jacques Lacan, *The Seminar of Jacques Lacan VII: The Ethics of Psychoanalysis* (New York: Norton, 1992), 102.
52. "It is noteworthy that Freud never speaks of representations or affects." Green, *Life Narcissism and Death Narcissism*, 94.
53. Lacan, *Seminar of Jacques Lacan VII*, 102.
54. Lisa Cartwright, *Moral Spectatorship: Technologies of Voice and Affect in Postwar Representations of the Child* (Durham, NC: Duke University Press, 2008).
55. See Lucy Lippard, "Vorwort", in *Valie EXPORT: MAGNA. Feminismus: Kunst und Kreativität* (exhibition catalog) (Vienna: Galerie Nächst St. Stephan, 1975).
56. VALIE EXPORT, "womans art. manifest zur Ausstellung MAGNA" (arbeitstitel frauenkunst) eine ausstellung, an der nur frauen teilnehmen, in *Neues Forum*, 228 (1972), 47.
57. Laura Mulvey, "Visual Pleasure and Narrative Cinema", in *Screen*, 16.3 (1975), 6–18 .
58. Luce Irigaray, *Speculum of the Other Woman* (1974) (Ithaca, NY: Cornell University Press, 1985).
59. Ibid., 33.
60. See Luce Irigaray, *This Sex Which Is Not One* (1977) (Ithaca, NY: Cornell University Press, 1985).

61. See Marie-Luise Angerer, "Expanded Thoughts. Zu Valie EXPORT", in *LAB, Jahrbuch für Künste und Apparate* (Cologne, Germany: Art Academy of Media, 2006), 11–25.

62. See Angerer, *Body Options*, especially 94–119.

63. Jacqueline Rose, *Sexuality in the Field of Vision* (London: Verso 1985), 136–38.

64. André Green, *Le discours vivant. La conception psychanalytique de l'affect* (Paris: PUF, 1973).

65. Julia Kristeva, *Revolution in Poetic Language* (New York: Columbia University Press, 1984).

66. See Julia Kristeva, *New Maladies of the Soul* (New York: Columbia University Press, 2005), 7.

67. Jacqueline Rose, "Julia Kristeva—Take Two", in Rose, *Sexuality in the Field of Vision*, 141–64, here 152.

68. Ibid.

69. André Green, *The Chains of Eros: The Sexual in Psychoanalysis* (London: H. Karnac, 2001).

70. Unlike Freud, Winnicott never accepted a death drive and, unlike Melanie Klein, he also rejected the model of drives.

71. Antonio R. Damasio, *Looking for Spinoza: Joy, Sorrow, and the Feeling Brain* (New York: Houghton Mifflin, 2003).

72. As proof of this, Damasio points to a number of publications in neuroscience that all refer to Spinoza or stress his importance to the new brain research. See ibid., 309, note 8. Slavoj Žižek has made fun of this widespread enthusiasm for Spinoza, asking, "Is it possible not to love Spinoza? [. . .] One of the unwritten rules of today's academia, from France to America, is the injunction to love Spinoza." Slavoj Žižek, *Organs without Bodies: Deleuze and the Consequences* (London: Routledge, 2012), 29.

73. Antonio R. Damasio, *The Feeling of What Happens: Body and Emotion in the Making of Consciousness* (New York: Harcourt Brace, 1999), 51.

74. Ibid., 317f.

75. Benedictus de Spinoza, *A Spinoza Reader: The Ethics and Other Works* (Princeton, NJ: Princeton University Press, 1994), 154.

76. Damasio, *The Feeling of What Happens*, 30f.

77. See Alexander Kochinka, *Emotionstheorien. Begriffliche Arbeit am Gefühl* (Bielefeld, Germany: Transcript), 213–15.

78. "Let us imagine that you recall a landscape dear to you, one whose evocation puts you in a state of great serenity, for example the image of those beautiful, fertile Tuscan hills where cypresses, olive trees, and vineyards weave a supple tapestry to the horizon." François Ansermet and Pierre Magistretti, *Biology of Freedom: Neural Plasticity, Experience and the Unconscious* (London: Karnac, 2007), 97. In his examples, Damasio, too, describes the beach and the sea, the soft sand, and the blue sky.

79. Ibid., 93.

80. Ibid., 107f.

81. Ibid., 114.

82. Ibid., 111f. The passage relating to the blouse (taken from the time of Freud and unquestioningly implanted into the present!): "When he is a little older, the child will discover sexuality with the nanny who also often wears a pink shirt. This time the experience of satisfaction will clearly be of a sexual nature." Ibid., 118.

83. Damasio, *Looking for Spinoza*, 208.

FOUR

Virtual Sex and Other Metamorphoses

This chapter examines the development of the digital space that has become all pervasive in the course of the last quarter century. This space may not have triggered the affective turn, but it significantly amplified it. Initially, "cyberspace" held the promise of a new realm of freedom, allowing people to adopt new roles, make new contacts, and anonymously turn their fantasies into reality. Today, these expectations sound naïve, as the reality of the virtual space has become increasingly clear: from surveillance (drones) to aggressive commerce (from porn to book selling) to self-exposure on social media platforms, it has become apparent that the promise of the digital means not more freedom but above all a radical transformation of the psychological, social and economic spheres.

In 2000, under the motto "Next Sex", the Ars Electronica Festival[1] invited artists, biologists, and theorists (from the natural sciences, psychiatry, and evolution research), whose contributions on the theme of "Sex in the Age of Its Procreative Superfluousness" ranged from Nobuya Unno's artificial womb to Randy Thornhill's abstruse theory of rape as part of evolution to Carl Djerassi's antibaby pill. It soon became clear that "Next Sex" understood sex purely in terms of procreation, but as the example of artificial insemination (unintentionally) reveals, more is at stake here than just the specific procedure. The question of why some people wish to have children, why others have none or abort pregnancies, why women and men go to extreme technical lengths to have a child of their own—all of this is embedded in a symbolic-imaginary order through which sexuality comes into being. From Freud to Lacan, sexuality has never been about the satisfaction of needs alone, but rather in order to be considered as sexuality, it has always also included the dimensions of demand and desire.[2]

As Jean Laplanche and Jean-Bertrand Pontalis have explained, this is because "human beings have lost their instincts, especially their sexual instinct and, more specifically still, their instinct to reproduce. [. . .] Drives and forms of behaviour are plastic, mobile and interchangeable. Above all, it foregrounds their [. . .] vicariousness, the ability of one drive to take the place of another."[3] The plasticity, malleability and adaptability to any new condition posited by Laplanche and Pontalis as characteristics of human sexuality are now undergoing an interesting shift or renaissance in the plasticity of the brain and of the affects.

But while theorists like Paul Virilio describe the digital space in pessimistic tones, cinema and art have long since addressed the theme of living simultaneously in real life (RL) and in virtual reality (VR). In his remarks on digitization, Virilio used the term *tele-action*, defining the transition from direct to remote action in pessimistic terms. In his view, acting, communicating, and feeling at a distance in this way would lead, in the long term, to total disorientation:

> *To be* used to mean to be somewhere, to be situated, in the here and now, but the situation of the essence of being is undermined by the instantaneity, the immediacy, and the ubiquity which are characteristic of our epoch. [. . .] From now on, humankind will have to act in two worlds at once. This opens up extraordinary possibilities, but at the same time we face the test of a tearing-up of the being, with awkward consequences. We can rejoice in these new opportunities if and only if we also are conscious of their dangers.[4]

Today, rather than any talk of danger, the fact that it is now possible to be everywhere at once is seen as a new stage in a media theory of global consciousness. Brain and environment communicate via signals; people and their surroundings act and react interactively, spontaneously, affectively.

This theme has been strikingly addressed by filmmakers like Kathryn Bigelow and David Cronenberg. In Bigelow's *Strange Days* (1995), the connection between humans and their brains is established via a "squid". What someone thinks and feels is recorded by this device, and these stored feelings can be accessed via the squid (as "feelable" images) by someone else. Stored on a chip, another person's wishes and longings, fears and joys, can be appropriated. In *Scanners* (1980), *Videodrome* (1982) and *eXistenZ* (1999), Cronenberg deals with the hypothetical linking of man and media. In these films, people are sucked up via communications wires (telephony, telepathy), media signals, and television pictures, as reality and simulation become impossible to tell apart. Elsewhere, the line between man and machine disappears. Chris Cunningham's video for Björk's song "All Is Full of Love" (1999) is built around a cyborg who turns to a clone (of herself) in her loneliness. Artificial (machine) beings, too, it seems, live and love better in couples.

Another form of the breaking-down of boundaries is staged in *Dandy Dust* (1998) by Austrian filmmaker Hans Scheirl. Although the film doesn't deal directly with cyberspace or the figure of the cyborg, it is all about other existences in other spaces, monstrous hybrids, mechanically extended bodies, about desire without sexual orientation and perverse desires. As Rachel Armstrong writes, cyborg identities "have much to offer. They physically demonstrate that it is possible to defeat obliteration, annihilation, or replacement by the encroachment of the dominant patriarchal, social, technological or medical pressures on the body, and interpret them as survival technologies."[5]

Man and machine merge in order to blow each other apart, or they join together in order to advance into deep emotional dimensions that cannot be reached without electronic assistance. But these alliances underline an aspect that, consciously or unconsciously, is played out in all of the previously mentioned examples from art and cinema: a failure to come to oneself in the other. Whether it is demonstrated on the level of content or explored in camera shots, editing and sound, the element of electronic amplification always shows that the place of Being and the essence of Being are not always identical (contrary to what Derrick de Kerckhove[6] has claimed).

Outside of cinematic and artistic realities, too, the playful adoption of identities has played a noticeable role in recent years. But the concept of "metrosexuality" introduced into academic debate by Marjorie Garbner[7] is misleading, confusing "role-play" with an "imperative" concerning sexuality and gender identities. When media, music and the cyberworld operate with ambiguity, fluid sexual orientations and the mixing of male and female, suggesting a form of queer joie de vivre, then they fail to appreciate their own part in producing imaginary settings that make this play with sexual identities desirable.[8]

As this makes clear, sexuality in the sense of the primarily sexual (i.e., prior to conscious organization controllable by the ego) is not a human faculty but, as Charles Shepherdson has written, an imperative resulting from Freud's distinction between drive and instinct. Stressing this imperative character means insisting on the structural inevitability of representation that characterizes sexuality. Rather than being any kind of return to corporeal nature or natural corporeality, this is a reminder that, in the psychoanalytical view, sexuality is neither sex nor gender, and the body is neither biological fact nor social construct. Instead sexuality is understood as being constitutively denaturalized, "organized by the image and the word".[9] Gender, on the other hand, can be understood as a role, consisting as it does of rules, norms, and rituals, as well as transgression and constant repetition. From a psychoanalytical point of view, this means that the euphoric conquest of cyberspace as a playing field for gender roles has always had to repress the imperative of the sexual in order for the play to get underway.

UNCONSCIOUS SEXUALITY AND VIRTUAL GENDER

In my 1999 book *Body Options*, I emphasize the differences between Judith Butler's *Gender Trouble* and Donna Haraway's *Manifest for Cyborgs* while nonetheless trying to relate their approaches because it seemed to me that their simultaneous appearance was not an accident. Butler and Haraway themselves have never shown any interest in getting in touch, however, and their euphoric reception in the early 1990s only contributed to a further systematic misapprehension of the basic differences between the concepts of the cyborg and "doing gender". Whereas Butler placed a political emphasis on the unconscious dimension of identities, Haraway rejected this concept entirely, instead advocating action by subjects defined as always already political. Nonetheless, it would have been interesting, at the height of the gender and cyborg debate, to combine the two positions rather than developing them further and further in separate directions—interesting because cyborgs in literature, in cinema and in computer science always work toward becoming more human. Cyborgs must learn something that the human subject neither has nor knows: the unconscious dimension that guides the *doing* of *gender* without knowing what gender is about. From the outset, however, the theorists and inventors of the cyberspheres entered a "post-gender world"[10] in reaction to a politics that had long since begun to view gender identities as passé, and this although the cybernetic basis of the cyborgs could have facilitated a direct connection to the unconscious of the subject. But this, too, had long been forgotten by cybernetic media theory, gender theories drawing on Lacan, and theories of technology operating with Haraway.

I am alluding here to Lacan's relationship with cybernetics, which certainly permitted links between the two fields. The unconscious is a supplement that is neither biological nor mathematical nor metaphysical but produces itself through language and, as Annette Bitsch puts it, "can only be introduced into the black boxes of cybernetics" and that an "amazed, alert and fascinated" Lacan "linked to the cybernetic machines".[11] A large distance exists between the circuitry of cybernetics and today's neurobiological representation of the unconscious via visual localization procedures in the brain. But this step must also be viewed alongside Haraway's dismissal of Freud, Lacan, and Foucault. In her eyes, psychoanalysis and *The Birth of the Clinic*[12] were no longer adequate, failing to do justice to the politics and economy of the day. Instead, Haraway appealed to women to develop a hybrid being (through cyberpolitics and cybertheory) that would be a satisfactory model for thinking about the requirements for survival in the postmodern world. Conceived of as pure surface with no spiritual depth, it refuses the old psychoanalytical story of papa and mama. Its identity bears neither the marks of family tragedy nor the scars of repressed desires. Neither traditions nor norms, neither gender identities nor boundaries of class or colour, are its essentialist identity markers. Instead, it is marked with open options. In this context, Haraway speaks of a "post-gender world", stressing that gender as a category can be charged with new meanings. Rather than being points of departure, gendered identities are now markings that can be used or not depending on the situation, signaling a rejection of conventional definitions—a rejection of heteronormativity, genital sexuality and the bipolarity of gender.

Astrid Deuber-Mankowsky has studied this situation with regard to computer games, pointing out the resulting paradox:

> With the computer, we thus find ourselves in the paradoxical situation of being faced with a virtual machine that is only accessible to us indirectly via symbolic characters, a medium for which the gender of its users is of no significance, but which at the same time functions as a wish-fulfilment machine, a function in which it promises—like an erotic encounter—to undermine or suspend the mediated dimension that makes communication and interaction possible in the first place. As if there were an appetite for unmediated contact on the level of pure appearances, an appetite only the digital signal were capable of satisfying.[13]

This constellation has parallels with Ovid's Narcissus, of course, who falls in love with his mirror image reflected in the water's surface and who, unable to forget this image, commits suicide to get rid of it. But computer games, chat rooms, and other forms of computer interaction still operate on the safe basis that the power of the imagination will continue to work for as long as the device remains switched on and the connection to the other person is unbroken.

Donna Haraway's successors Zoe Sofoulis and Sadie Plant[14] were attracted above all to the utopia of a new zone, what Sofoulis called a still "unnamed zone".[15] Initially, this zone was declared to be genuinely female because women as nonsubjects of a long-standing patriarchal society are, as the first cyborgs, predestined to inhabit the new territories. This was followed, in a second step, by the acknowledgment that, if the "Manifesto for Cyborgs" was meant to be taken seriously, then "female" could not be a selection criterion. So Sadie Plant spoke in favour of microorganisms, of clouds, cells and bacteria, of anything yet to attain any culturally recognized status.[16] They were to become the true inhabitants of cyberspace, using it as their base for subversive attacks on other worlds. Male and female would then no longer be distinct units; animals, machines and humans would no longer be strictly separate, displaying only gradual differences.[17] These are the first signs of what would later become a united front against Butler's *Gender Trouble* in the name of Deleuze and Guattari, using their "intensities" to free the data flow of the networks of its burden of history, including its sexual history. At the end of her study, Deuber-Mankowsky writes that both the academic discourses of cyberfeminism and the reality of computer games and their players show "that a profound change is currently taking place with regard to relations between the sexes that is as far-reaching as the dissociation of sexuality from reproduction a century ago".[18] But perhaps this diagnosis is too close to discourse, too close to the phenomenon itself, for any suitably distanced view of what it abandons and reveals.

In her provocative notion of a "digital feminism",[19] Claudia Reiche states that "woman", "language" and "digital medium" are generated exclusively out of their radical difference, thus arguing against a literal implementation or equation of cyberfeminism with the Lacanian formula of the nonexistence of sexual relations. The basic opposition is between the digital base mode of zero/one, translated as absence/presence, which plays no part in the unconscious. This means that cyberspace does not embody this unconscious, acting instead as a further arena for its interventions. In spite of this, a misunderstanding has become entrenched in the discussion about posthuman cyberidentities with regard to virtual genders. The mobility of drives and the interchangeability of their objects, defined by psychoanalysis as an insatiable desire, is transformed within digital networks into gender swapping and the phantasm of what is physically possible using plastic surgery and hormones. In *Gender Trouble*, Butler does not speak of swapping roles. The "trouble" in question refers to the fact that the body must always be traversed by gender, that any morphology always has an imaginary dimension. In the gender swapping popularized by cyberhype, this aspect was lost: Haraway's declaration of a "post-gender world" as a world where identities are multiple excluded sexuality as a basic category of the human. And the consequences of this are now beginning to emerge in the focus on affect as the primordial system of motivation in humans.

METAMORPHOTIC MOVEMENTS

These developments are also addressed by Rosi Braidotti in her book *Metamorphosis.*[20] As a proponent of nomadic cyborg theories herself, she sided with Deleuze and Guattari, asking how it might be possible, instead of refusing or ignoring the unconscious, to free it from the clutches of the oedipal. What she proposes is a "sort of becoming-animal: the cyborg, the coyote, the trickster, the onco-mouse produce alternative structures of otherness."[21] But how do these alternatives manifest themselves? What do they look like? The OncoMouse, which also became popular in cultural studies, was patented at Harvard University in 1988 and was destined for use in cancer research. It is a transgenetic animal into whose genome a human oncogene was inserted.

In their list of options for "becoming other", Deleuze and Guattari gave a prominent position to "becoming animal". What they had in mind, however, is unlikely to have been an OncoMouse. Instead, it must be assumed that they conceived of becoming-animal in the sense of Franz Kafka's *Metamorphosis*: waking up and no longer being able to stand on two legs, wriggling helplessly on one's armour-plated back. Or perhaps they were thinking of a Robinson Crusoe who gradually mutates into the lover of his island. Their main focus, in any case, was on that aspect within the human that resists, refusing to be reduced to the merely human—the same nonhuman, machinic core that Braidotti equates with *zoe* in opposition to *bios*. In contrast to Agamben's version, "bare life" for Braidotti is something she would like to recapture, to love, and to give back the attention it has lost. In this way, she transforms the nonhuman part that has been excommunicated from the symbolic order into a collective female subjectivity:

> What attracts me to *zoe* is the part of me that has long become disenchanted with and disengaged from the anthropocentrism that is built into humanistic thought. That in me which no longer identifies under the dominant categories of subjectivity, and which is not yet completely out of the cage of identity, that rebellious and impatient part, runs with *zoe.*[22]

What Braidotti wishes to recapture is that part of her sexual identity that has been sidelined in the phallogocentric discourse of humanism. In Braidotti's equation, then, the feminine as Other corresponds to Agamben's "bare life": "In the political economy of phallogocentrism and of its anthropocentric humanism, which predicates the sovereignty of Sameness, my sex fell on the side of Otherness, understood as pejorative difference, or as being worth-less-than."[23]

Hence the affinity of the feminine with the animal, the insane, the foreign, and so on. This reframes Agamben's pair of concepts, equating "bare life" with the female and the nonhuman (whereas in Agamben's version bare life defines the political moment that rules over life and marks its exclusion from society). For Braidotti, "bare life" is not the excluded, wild, uncivilized, threatening Other, but that part of human existence that must face sovereign power. Her definition mixes bare life and sexuality, whereas sexuality is not mentioned explicitly by Agamben. But Slavoj Žižek's charge that western philosophy has only ever dealt with sexuality in superficial terms may provide a kind of missing link here. For Žižek, philosophy never conceived of the subject as sexual, with "sexualization only [occurring] at the contingent, empirical level, whereas psychoanalysis promulgates sexuation into a kind of formal, a priori, condition of the very emergence of the subject."[24] Can this definition of sexuality shed a different light on the distinction between sovereign power and bare life? As the limit of the body that is not the body's own but that nonetheless inscribes itself into it?

As an example, I would like to use the same work also quoted by Agamben in *Homo Sacer*, de Sade's *Les cent vingt journées de Sodome* (on which Pier Paolo Pasolini's film *Salò or the 120 Days of Sodom* is also based). In Agamben's view, the book shows the confrontation between sovereign power and bare life down to the last detail—digestion, excrement, genitals, every aspect of the body, including its insides, is controlled by the masters. "Sade's modernity", Agamben writes,

> does not consist in having foreseen the unpolitical primacy of sexuality in our unpolitical age. On the contrary, Sade is as contemporary as he is because of his incomparable presentation of the absolutely political (that is, 'biopolitical') meaning of sexuality and physiological life itself. Like the concentration camps of our century, the totalitarian character of the organization of life in Silling's castle—with its meticulous regulations that do not spare any aspect of physiological life—[. . .] has its roots in the fact that what is proposed here for the first time is a normal and collective (and hence political) organization of human life founded solely on bare life.[25]

For Žižek, sexuation is the deferred precondition for the human. The path to the extinction of the human goes via the extinction of the sexual, leading to a merging of the Real and reality.

In contrast to this, Braidotti's wish to recapture *zoe* tends increasingly toward a reclaiming of affect. For in Brian Massumi's definition, affect is the moment between "not yet" and "no longer", it is the asocial part that always remains outside, for as soon as it is captured by an ego or consciousness, it will be past. But other definitions of affect also raise the suspicion that Braidotti's concept of *zoe* aims to reclaim the unconscious as part of the body. This is a similar move to that undertaken by Katherine Hayles when she interprets the loss of penis in *The Fly* as the character's transition to a posthuman stage, thus unwillingly falling into the castration trap. This is exactly the moment where Žižek insists that sexual difference belongs to the Real, as the difference between human, machine and animal, and that the Turing test does not so much distinguish between man and machine as between man and woman. The successful imitation of a woman's answers by a man (or vice versa) proves nothing because sexual identity does not depend on sequences of symbols, while the successful imitation of a human by a machine proves that this machine thinks, as thinking is finally no more than the correct sequencing of symbols: "What if," Žižek asks, "the solution to this enigma is much more simple and radical. What if sexual difference is not simply a biological fact, but the Real of an antagonism that defines humanity, so that once sexual difference is abolished, a human machine effectively becomes indistinguishable from a machine?"[26] Sexual difference should not be understood here as the simple difference between man and woman but as the marking of a disconnect—the relation between male and female is skewed:

> Sexual difference is not the ultimate referent which posits a limit to the unending drift of symbolization, insofar as it underlies all other polarities and provides their 'deep' meaning [. . .] but, on the contrary, that which 'skews' the discursive universe, preventing us from grounding its formations in 'hard reality'—that on account of which every *symbolization* of sexual difference is forever unstable and displaced with regard to itself.[27]

CUTS

In 1991, when the cyberfeminist manifesto was written in Australia by the artist collective VNS Matrix,[28] French performance artist Orlan had already presented her first spectacular operations on camera. In *La Réincarnation de Sainte Orlan* and in the seventh operation, *Ceci est mon corps . . . ceci est mon logiciel: Omniprésence*, she had her face remodelled using incisions and implants to make it resemble classical models from art history. During this procedure, she recited passages from the works of French psychoanalyst Jacques Lacan as a way of highlighting the existential dimension of what she was doing. The self is nothing but an image and a deceptive one at that, which we always misjudge so that we never perceive ourselves as we really are but always as we would like to be seen. In other words, the skin is all we have; there is nothing underneath, no ego, no soul, no truth. But even this skin is not unique; it can be shaped and altered. In the words of French psychoanalyst Eugénie Lémoine-Luccioni:

> Skin is deceiving—in life, one only has one skin—there is a bad exchange in human relations because one never is what one has. I have the skin of an angel but I am a jackal, the skin of a crocodile but I am a poodle, the skin of a black person, but I am white, the skin of a woman, but I am a man, I never have the skin of what I am. There is no exception to this rule because I am never what I have.[29]

With her body-cutting performances, Orlan staged something in the art world that can be watched every day on television: makeover shows, a series like *Nip/Tuck*, counselling sessions with cosmetic surgeons and beauty therapists. As Orlan has drastically shown, the cut brings nothing to light, leading instead, as many viewers of her operations can report, to nausea, disgust and horror. Something is coming apart at the seams here that can be compared with Gregor Samsa's horror in Kafka's *Metamorphosis* when proportions, viewpoints, and perspectives no longer converge but go their own way and take on anamorphotic qualities.[30]

Something different occurs in the case of *Strange Days*. When Lenny puts on his squid and immediately, as a woman, becomes the victim of a lethal rape, the twitching and wriggling of his body and his stammering are not expressions of surprise at suddenly finding himself "in a different film" but an indication of his being overwhelmed in the image as an image. The surprise of Lenny's customer who suddenly, thanks to another squid, finds himself an eighteen-year-old woman in the shower can also be attributed to the fact that, for a few moments, the borders between different realities are no longer perceived: The other body is experienced via one's own body and its movements; it is strange and familiar at the same time, which is what makes the whole thing so uncanny.[31]

Some years ago, the Slovenian cultural theorist Renata Salecl provocatively drew attention to the link between body art and female circumcision.[32] Why, she asks, is something art in the west but a horrific mutilation in Africa? Why are Orlan's cuts art while women who perform clitoridectomy on their daughters and granddaughters are inflicting bodily harm? Because, she answers, the different rituals and practices are governed by different laws. While a law in Africa requires the "circumcision" of girls to make them more fertile, more faithful and more beautiful, different symbolic conditions lead to the practices of body art and cosmetic surgery. But are the two really comparable? Are the art cuts always body incisions and thus also always sexual cuts?

Increasingly, Salecl stresses, clitoridectomy is not restricted to Africa, also becoming a problem in western cultures. Both forms of cutting (body art and female genital mutilation), she continues, highlight a phenomenon in postmodern societies where the big Other (the law, the symbolic order) breaks down and forfeits its authority. The word has forfeited its authority, and faith in the law has been lost, allowing the visual to become self-evident. Only what can be seen is credible, be it Orlan's sliced face or reality TV, docu-soaps, talk shows, and other television formats based on unfettered emotional outpourings. Consequently, the implosion of the symbolic order brings the cuts back into society by force as something literal, material, and physical—be it self-harming among adolescents, attacks based on skin colour, or cosmetic surgery and body art that not only cut but also constantly break other taboos and body boundaries.

DRAWING LINES

In the early 1990s, Slavoj Žižek introduced the concept of "interpassivity" to draw attention to a phenomenon that plays an important part in a media society: the chorus in classical drama had the function of reacting in place of the audience; the same can be said of the wailing women at funerals who mourn in place of the family; and in television, canned laughter stands in for the laughter of the viewers. In all of these cases, Žižek says, we allow ourselves to be represented and derive our enjoyment in this indirect way.[33] A few years later, however, Žižek described a new scenario in which the relationship between user and computer has an entirely different impact, capable of generating a state prior to any sexuation of the subject, a state before all sexual differentiation that is therefore pure enjoyment, pure autoeroticism.[34] Another three years later, however, in *Plague of Phantasms*, he writes again of counterforces that try to check this boundless state of enjoyment. First and foremost, he observes, the subject denies itself this enjoyment: "Is not one of the possible reactions to the excessive filling-in of the voids in cyberspace therefore *informational anorexia*, the desperate refusal to accept information, insofar as it occludes the presence of the Real?"[35]

A similar paradox in the fundaments of postindustrial society is described by Paul Verhaeghe. Such societies claim to allow everything while at the same time forcing the individual to have everything, to be everything, to enjoy everything. But instead of boundless happiness, this results in the spread of boredom, fatigue and depression. Fewer and fewer people are capable of engaging with someone or something else. Instead, as Verhaeghe explains, one can observe a hysterical search for new taboos, new leaders, new rules and new rituals. Such great freedom, such boundless enjoyment, communication and sexual contact thus lead to a tedious void. Demarcations, restrictions, decrees and laws are clearly necessary in order to keep alive the force referred to by psychoanalysis since the early twentieth century as the sex/death drive and that, since Lacan, has driven the subject before it as desire. In the theories of Kant and de Sade, Bataille and Lacan, desire requires the categorical imperative (moral law) in order to appear as desire.[36]

Against this backdrop, Tim Dean's argument that Lacan's theory of desire is far more radical than the nomadic liberation advocated by Deleuze and Guattari makes sense. By depersonalizing desire and locating it in the real, Dean writes, Lacan shook up sociality far more radically in theory than *Anti-Oedipus* does in political practice. By misunderstanding Deleuze and Guattari's critique of representation as a form of oppression, political movements, the new swarms and multitudes, simply reject the symbolic order. The problem with this approach, Dean claims, "appears as soon as they propose liberating desire—conceptually and in reality".[37] Not only the notion of primary forces being given free reign in society without any representation or regulation but also Deleuze and Guattari's definition of schizophrenia as a utopian expression of social and mental processes now appears quite prophetic, as I will show in chapter 6.

VIRAL BEINGS

In spite of all this, Deleuze and Guattari stand today for the liberation of the subject, of the human, of animals, and of society in the name of a desire that affects the body and drives it on in the process of becoming. Like Rosi Braidotti, many refer to the philosophers of "machinic desire" while trying not to overlook or ignore the gap that must necessarily open up between philosophy/theory and practice/politics.

Although Deleuze and Guattari were strangely blind regarding the sexually marked body, their approach can still be opened up for the linking of the sexuated body and its corresponding subjectivity, as Elizabeth Grosz has shown in *Volatile Bodies*. In her view, the merits of Deleuzian philosophy for a feminist analysis are: the psychical and the social are not opposed; there is no duplication of the real by representation, no mediation or production of reality by the symbolic order; subject–object relations are broken down into intensities and microprocesses, beyond which the Deleuzian model refuses any explanatory paradigm that might install relationships of causality. Key terms listed by Grosz in this context are fluid, flows, elasticity, and indeterminacy:

> The fluidity and indeterminacy of female body parts, most notably the breasts but no less the female sexual organs, are con-

> fined, constrained, solidified, through more or less temporary or permanent means of solidification by clothing or, at the limit, by surgery. This indeterminacy is again not a fact of nature but a function of the modes of representation that privilege the solid and the determinate over the fluid.[38]

In the meantime, Grosz has gone one step further, or rather one step back, to Darwin's theory of evolution, where, she argues, a diversity of sexual phenomena is already confirmed—a diversity and openness that she also finds in the empirical studies conducted by Alfred Kinsey in the 1950s, which she contrasts with feminist positions, especially those of the 1970s and '80s.[39]

In this light, the net art projects of Australian artist Melinda Rackham can be imagined as early examples of "bodies without organs". Rackham produces digital life forms that she uses to portray all manner of movements, migrations, transmissions, affections, amorous states, viral symbioses, and transformations: pulsating, glowing, starfish-like structures that glitter and flicker as in an aquarium. Her *Empyrean* project features a parallel universe that is an arena beyond space and time, expressing a great longing for potentialities, a world of breaks and intervals in which visitors move about as avatars. *Carrier*, on the other hand, visualizes a symbiotic ecology arising as a result of a love story between a male and female user via the Hepatitis C virus. This viral love story is described by Yvonne Volkart in precisely the same terms used by Elizabeth Grosz for a Deleuzian feminism:

> The body as a dynamic flow of information, as a molecule, a virus, an intelligent agent, as a fluid gender outside the gender dichotomy, but one that nonetheless seems to tend towards being feminine—this is also the concept of body and subject that Melinda Rackham presents in [*Carrier*], a Network created in 1999. The virus is called 'sHe', i.e. it is a being that is both genders at once and yet possibly more universally feminine, because the 's' that denotes femininity is contained in the word 'sHe' and pronounced, while the capital 'H' remains silent. The fact that it tends towards a 'she' is also shown in the feminine personal pronouns that follow, such as her swarming consciousness.[40]

This refusal of the *she* and the attachment of an *s* to the *He* can also be read as an allusion to Haraway's female cyborg that refuses to become a woman, remaining indeterminate with a slight tendency toward being a girl.

Brian Massumi once proposed to think the "body without organs" as a body situated outside any determination, as a body that adopts the viewpoint of the virtual, the potential.[41] But we come closer to what Deleuze and Guattari had in mind if we translate this body "without organs" as a body "without organization". It is a body that exists simultaneously alongside the organized (fixed, arranged, subdivided) body that threatens to subvert the organization of the one body (and that sometimes, in cases of madness, drugs, and illness, actually does so) or, as in the films of David Cronenberg, in *Shivers* (1975) and *Naked Lunch* (1991), explodes the body, either quietly, with discretion, or resoundingly killing the host. Based on this reading, Rackham's agents reveal themselves as not translations of this "body without organs" but as beings that already tend in the direction of *abstract sex*.

Luciana Parisi structured her book *Abstract Sex* as a comprehensive dismantling of philosophy and biotechnology where sex is dealt with on three levels—biophysical, biocultural and biodigital. Over millions of years, she writes, a biodigital level has taken shape on which sex now takes place only in the form of cloning and cybersex. Parisi neither mourns the disappearance of natural sexuality nor celebrates virtual sex. Instead she proposes a third path that links the latest phase (the biodigital) with an older developmental stage (the biophysical): "linking these mutations to microcellular processes of information transmission that involve the unnatural mixtures of bodies and sexes."[42] In the next chapter, I look in more detail at the consequences of this vision of sexuality as "affective contagion".

When cybernauts are equated with Deleuzian nomadic subjects, when Deleuze's lines of light are grasped as network channels and the network itself as the Lacanian Real, then specific differences are lost that are partly responsible for the tedious void mentioned earlier. What manifests itself in the development from cybersex to abstract sex is a decomposition that has less to do with the subjects and their real bodies than with a specific twist in the definition of sexuality as something that has nothing (more) to do with the Other: "Sex is a genetic mixing in organisms that operates at a variety of levels; it occurs in some organisms at more than one level simultaneously."[43]

NOTES

1. Ars Electronica was founded in 1979 in Linz, Austria, and is now one of the annual highlights on the international media art festival circuit, www.aec.at/about/geschichte (retrieved 19 June 2014).
2. Using the example of anorexia, Charles Shepherdson has analysed the distinction between need, demand, and desire in his essay "The Gift of Love and the Debt of Desire," in *Differences* 10 (1998).
3. Jean Laplanche and Jean-Bertrand Pontalis, "Fantasy and the Origins of Sexuality," in Victor Burgin, James Donald, and Cora Kaplan (eds.), *Formations of Fantasy* (London: Routledge, 1986), 5–34, here 29f.
4. Paul Virilio, in conversation with Carlos Oliveira, "Global Algorithm 1.7: The Silence of the Lambs: Paul Viriolio in Conversation," in *CTheory.net* (12 June 1996), http://www.ctheory.net/articles.aspx?id=38 (retrieved 19 May 2014).

5. Rachel Armstrong, "Cyborg Film Making in Great Britain," in Andrea B. Braidt (ed.), *[Cyborgs.Nets/z]*, catalog accompanying the film *Dandy Dust* (Vienna: Eigenverlag, 1999), 29.

6. According to de Kerckhove, location and place of being coincide. Space itself becomes interactive and revolves around us. But this would mean a second Copernican revolution. Summarized in Simone Mahrenholz, "Derrick de Kerckhove—Medien als Psychotechnologien," in Alice Lagaay and David Lauer (eds.), *Medien-Theorien. Eine philosophische Einführung* (Frankfurt, Germany: Campus, 2004), 87.

7. Marjorie Garbner, "Some Like It Haute," interview with Hannah J. L. Feldman in *World/Art*, 1 (1995), 30–33.

8. Mark Simpson, who originally coined the term *metrosexual*, has now identified a new generation, the "spornosexuals" (sport and porn), for whom body grooming (rather than clothes and cosmetics) is the key to being admired; Mark Simpson, "The Metrosexual Is Dead. Long Live the 'Spornosexual'," in *The Telegraph*, (10 June 2014), http://www.telegraph.co.uk/men/fashion-and-style/10881682/The-metrosexual-is-dead.-Long-live-the-spornosexual.html (retrieved 10 June 2014).

9. Charles Shepherdson, "The Role of Gender and the Imperative of Sex," in Joan Copjec (ed.), *Supposing the Subject* (London: Verso, 1994), 158–84, here 170.

10. Haraway describes the cyborg as a figure in a "post-gender world", thus underlining the end of a politics of origins. See Donna J. Haraway, "Cyborg Manifesto: Science, Technology, and Socialist-Feminism in the Late Twentieth Century" (1983) in Donna J. Haraway, *Simians, Cyborgs, and Women: The Reinvention of Nature* (New York: Routledge, 1991), 149–81, here 150.

11. Annette Bitsch, "Kybernetik des Unbewussten, das Unbewusste der Kybernetik," in Pias (ed.), *Cybernetics | Kybernetik, The Macy Conferences 1946–1953, Essays & Dokumente, Vol. II* (Zurich, Switzerland: diaphanes, 2003), 153–68, here 157.

12. Michel Foucault, *The Birth of the Clinic* (1963) (London: Tavistock, 1973).

13. Astrid Deuber-Mankowsky, "Das virtuelle Geschlecht. Gender und Computerspiele, eine diskursanalytische Annäherung," in Claus Pias and Christian Holtorf (eds.), *Escape! Computerspiele als Kulturtechnik* (Cologne, Germany: Böhlau, 2007), 85–104.

14. Sadie Plant, "The Future Looms: Weaving Women and Cybernetics," in *Body & Society*, 1.3–4 (1995), 45–64.

15. Zoe Sofoulis, "Contested Zones: Artists, Technologies, and Questions of Futurity," in *Leonardo*, 29.1 (1996), 59–66.

16. "Complex interactions of media, organisms, weather patterns, ecosystems, thought patterns, cities, discourses, fashions, populations, brains, markets, dance nights and bacterial exchanges emerge. [. . .] You live in cultures, and cultures live in you. [. . .] Without the centrality of agency, culture is neither high, nor ordinary, but complex." [Sadie Plant, "The Virtual Complexity of Culture," in George Robertson, Melinda Mash, Lisa Tickner, Jon Bird, Barry Curtis, and Tim Putnam (eds.), *FutureNatural, Nature/Science/Culture* (New York: Routledge, 1996), 203–17, here 214].

17. See Marie-Luise Angerer, *Body Options. Körper.Spuren.Medien.Bilder* (Vienna: Turia & Kant, 1999), especially the section "Space Does Matter," 132–58.

18. Astrid Deuber-Mankowsky, *Lara Croft: Cyberheroine* (Minneapolis: University of Minnesota Press, 2005).

19. See Claudia Reiche, *Digitaler Feminismus* (Hamburg, Germany: Thealit, 2006), 111–40.

20. Rosi Braidotti, *Metamorphosis. Towards a Materialist Theory of Becoming* (Cambridge, UK: Polity, 2002).

21. Ibid., 139.

22. Rosi Braidotti, "Between No Longer and the Not Yet: On Bios/Zoe-Ethics," in *Filozofski vestnik*, 23.2 (2002), 9–26, here 16.

23. Ibid.

24. Slavoj Žižek, "Four Discourses, Four Subjects," in Slavoj Žižek (ed.), *Cogito and the Unconscious* (Durham, NC: Duke University Press, 1998), 74–116, here 81.

25. Giorgio Agamben, *Homo Sacer: Sovereign Power and Bare Life* (Stanford, CA: Stanford University Press, 1998), 135.

26. Slavoj Žižek, *On Belief* (London: Routledge, 2003), 43.
27. Slavoj Žižek, *Plague of Fantasies* (London: Verso, 1997), 216.
28. See Angerer, *Body Options*, 152f.
29. Eugénie Lémoine-Luccioni, quoted in David Moss, "Memories of Being: Orlan's Theatre of the Self," in *Art + Text*, 54 (1996), 67–72, here 68f.
30. Parveen Adams has described Orlan's operations as an "anamorphosis of space which bears upon sexual difference." Spatial arrangements depend on basic assumptions. When one of these is not fulfilled, the subject may fall out of his or her perceptive framework. Inside and outside must be clearly separated and fit together properly; inside and outside must be isomorphic, meaning that they match in a simple way. This isomorphism applies not only to inside/outside, however, but determines the whole list of oppositions that characterize western thought: body/mind, essence/appearance, subject/object, male/female, and finally phallic/castrated. If these processes undergo an anamorphotic process, then it becomes clear that "each term of the pair is not in contradiction to the other term and the extent to which the relations between them, far from conforming to a clean-cut isomorphism, are strewn with strange thresholds and hybrid forms." With Orlan's opening of the skin, the border between inside and outside is violated, thus destroying the semblance of "true" depth. See Parveen Adams, *The Emptiness of the Image* (London: Routledge, 1996), 141.
31. Sigmund Freud describes the uncanny as far closer than it first appears. It is something deeply familiar that must nonetheless remain hidden. Unconscious wishes that push their way to the surface become threatening and eerie—uncanny. See Sigmund Freud, "The Uncanny" (1919), in *The Standard Edition of the Complete Psychological Works of Sigmund Freud, Vol. 17* (London: Hogarth Press, 1955), 219–52.
32. See Renata Salecl, "Sexuelle Differenz als Einschnitt in den Körper," in Jörg Huber and Martin Heller (eds.), *Inszenierung und Geltungsdrang, Interventionen* (Zurich, Switzerland: Museum für Gestaltung, 1998), 165–85.
33. See Slavoj Žižek, "Is It Possible to Traverse the Fantasy in Cyberspace?" in Elizabeth Wright and Edmond Wright (eds.), *The Žižek Reader* (Oxford, UK: Blackwell, 1999), 102–24.
34. See Slavoj Žižek, "Lacan with Quantum Physics," in George Robertson, Melinda Mash, Lisa Tickner, Jon Bird, Barry Curtis, and Tim Putnam (eds.), *FutureNatural, Nature/Science/Culture* (New York: Routledge, 1996), 270–92.
35. Žižek, *Plague of Fantasies*, 155.
36. See Verhaeghe, *Love in a Time of Loneliness: Three Essays on Drive and Desire* (New York: Other Press, 1999), 63f.
37. Tim Dean, *Beyond Sexuality* (Chicago: University of Chicago Press, 2000), 242.
38. Elizabeth Grosz, *Volatile Bodies: Toward a Corporeal Feminism* (Bloomington: Indiana University Press, 1994), 205.
39. See Elizabeth Grosz, *Time Travels: Feminism, Nature, Power* (Durham, NC: Duke University Press, 2005), 198–214.
40. Yvonne Volkart, "Physicalization in Networked Space: Melinda Rackham—Visualization of Identity and Subjectivity in Cyberspace," in *Springerin*, 1 (2000), http://www.springerin.at/dyn/heft_text.php?textid=868&lang=en&pos=1 (retrieved 20 June 2014).
41. See Brian Massumi, *A User's Guide to Capitalism and Schizophrenia: Deviations from Deleuze and Guattari* (Cambridge, MA: MIT Press, 1993), 70.
42. Luciana Parisi, *Abstract Sex: Philosophy, Bio-Technology and the Mutations of Desire* (London: Bloomsbury Academic, 2004), 4.
43. Lynn Margulis, quoted in Matthew Fuller, "Luciana Parisi Interview," (28 October 2004), http://www.nettime.org/Lists-Archives/nettime-l-0410/msg00054.html (retrieved 16 May 2014).

FIVE

Sexualizing Affect

The preceding chapters concentrate on specific shifts, omissions, and parallels in the history of thinking the human being. The most striking aspect of all these various approaches, I have argued, is their desire to free the human from the clutches of psychoanalysis and its specific linguistic definition of the subject. As we have seen, very different scientific disciplines (neurology, biology, philosophy, cultural and media theory) and diverse fields of activity (from politics to the economy to universities and the online world) are involved in this reformulation. This chapter presents a specific debate that goes deeper still in its attempt to dislodge the human subject at its very core, assailing the unconscious and the sexual in a move that leads ultimately toward a possible extinction of the sexual.

TRANSITIONS

Feminist philosopher Rosi Braidotti has called for an end to the anthropocentric thinking in which desire and life are conceived of in purely subject-centered terms. With reference to Gilles Deleuze's "Nomadology" she wishes to understand "life as subject", an argument that calls for a dynamic view of nature, life, and man. All psychoanalytical and language- and structure-based approaches are rejected as no longer adequate: "What if the subject is 'trans', or in transit, that is to say no longer one, whole, unified and in control, but rather fluid, in process and hybrid? What are the ethical and political implications of a non-unitary vision of the human subject?"[1]

British cultural theorist Luciana Parisi translates Braidotti's demand into a radical model, developing a definition of sexuality (abstract sex) that links Deleuzian concepts with a molecular-biological approach (Lynn Margulis's theory of endosymbiosis[2]). In this view, sex has nothing to do with gender or bodies in the actual sense, being instead a matter of exchange, combination and remodelling on various levels of life—inorganic, organic, climatic, geological, and so on.[3]

In the following, I want to highlight the consequences of these two approaches—Braidotti's version of desire and Parisi's of sexuality. However, psychoanalysis (which is subjected to a thorough critique by these two writers, among many others) is itself making first steps toward neurobiology in order to regain some ground via the kind of biological underpinning Freud himself is said to have wished for.

Within media, art and cultural studies, too, the focus has moved away from the fantasmatic identification of the viewer with visual models, shifting conspicuously toward affective image–viewer relationships. In this context, audiovisual signals and physical reactions are once more being recorded, measured and examined image sequence by image sequence, in order to explain which images and sounds allegedly trigger which emotions. This development was also promoted by the "pictorial turn",[4] which gave rise to discussions within the new discipline of visual studies concerning the nature of images in a "post-media" age.[5] Today, the argument goes, images are strictly speaking no longer images but algorithmic productions whose surfaces are still legible but whose basis is no longer a visual one.

These shifts and dislocations are underpinned by the (often implicit) assumption that the development toward a posthuman (or transhuman) social order, the first signs of which are already emerging in today's postindustrial society, is the predominant one.[6] Within these developments, the figure of *anthropos* as we have come to know it has been destabilized, its much-mooted demise now widely considered a foregone conclusion: the modern era with its ideological state apparatuses is over, and in retrospect the postmodern era emerges as the final phase of its hollowing out. In this "post-ideological era", as Brian Massumi, among others, has called it, there is a focus on affect as the dimension where ideology now operates: "It seems to me that alternative political action does not have to fight against the idea that power has become affective, but rather has to learn to function itself on that same level—meet affective modulation with affective modulation. That requires, in some ways, a performative, theatrical or aesthetic approach to politics."[7]

At first glance, this corresponds to the developments in politics, art, and the media discussed earlier, with the emphasis not on *what* but on *how*, not on a critique of representation (in art, for example) but on events, co-presence and the space of experience. But what do digital images have in common with affect? Why is there such a strong sense that the new technical production of images (and media in general) is intimately connected with what I have called the "*dispositif* of affect"? As discussed in chapter 1, the digital images are associated, like affect, with the desire for a direct, unmediated link to the brain or organism. This may seem harmless enough, but it has far-reaching implications.

In his book *Kybernetische Anthropologie*, Stefan Rieger names this desire clearly when he writes that the ultimate objective is to implant a kind of unconscious into cybernetic machines so that they acquire the competence that characterizes the human brain and perceptive apparatus—the ability to overlook and overhear. For, he continues, it is broadly agreed "that human efficiency is based on overseeing and overhearing, thus always taking place where consciousness is not or is not yet."[8] The unconscious is portrayed here as something that functions more efficiently than its counterpart, consciousness. Although this reflects an "erroneous" understanding of the unconscious (with regard to psychoanalytic definitions), it shows the direction in which both machines and humans are being examined, explored and manipulated: as automata that react correctly without knowing because their spontaneity communicates directly with their surroundings. A number of parallels can be drawn between the significance of the unconscious in cybernetic research and the current focus on affect. First, both the unconscious and affect are viewed as the site of a truth not of the human but of the body, a truth that goes beyond consciousness. And second, the construction of the digital can be compared with the system of consciousness. As a result, the four poles—consciousness, the unconscious, the digital, affect—are variously interconnected. Having focused so far on affect and its links to the digital, we will now also consider sexuality as intrinsically linked to affect.

In his 1973 book *Crash*,[9] J. G. Ballard, whose science-fiction novels often centre on human sexuality and its modification, wrote that technology would hollow out sexuality: here, erotic arousal only arises where the human body is broken, injured, wounded; sex and eroticism can only be integrated into a violent logic via a mechanical apparatus. In his dissertation, Matt Smith describes Ballard's oeuvre as the unfolding story of the demise of affect. In Ballard's eyes, the late twentieth century is marked by the death of the emotions and the triumph of the imaginary; sex, paranoia, voyeurism, self-loathing (all these ailments of the previous century) are now culminating in the "death of affect"[10] as the most horrific phase of this development.[11]

FROM THE UNCONSCIOUS TO DESIRE

Long live the radical constructivism of the unconscious.[12]

With this rallying cry, Clausberg and Weiller campaign against a purely functional understanding of unconscious images, arguing that images are more than mere neurobiological data. Antonio Damasio has reintroduced the notion of inner, mental images to explain the nature of consciousness. Bergson speaks of the body as an inner image, connecting with a tradition that also includes such figures as Ernst Mach with his theory of sensations.[13] Consciousness had been the object of suspicion for a long time, then, before Freud reluctantly reintroduced it into his concept of the psychical apparatus. The unconscious, on the other hand, is credited by Freud with a dynamic potential that surpasses the individual but without being subsumed into a "collective" unconscious. Instead, he uses the term to describe unconsciousness as a "regular and inevitable phase in the processes constituting our psychical activity; every psychical act begins as an unconscious one, and it may either remain so or go on developing into consciousness, as it meets with resistance or not."[14]

In historical terms, an unconscious that could claim a scientific-empirical status was first acknowledged in the nineteenth century. This also marked the beginning of its period of conceptual and systematic differentiation within the fields of physiology and philosophy. Today we are experiencing a new struggle over definitions of the unconscious, as neurobiology and posthuman models postulate its end.

In discussions of affect, feeling and sensation, the unconscious plays a smaller part than consciousness, as the basic questions are, How do bodily processes give rise to conscious, mental ones? How does matter develop into mind? A key issue here is the transition, the process of translation, and the zone where this translation occurs. In Freud, we find the concept of the threshold with regard to his concept of the drives, but it can be inserted between the unconscious and consciousness more generally, as Mai Wegener has shown in her history of concepts of the unconscious.[15] A central role is played here by Gustav Theodor Fechner's *Elements of Psychophysics* (1860) in which he defines a "psychophysical threshold"[16] located where sensations enter consciousness. Here, unconscious sensations and mental images are recognized—as "ultimately [. . .] quantifiable conditions".[17] Today, these conditions are of interest once more as biological ones that, in tandem with new recording technologies, offer insights far greater then Fechner would ever have dared to imagine (giving an idea of the scale of the break that Freud would make with his psychophysical arrangement). But regarding aesthetic perception, Fechner's comments have become highly topical again, as he posits aesthetic perception as being based on unconscious associations. This refers back to Hermann von Helmholtz, whose *Treatise on Physiological Optics* assumes that unconscious perception is a key shaping influence on our aesthetic sensitivity.[18] With Nietzsche, however, there emerged for the first time the notion of an unconscious induced by language, which led to his call for a "language of signs [. . .] that is capable of 'making conscious the unconscious'."[19] When Nietzsche states that the unconscious appears as dark and inaccessible because consciousness is unable to perceive or comprehend it, he opens up two paths of thought—the psychoanalytical project of gaining access to the unconscious, and its celebration as a positive force by the Surrealists. Much of this was later to be echoed by Deleuze and Guattari in their remarks on desiring-machines and lines of light.

Freud developed a practice of the unconscious that differed radically from everything that went before both in its approach and in its theoretical concepts. The unconscious "shows" itself in symptoms whose language must be unravelled like a rebus. In language itself, the unconscious communicates what must then be accessed by listening and making associative links. In dreams, the subject's story is told with the aid of various mechanisms (condensation, displacement, considerations of representability, secondary revision), a story in which the dreamer is a guest, protagonist, observer, rhythm, colour, music, spectacle, all of these at once, or absent. In *The Interpretation of Dreams*, Freud analyses the laws of the unconscious. The primary processes shaping the unconscious never show themselves as they truly are, instead always representing compromises resulting from the impact of censorship (by the super-ego and the ego) on wishes and the satisfaction of drives. The unconscious itself knows no negation, no contradiction and no time. In the course of the development from infant to child to adult, it is shaped by traumatic experiences of satisfaction and pain, including the discovery of the difference between the sexes.[20]

This is why Joan Copjec keeps asking "What is a body?" and why she insists that, although there are many definitions that try to prove that the body "matters" (Judith Butler), the body we have is one that obeys rules to which we have no access, which in turn prompts another question:

> Why do we find ourselves constantly overeating or starving ourselves, cutting up other bodies into little pieces or prostrating

> ourselves at another's feet? In other words, why, even in their 'basic' pursuits of nourishment and sex, are human bodies given to compulsion, inhibition, sadism, idealization? Animals have bodies, too, but not such exotic pleasures, such perverse tastes. Their instincts, like our drives, are a kind of nonconscious knowledge of what they must do.[21]

But what is this nonconscious knowledge of the drives that makes us do things without knowing what we are doing (or that we are doing it)?

Jacques Lacan has defined this nonconscious knowledge as desire that articulates itself in and through language. Lacanian *jouissance* is a desire that, like the wish in Freud, goes beyond the sexual.[22] Lacan's rewriting of psychoanalytical theory is characterized by two striking breaks: the central position he accords to the symbolic and his definition of *desire* as desire for the Other. This desire is experienced in the Other as lack. For Lacan, the reality of the unconscious is sexual, meaning that the development of the human subject unfolds between misrecognition (*méconnaissance*) and lack-in-being (*manque à l'être*). Others, like Deleuze and Guattari, have argued against this dramatic dimension of the subject (see chapter 2), centring their theories on a becoming that gives a decisive turn to Lacanian lack-in-being as a saturatedness that drives the subject forward.

Whereas Freud famously omitted cinema, the medium of his age, from his work, in Lacan the visual is present early on in his theory of the "mirror phase" and in his "eye-gaze theory".[23] I refer here deliberately to the visual and not to media, as Lacan's approach is certainly not based on media theory or visual studies. Instead, his theory of a separation of seeing and looking refuses to offer any coherent notion of desire that might be located in the visual. The Lacanian desire for pleasure (*jouissance* = ecstasy as opposed to enjoyment) that takes place outside the symbolic order can thus be specifically related to the cybernetic definition of the unconscious. Lacan was so taken with the algorithmic construction of this "reality" that his theory of the unconscious became more and more mathematical, its functioning illustrated in equations and formulas. His application of cybernetics to psychoanalysis follows a programme inherent in cybernetics, that of the "black box", as Annette Bitsch has shown. Lacan, she writes, profited from cybernetics and its objects of study because they, like the unconscious in psychoanalysis, belong to the realm of the real: "They can only be examined in their functional and operational relations, interactions and effects: black box."[24] And she continues: "With cybernetic cheer, Lacan benefits from the fact that the primal scene of psychoanalysis is the testimony of a loss, the loss of truth, of the object, of being, both metaphysically and physically."[25] Due to this splitting by language, the subject enters a media state whose core truth is a technology that owes its effectiveness to the regulatory circuit of the symbolic. For all this focus on language and "mathemes", however, one should not overlook the degree to which the body is taken seriously in Lacan's theory as an organism, as something real. Lacan first focused on the body as the Other of the subject in *Seminar XI*, shifting his attention from the signifier and desire to the real and *jouissance*. With this shift, Lacan shows how the concepts of the unconscious, the real and the body (as organism) are interchangeable. In the process, a new opposition arises—that between the enjoying organism and the sexually marked body whose phallic pleasure resists the enjoyment of the organism.

Paul Verhaeghe states, "The Real of the organism functions as a cause, in the sense that it contains a primordial loss which precedes the loss involved in the chain of signifiers. [. . .] It is the loss of eternal life, which paradoxically enough is lost at the moment of birth as a sexed being."[26] Sexuality, then, is always inscribed with loss of a oneness that was asexual. With sexuality as the birth of a gendered subject, the body as organism is lost and a desire is gained that makes the body reappear for moments of desire for the Other, briefly overcoming the organism's division: "Orgasm is the only conceivable way in which this gap can be closed: a stitching up (*suture du sujet*) by which the subject joins his own body for a moment along with the body of another."[27] Immediately afterwards, the gap is reinstated and a sadness (*la petite mort*) sets in: "What comes before and after this teaches us something about *affect* [my emphasis]. Before, there is desire and anxiety because the subject has to disappear from the scene. Afterwards, there is sadness because the union with the object disappears."[28]

The radical breach between subject and body is readily apparent here. But affect in this sense has little to do with the affects and emotions discussed in the previous chapters, instead being an inscription of the first Other, the mother and her "lalangue",[29] that leaves traces on the body of the child that can no longer be accessed by language. Lacan perceived and addressed these affects, but he also warned against confusing them with the real of the subject: "It is not a matter of denying the importance of affects. But it is important not to confuse them with the substance of that which we are seeking in the *Real-Ich*, beyond signifying articulation of the kind we artists of analytical speech are capable of handling."[30]

In *The Transmission of Affect*, Teresa Brennan examines the relationship between affect and language, presenting them both as (ideally) communicating with one another. But her approach is greatly at odds with Lacan, who accords no language to the body—neither the biological nor the hormonal nor the genetic code speak.

Instead, an unbridgeable divide exists between language and communication as information transmission, assigning them to different orders. The fact that Lacan found cybernetics and its systems of rules attractive as a way of underlining the radical otherness of the body from the subject should not cause us to overlook the fact that he always opposed the notion of language as communication. Brennan, on the other hand, attempts to heal, to *suture*, as a way of bringing language—which she describes as developing out of the body and then functioning as a separate code—into harmony with the previously mentioned body codes. At the end of her book, she paraphrases Wittgenstein: "Of that we cannot speak, thereof we must learn."[31] Her theory thus centres on a kind of reeducation programme intended to bring the senses, genes, hormones and human language closer together again so that the languages of the body and human communication can understand one another.

Lacan's version is far removed from any such striving for harmony. In his view, language is inhuman (i.e., not a human faculty), making it appear closer to the other codes. But as transmitters of information, the biological, physical and neurological codes are completely different in quality to language as articulation. Instead, with every developmental step in human life, Lacan postulates an opening and a closing in which an alienation is produced that is captured in language. In this context, he speaks of "aphanisis", what he also calls a "fading" of the subject. For Lacan, the subject first appears in the Other "in so far as the first signifier, the unary signifier, emerges in the field of the Other and represents the subject for another signifier, which other signifier has as its effect the *aphanisis* of the subject."[32] The subject is thus so radically divided by language and representation that "when the subject appears somewhere as meaning, he is manifested elsewhere as fading, as disappearance".[33] Lacan locates desire in this "interval between these two signifiers", relating this back to the desire of the first Other, the mother: "It is in so far as his desire is beyond or falls short of what she says, of what she hints at, of what she brings out as meaning, it is in so far as his desire is unknown, it is in this point of lack, that the desire of the subject is constituted."[34] Paul Verhaeghe has described these openings and closings with a sequence of specific bodily developments/events as follows: first, the "advent of the living—the opening and closing of life at birth" (marking the difference between eternal and individual life); followed by "the advent of the I" as development opens up the body as the individual's own and separates it from the body of the mother ("the opening and closing of the body")—at this stage, the body is perceived as ego in the mirror stage and misrecognized; only with its entry or acceptance into the symbolic order does the subject arrive ("advent of the subject"), which, as Lacan also states, takes place as "the opening and closing of signifiers". This entry into the symbolic order is accompanied by "the advent of gender" as a sexed identity of position.[35]

This development clearly shows the different relations between body and ego, body and subject. The site of the subject is language, whereas the ego "dwells" on the body (developing out of what Freud calls the "projection of a surface").[36] The primary drives draw the line between zoe and bios, between individual and eternal life. In the course of the mirror stage, a sexless and gender-free ego emerges on the foundation of an initial alienation—the break between Being and a speaking being is concealed at the cost of the disappearance of the subject. The secondary and partial drives (the phallic drive) introduce a further phase of subjectivization that enthrones the order of gender and, with this "closure", installs the *objet petit a* that points to the gap between ego and subject: "The *petit a* never crosses this gap. [. . .] This *a* is presented precisely, in the field of the mirage of the narcissistic function of desire, as the object that cannot be swallowed, as it were, which remains stuck in the gullet of the signifier."[37] The tragedy insisted on by Lacan consists in the constant attempt by individual life to become reunited with eternal life (Freud's life and death drive), which is why human sexuality belongs to a different order than animal reproduction. In and with human sexuality, the trauma of the cut (of separation and alienation) is repeated.

In chapter 4, I quote Renata Salecl, who links the cut with female genital mutilation and body art in order to show that the symbolic order, the law, and language have forfeited a degree of power and influence. Instead of language making the cut, a real cut is made, an incision that places the body within the (hierarchic) order. Verhaeghe makes a similar observation, but he links it explicitly with the rise of (neuro-)biology as a hegemonic form of knowledge production, translating Butler's sex–gender split back into a simple bipolar man–woman model: "Today we are facing a strange backlash towards sex and gender, man and woman. The paradoxical scattering of gender identity by Butler has recently led to a return to the classic, safe male/female opposition within the biology of sex. Today in biology, genetics, brain studies, voices are heard everywhere defending this binary opposition."[38]

Rather than physical cuts, gender difference is upheld by referring to different brain signals, affective reactions and hormone levels. Deleuze, too, describes this drama of biological life, not as a tragedy but as a comedy in which the protagonists are driven by the machinic (language, the media). In this view, however, individuals experience themselves via overwhelming superabundance and not via a lack of being.

At first glance, one might think that precisely this machinic quality could be linked to the language-based subject of psychoanalysis, namely (as mentioned several times earlier) on the level of the affects, which, in Deleuze's philosophy, occupy the position of the "partial objects".[39] Slavoj Žižek makes this comparison in *Organs without Bodies,* but as we have already seen in the discussion of Hansen's critique of Deleuze's concept of affect, rather than assigning affects to a specific subject, Žižek locates them on a preindividual level. They are "freefloating intensities" that "circulate at a level 'beneath' intersubjectivity".[40] They belong to the virtual (as opposed to the actual) and emerge only as a blockade, as an entity, as a molar fixing. Žižek tries to show here that this definition brings Deleuze dangerously close to an empiriocritical position—"the flow of feelings *precedes* the subject".[41] Žižek, following Badiou's reading, does not consider Deleuze to be an advocate of psychophysical parallelism, however, seeing his thinking instead as an intersection between the logic of being and the logic of becoming, as the production of being emerges from the immaterial.[42] This emergence takes place without negativity; everything strives for a complete actualization that can only be slowed, prevented, and diverted from outside. (In Spinoza's model, the body is only ever affected by other bodies, resulting in its current form, which changes with each further affection.) The affective, preindividual body is thus affected, treated, and modulated from outside. In the psychoanalytical model, this affirmative striving for life is given a very different interpretation. Even if the life drive (or the libido) keeps the organism alive, life is always directed toward death, defined in opposition to eternal (biological) being. In this in-between position, sexuality operates as preservation and loss, as desire for a pleasure that is impossible because it means extinction. Freud accords sexuality the function of forming an *impasse,* a blockade, preventing the body and the symbolic order from intersecting or overlapping. According to Žižek, sexuality represents an "inherent impasse"[43] because "sexuality is the only drive that is, in itself, hindered and perverted, being simultaneously insufficient and excessive".[44] This allows sexuality to function as a "co-sense" that can dock onto any (neutral, literal) meaning because it is itself empty of meaning.[45]

Language generates the surface of the body as a sexual subject, causing it to split into a knowledge-body and a pleasure-body. The latter is addressed by psychoanalysis as radically nonbiological, nonanimal—as an "uncoordinated plurality of erogenous zones".[46] If one compares this "plurality of erogenous zones" with Deleuze and Guattari's "body without organs", their respective concepts of the unconscious and the virtual must be taken into account in order to understand the decisive difference between the two. In Žižek's comparison, affects and partial objects are named as the nonhuman appendages of the body that signal its intrinsic laws. But the two views of the body have different agendas: Partial objects point to a radical nonorganization of the sexual, to the potentiality of erogenous associations and pleasures, whereas affects strive for connections and new relations in order to further fold the virtuality of being. The affects stand for the "splendour of the pronoun 'one'"[47] (in the sense of one lives, one loves, and one dies). The body without organs eludes identity, refuses production, is pure intensity, allows events to take hold of the subject from the depths of the body. Although this model based on intensity and the senses depends on a subject that knows and can say what it feels, a difference is inscribed here that is linked to this knowing and saying. The subject of psychoanalysis does not know what it feels; however deeply it exposes itself to the unconscious of its body, it will always come up against the "pure surface of a fantasmatic screen".[48] In neurobiology, on the other hand, affect and emotion no longer need a subject that does or does not know, that can or cannot speak.

THE PHANTASM OF LIFE

The various models cited earlier speak of life (being) as an organism, as virtuality, as something vital, as the opposite of understanding. Access to this life is barred in various ways: by language, by politics, by the essence of the human. This life has been referred to as "sacred life", then as "eternal" as distinct from biological. Agamben describes *zoe* as sacred, bare life from which man as a political being has distanced himself, placing it in political quarantine. According to Agamben, however, bare life has become a constituent part of a modern politics that is showing itself perhaps more clearly and more cynically in today's late capitalism. Capitalized through and through, politics divides people cartographically into bare (worthless) and full (valuable) life, forcing the latter into apparatuses based on techniques of the self that produce self-responsible subjects.[49]

Agamben's bare life is not identical with Verhaeghe's eternal life toward which the biological life of the individual strives, wishing (unconsciously) to be reunited with it. Eternal life here is that primal, unbroken state that undergoes a first separation at birth.

Rosi Braidotti gives her concept of zoë a different definition again, opposing Agamben's definition with the claim that this bare life has always been treated as feminine. This idea can of course also be applied to eternal life as feminine/motherly (as defined by Verhaeghe) in the sense that the repressed (the idealized primal state) is always conceived of as feminine. This situation, as Braidotti writes, is being altered and reordered by a politics of life (biopolitics, life science):

> We need to attend to the forces of life and matter that are traversed by and not exhausted by politics. This implies giving centre stage to *zoe* as relations or flows of interaction; production or generative power and the inhuman. Accepting the bio-egalitarianism of *zoe*-politics means that each subject, no matter the sex, race or species, has to be rethought according to the positivity of difference, i.e. the notion of difference as the principle of non-One as zero-institution.[50]

Braidotti develops (or moves away from) Foucault and Agamben's concept of biopolitics, considering that they defined it as nothing but loss. In contrast to this, Braidotti emphasizes the positive power of *zoe*, focusing on the possibility of a-human, not-yet-subject-centred connections. *Zoe* means a world in which no difference exists between the socialized forces of body politics and the forces of the body itself. The difficultly here however, as Braidotti remarks, consists in explaining the synthesis of subject-bound and prepersonal forces. What drives these forces? What is the primal force? To find an answer to these questions, she refers to *conatus*, the term used by Spinoza to describe the life force as a virtual potentiality. But in fact, as Braidotti writes with regard to Deleuze, people wish to immerse themselves in this flow of life; they want to submerge and dissolve. Lacan, she notes, cynically referred to this as becoming one with the body. In her eyes, however, this is not an ontological implosion but a fading away of

> subjects [that] are enfleshed entities [. . .] immersed in the full intensity and luminosity of becoming. [. . .] This, therefore, is the glorious expression of the life force that is *zoe*, and not the emanation of some divine essence. Radical immanence as a mode of thinking the subject [. . .] deflates the pretence of grandiose eternity. [. . .] Life is eternal, but this eternity is postulated on the dissolution of the self, the individual ego. [. . .] The life in me does not bear my name: 'I' inhabits it as a time-share.[51]

Braidotti continues in euphoric terms, describing how the self as a stopping point in the process of becoming can be overcome in order to culminate, in a radical reversal of all negativity, in the body without organs ("the cosmic echoing chamber of infinite becomings").[52] Her stated aim is to leap over the ruins of metaphysics—not as a utopia but "in a very embodied and embedded way",[53] rooted in the here and now: "just a life".[54]

But what is "just a life"? One with no beginning and end? With no breaks in the sense of a signification? Braidotti knows that life, like the body, cannot appear without signification. As quoted earlier, Elizabeth Grosz expressed this clearly twenty years ago in her weighing-up of a Deleuzian feminism. At the time, Grosz states that decisive steps had yet to be taken in order to overcome the blindness of Deleuze and Guattari concerning the sexual body, a body that is always sexually marked.[55]

Whereas in the mid-1990s the focus was still on the body and its gendered and ethnic markings, today, in an advanced state of capitalism, life as such has detached itself from these markings. This disconnect, Braidotti argues, has been driven by genetic engineering: "Genetic engineering and contemporary molecular biology have located the markers for the organization and distribution of differences in micro-instances like the cells of living organisms. [. . .] We have moved from the bio-power that Foucault exemplified by comparative anatomy to the sort of molecular *bios/zoe* power of today."[56]

Just as digital images have lost their frames (see chapter 3), human existence in advanced capitalism has forfeited its framing, prompting calls for a new ethics of difference (as a framework and, in practical terms, as an aid to orientation).

It is not surprising, then, that Braidotti responds to Deleuze's blind spot on sexuality by citing Luce Irigaray, placing her *Ethics of Sexual Difference*[57] alongside Deleuze's nomadic doctrine. In this way, another woman theorist who fell out of favour within feminist discourse in the 1980s is revaluated. Irigaray fell from grace because she tried to establish an ontological basis for femininity that was at odds with that of masculinity. But this is not what Braidotti is interested in here. Instead, she argues that Irigaray's feminist critique of patriarchy should now be integrated into Deleuze's critique of western metaphysics. For according to Braidotti, this tradition of feminist thinking (in which she also includes Haraway) can be seen as the missing link in the relationship between theory and practice or philosophy and politics, and it is also lacking in the philosophy of Deleuze.

Describing her model of Deleuzian feminism, Elizabeth Grosz writes that she will "explore the corporeal styles, the ontological structure, and the lived realities of sexually different bodies",[58] an argument that takes her very close to Moira Gatens's philosophy of the body. In her work on *Imaginary Bodies*,[59] Gatens defines *gender* as an organization of typical affects on the intensive axis and *sex* as a body organization on the extensive axis, taking this as the basis for opening Spinoza up for feminist debate.[60] She thus became one of the early feminist Deleuzians, while Braidotti, Grosz and others remained ardent Lacanians. Braidotti cites this attempt to combine feminism and Deleuze as the point of departure for a concept of the subject that does justice to a globalized mode of existence, falling neither into the trap of a reawakened essentialism nor into that of a mystic spirituality.

For many people today, "sexual difference" sounds like an anachronistic category that lags hopelessly behind what the body is capable of. After all, the breaking down of physical references described by Braidotti also applies to the differentiation of gender. But how does she deal with the connection between body and sexuality when it is no longer strung between a male and a female pole? Braidotti makes the connection as follows: *Desire* is defined as *potentia*, as a positive power (what Spinoza called *conatus*), and this power or force drives the body to multiple forms of becoming. What Derrida refers to as "supplementary delay",[61] thus smuggling sexual difference in as the original-deferred difference that makes a life (in the sense of an arrival) possible, is understood by Braidotti, with her Spinozan-Deleuzian background, as qualitative shifts of subjectivity.[62] The difference between her position and Derrida's, as well as Irigaray's ontological positing of the female versus the male body, is (a) that life is no longer conceived of as a trace and (b) that the ontological postulate forfeits its universality to become a positive, vital force. Braidotti presents a transversal subject whose relational ties affect its body, thus determining its consciousness: "Transversal and interconnecting entities, defined in terms of common propensities. They are intelligent matter, activated by shared affectivity."[63]

DESIRE OR INTENSE LIVING: NEOSEXUALS

In her nomadic ethics, Braidotti switches between theoretical and literary analysis, according equal value to both types of text and developing a theoretico-fictional toolkit. Virginia Woolf's diary, in which she describes her relationship with Vita (!),[64] serves Braidotti as the basis for her definition of a construction of desire that has freed itself from the coordinates of woman/man, hetero-/homosexuality, physical/mental. Braidotti reads the homosexual relationship between Woolf and Vita not as a lesbian one but as an ethical model "where the play of sameness-difference is not modelled on the dialectics of masculinity and femininity; rather it is an active space of becoming, which is productive of new meanings and definitions."[65] The blurring of the line between self and other also moves towards a subject that no longer conceives of itself as a single entity—instead, the depersonalization of the self can be read as a surpassing of the ego and a merging of internal and external forces.[66] And finally, Braidotti cites a desire that drives and performs the work on these connections and encounters. It is described as a horizon toward which life strives. Desire pioneers possible formations of a becoming-other, intersecting with sexuality as a temporary fixing, a kind of node that may be dissolved and reformed under the influence of different, more intense affects. This desire is defined as "between the no longer and the not yet",[67] thus coinciding with Massumi's definition of *affect*.[68] This seems to confirm my often-stated suspicion that against the background of a Deleuzian philosophy desire is equated with affect. Even if Braidotti does not totally reject a concept of the subject, linking her nomadic ethics with a feminist-materialist philosophy,[69] she cannot stop the consequences of its development. Among other things, it leads to "abstract sex", where desire no longer even has the status of affect, being relegated instead to the level of exchanging, moving and sharing.

I would like to deal briefly here with an interesting phenomenon. In recent times, many surveys have been published that reassess the sexual behaviour of groups within society. As well as sexuality in old age, "asexuality" is also being discussed. "It is an act of emancipation", writes Volkmar Sigusch,

> when men and women who have no sexual desire openly profess this fact. For the lack of sexual appetite now observed by sexologists among countless women and increasing numbers of men has far more to do with the cultural transformation of the old, supposedly natural, constant fount of (endogenous-instinctive) sexuality than with any technically watertight diagnosis of a sexual disorder.[70]

Sigusch analyses changes concerning sexuality and notes that, for both men and women, sexuality no longer possesses the same identity-forming power as it did in the 1960s and '70s. Today, sexuality has become a question of lifestyle, part of an ensemble of everyday organization, leisure, income, interests, peer groups, age and life phase. Sexuality is for pleasure, for relaxation, it is a kick and a thrill, making it subject to corresponding processes of wear and tear and mechanisms of reactivation.[71] Sigusch not only concurs here with Paul Verhaeghe's verdict that *Love in a Time of Loneliness* seeks out new rituals and taboos in order to reinstall something that was lost in the implosion of the grand narratives, but also affirms images whose presence in the media is currently being boosted by queer culture: male and female have broken loose of their rigid dichotomy to explore new combinations of homo-, hetero-, bi- and transsexuality. Men wear dresses without drawing horrified stares, women wear beards and use dildos not only as a caricature of the dominant position of the phallus but also as a way of actually sidelining it.[72] Between omnisexual and asexual, then, a whole range of possible sexualities can now be manipulated and consumed.

How do these realities correspond with a radically different form of sexuality that has completely abandoned its symbolic-imaginary framing and been redefined without it? As discussed earlier, Luciana Parisi has merged Deleuzian concepts with molecular biology to create an evolutionary model in which sexuality has overcome itself and thus the position of the subject. It is no coincidence that theorists of transhumanism often refer to Nietzsche and his notion of the superman in order to underline the fact that it will not be Darwin but a form of being beyond or above man that will shape the future. Keith Ansell Pearson, for example, defines the transhuman condition as an interplay or collision of the human and the inhuman via new technologies. In his view, neither human nor inhuman will survive under advanced global capitalism. Instead, he refers to Baudrillard's notion of "anthropological deregulation" (noted with regard to genetic engineering), proclaiming a general deregulation of the human.[73] What lies ahead is not a transcendence of the human but a nonteleological becoming in an immanent process. Once again, then, Deleuze's philosophy is employed to imagine a permanently evolving future. The "viroid" life described by Pearson as the basis for the transhuman condition is also taken by Parisi as the point of departure for her model of abstract sex: she advocates a radical rewriting of sexuality, whose functioning will no longer be human nor genital but cellular and anonymous, a-personal and subjectless.

Similar to Eduard von Hartmann's three-part model from the mid-nineteenth century concerning the "stages of the unconscious",[74] Parisi proposes three strata of sex—a biophysical, a biocultural and a biodigital level. "Human sex" is located on the biocultural level, but Parisi considers it relevant only for the period from the nineteenth to the mid-twentieth century, when it was still necessary for reproduction. Today, by contrast, we have "cloning" and a correspondingly polymorphous structure of sexuality ("molecular sex"), combined with constantly self-modifying "recombinant desire". The female's eggs are exchanged, carried, and used for cloning, causing their value to increase.[75] In an interview with Matthew Fuller, Parisi explains the potential dynamism and liberation offered by the "stratification of sex" she proposes:

> These levels of stratification constitute for Abstract Sex the endosymbiotic dynamics of organization of matter—a sort of antigenealogical process of becoming that suspends the teleology of evolution and the anthropocentrism of life. [. . .] Once we are forced to engage with the way layers collide in the human species—the way some biophysical and biocultural sedimentations rub against each other under certain pressures and in their turn the way they are rubbed against by the biodigital mutations of sensory perception for example—then the moral stances of optimism and pessimism no longer make sense.[76]

Whereas in Braidotti's approach we saw the concept of desire merging with (a Deleuzian reading of) affect, in Parisi's work we see desire mutating into pure energy. Representation as a form of access to the world (to life, the body, the organism) is rejected by Parisi on the grounds that it reduces all differences. In her view, the debates on cyberfeminism and cybersex have also failed to develop a genuine alternative to the mind/body problem, merely reiterating the distinction between biological presence and a discursive, absent body. Parisi therefore proposes a new metaphysics of the body and sex that has nothing to do with a binary logic of representation: Here, the body is understood as something more than a biological or organic whole, more than a closed self-sufficient system; it is traversed by various levels, from the microlevel of bacterial cells and viruses to the macrolevel of sociocultural and economic systems; the oppositions of nature/culture and sex/gender become intense connections, with nature and sex (anatomical-organic body) no longer functioning as "sources" to be viewed as reservoirs out of which gender identities and other sociocultural artifacts develop. As well as the binary division into sex as nature (anatomy) and gender as culture, undertaken in the 1960s as a progressive step, Parisi also rejects Judith Butler's position. In the early 1990s, Butler turned sex and gender on their heads, declaring that sex, too, should be understood as always already shaped by culture. Parisi introduces a further generation of concepts for this pair, defining them as parallels—"gender is a parallel dimension of sex entailing a network of variations of bodies that challenge the dualism between the natural and the cultural."[77] She justifies this move by referring to Spinoza's ethics, allowing both (sex and gender) to be understood as attributes of a single substance. As mentioned earlier, Moira Gatens had already proposed this at the time Butler presented her model. Today, the molecular-biological resurgence of the two concepts is being greeted with enthusiasm. In Parisi's words, "Desire is autonomous from the subject and the object as it primarily entails a non-discharging distribution of energy, a ceaseless flowing that links together the most indifferent of bodies, particles, forces and signs."[78]

All of this reinforces the arguments I have presented regarding shifts within the figure of *anthropos*. Can the interest in affect we have observed in examples from art, cyberspace, media theory and cultural studies be diagnosed as a transition to a radically subjectless formation of organic bodies? Is the euphoria surrounding emotion and affect in brain research and cognitive psychology to be understood in the sense that it is now possible, at last, to place humans on the same level as animals and intelligent machines? A species among other species, as Haraway puts it in her manifesto of "companion species"?[79] Can we finally bid farewell to the psychical dimension in which the twentieth century was so interested, henceforth vesting all responsibility in a vitalistic motivational force? Is the call to take "life as subject" seriously (as formulated by Braidotti) a first move in this direction?

AFFECT AND TRUTH

With reference to Foucault's *History of Sexuality*, I have tried here to frame affect as a new *dispositif* that bundles a variety of forces: the autopoietic system of cybernetics with the system of endosymbiosis, the affective body of the digital art space with the affective reaction in the process of media reception. This *dispositif* is theoretically underpinned and reinforced by a turn within academic discourses that have proved unable to withstand the pressure from neo-liberal politics and the knowledge industry.

But whereas in the three volumes of his *History of Sexuality*, Foucault was able to presume concepts of knowledge and truth that surround the human being, inserting it into a matrix of technologies of discipline, today knowledge and truth have been replaced by the data and evidence generated by digital recording and computing systems (technologies of control). What remains is affect as intensity, desire and life force, as an interval of time that eludes the subject at the same time as reactively inserting it into its world, as the new coordinator of perception and as a filter of the world, as a primal motivation system that drives us, adapts us and keeps us alive. However, these euphoric-sounding projects of Braidotti and Parisi have been corrupted by a drastic real-world remapping of people and geographical spaces. In a cynical reading, the "organic capital"[80] described by Parisi, for example, can be linked with the global trade in human organs, resulting not in a euphoric "body without organs" but a body that risks losing the organs it needs to survive (becoming a "body minus organs"). But this is just one aspect. Another is the anger or disappointment displayed by many writers who attack the system of representation as if it had let them down, as if it had deceived them and taken them for a ride. They behave as if they could now finally cast off an ancient yoke in order to take refuge, like a microbe, within some other unicellular organism. For two centuries, the erroneous doctrine of anthropocentrism made people believe they were something different, something better, on a higher level than Earth's other inhabitants. What Foucault described as the emergence of the figure of *anthropos* can be understood today as its disappearance, preceded by a watering-down of specific parameters (language, sexuality, politics). Foucault perceived the crisis of government (the management of people) at the end of the 1970s, anticipating the problematic transition from technologies of discipline to those of security long before 11 September 2001. Whereas disciplinary systems presume a prescriptive norm, the "starting point of security technology is the empirically normal, serving as a second-order norm and allowing further differentiations".[81] The technologies of security no longer distinguish between permitted and forbidden, instead defining an "optimum medium".[82] Applying Thomas Lemke's analysis of the *Government of Risks*[83] (in which he traces the development from eugenics to genetic governmentality) to the affective *dispositif*, it becomes clear that this *dispositif* installs an affective conjunctive that implies a divide between promise and reality. Media analyses, philosophical reformulations of the subject, and immersive or atmospheric experiences also promise to decode the truth of body, organism, and subject; "affectification as a strategy of power."[84] When Lemke writes that this promise of a truth "organizes an epistemological field of the seeable and sayable",[85] then where the affective *dispositif* is concerned we can identify a shift toward the seeable because the sayable now only "shows" itself (being evident). What this points to is a shift of the economy toward an "'inner colonization' (Feyerabend) that uses and exploits the body".[86] Jean Baudrillard's prediction of a "metaphysics of code" whose immanence will replace transcendence can be placed alongside the affective version of the subject, to which what Baudrillard predicted for society as a whole also applies: mutation as the basic movement of change and development. The immanence of code no longer permits an outside that might enable self-reflection; instead it generates a logic of affirmation (as a positive force).[87]

This lack (or negation) of an outside is also described by Ernesto Laclau in *On Populist Reason*, where he writes about the role of affects in constituting populist identities:

> The affective bond becomes more central whenever the combinatorial/symbolic dimension of language operates less automatically. From this perspective, affect is absolutely crucial in explaining the operation of the substitutive/paradigmatic pole of language, which is more freely associative in its workings (and thus more open to psychoanalytic exploration).[88]

Laclau's suggestion that affect might be explored by psychoanalysis is well meant, but it seriously underestimates the tendencies within political discourse that have been influenced by Deleuze and Guattari, long since switching to an affirmative stance concerning a politics of affect, whereas Laclau still views politics as a system of representation, albeit one that now increasingly operates with images of similarity (in the sense of an imaginary closure), thus disabling the differentiating function of language.

In order to fill the political void in media analysis, Maurizio Lazzarato has suggested that the politics of affect be coupled with digital data streams. This intensification of politics as an affective installing of body media or media body machines takes place, Lazzarato writes, as collective perception: "Not only do the digital *dispositifs* duplicate the world via images (television), but they are also the source of a new capacity for feeling and thinking, and they define a new materiality and spirituality. [. . .] A new power of metamorphosis and creation is at our disposal. From now on, new forms of subjectivity and materiality are possible."[89]

As if anticipating Laclau's remark that today's politics increasingly operates with images (of similarity), Lazzarato writes that a "positive ontology" (as pursued by Deleuze's model or, in Lazzarato's case, that of Henri Bergson) does not pass responsibility for the image to the lack because the image no longer represents the real, but that *"on the contrary, [the image] itself becomes the substance of being"*.[90] Does this not bring together all the various analyses undertaken in this book? The movement toward "just a life", toward the organism and the machine, toward affect? Tim Dean's remark, quoted earlier, that the concepts of Deleuze and Guattari fail as soon as they are translated into political theories, is confirmed by the political manifestoes of Antonio Negri and Michael Hardt, *Empire* and *Multitude*.[91] In *Empire*, as if to jovially sweep what we are talking about here from the table, they write: "Perhaps along with Spinoza we should recognize prophetic desire as irresistible, and all the more powerful the more it becomes identified with the multitude."[92]

Deleuze and Guattari were not the first to give a positive charge to concepts such as mob, swarm, current or affective force. But today, these models (especially the swarm) are attractive because they hold the promise of a truth that is embedded in an enjoyable shared memory.

SEXUALIZING AFFECT

I do not wish to introduce a new, additional theory of affect that accords a special place to the Freudian and Lacanian view of sexuality and desire. Instead, my aim is to bring affect into play as a component whose advance and displacement of other components has resulted in the emergence of a kind of "affective *dispositif*". This reflects a movement that cannot be explained in terms of affect alone, calling instead for a broader framework encompassing language, the "analytic of the man", cybernetics, art and the media, as well as the microlevels of academic discourse. In all of these fields, affect is displacing sexuality and its characteristic desire. As I hope the preceding chapters have made clear, however, sexuality and desire can be equated neither with the body, nor with language and its polysemantic levels, nor with the life of the organism and its inner and outer relations. It should also have become clear that sexuality does not mean an exchange of information, neither on the biophysical microlevel nor on the biodigital macrolevel. Instead, sexuality must be conceived of as the ungraspable reality of the unconscious, as the unbridgeable gap within the symbolic, a gap that should not be confused with the phase or time zone of affect that has been described as "not yet and already past" but that must rather be conceived of as "never entirely closable". Instead, it is the affective state, radically excluded from the ego, that transposes fear, happiness, excitement and arousal into images that mark the real. In the model of affective reaction, this dimension of translation that permits an opening of the body through language has been lost.

This brings us to the question of "desire after affect". In the field of affect, does desire still exist, and will it undergo similar changes as part of the reformulation of the human noted earlier? Deleuze and his followers would answer with a resounding yes, for as we have seen, in Deleuze's philosophy, desire is an energy that allows bodies to affect themselves, thus keeping them in motion. Freud and Lacan also locate the libido in the body, but in their view it requires representation, as it is not self-evident. For the theorists of affect, however, representation is a focus of criticism, being viewed as a mediator of the world and the subject that always interposes itself, thus obstructing access to reality.[93] Affects, on the other hand, are treated as spontaneous reactions of the body to its surroundings, signalling a direct connection between body and world or a kind of statement on behalf of the body itself concerning its condition.

But maybe the question we should be asking here is whether sexuality will survive under the reign of affect, if one understands sexuality not merely as the basis of reproduction or cell division. According to Parisi, there are many forms of sexuality that exist side by side, no longer attaching themselves to a specific subject formation. Can this still be referred to as sexuality? If sexuality is understood as a characteristic of the human condition, as a special form of loss and as a repetition of this loss in and through sexuality (as an intimation of death and simultaneously a denial of one's own mortality), then the answer must be no.

Lacan once said that animals were more humane than humans because animals have instinct but no desire, and desire complicates things by never being able to find satisfaction. This is because there is always something between subject and object—language, the symbolic order, the Other. As Lacan stresses, object and subject stand in a "mirror relation" to one another, meaning a relationship based on reciprocity that keeps the subject at a distance from its (mirror) image and from its inner tensions. This distance or irresolvable residue, however, should be understood not only as a lack but also as the stage of desire and fantasy. For if this distance collapses, then sexuality is revealed in its bare, basic state.

I would like to stress once again at this point that the affective *dispositif* outlined here is anything but homogenous, as shown by the survey of the various fields of (media) art and theory in the preceding chapters. The difference between the concepts of Brian Massumi and Silvan Tomkins, for example, could not be greater: while Tomkins refuses any sexualization of affect, for Massumi affect is prior to the subject, belatedly attaching itself to something that can be described or experienced as anger, shame or arousal.[94]

Consequently, it is more interesting to ask why so many academic and artistic groups today are embracing affect, contesting representation and language in its name. Or how shame, installed by Tomkins as the primary affect, is meant to be organized without sexual implications—followed by the question of why writers like Eve Kosofsky Sedgwick so vehemently defend a system of affect in which sexuality is dismissed as secondary.

In this light, *sexualizing affect* means reading affect as a symptom, as a node that resists something at the same time as allowing it to be enjoyed. In this way, it becomes possible to identify in the current resurgence of interest in shame something that is not allowed to appear without revealing a fundamental fear on the part of the subject. Focusing attention on shame thus both reveals shame and hides it from view. At the same time as Tomkins brought shame into play, Lacan defined fear as the central affect that arises when the subject's basic relationship to being is revealed. Conversely, shame is defined by Lacan as the ethical relationship of the subject to its own being and to that of others.

It may be no coincidence, then, that Joan Copjec, too, has been working in recent years on fear and shame. Driven perhaps, like Žižek, by the ambition of not giving in to the Deleuzians without a fight, she has instead pointed out early misapprehensions in order to make clear that psychoanalysis, and especially Lacan, who has faced such heavy charges from the theorists of affect, was always already in the place toward which they are now striving. As explained earlier, Lacan described affect as not repressed but as "unfastened" like a ship's cargo, subject to slippage. Copjec refers to this slippage and shows that Deleuze's earlier definition of affect was very close to Lacan's before he went on to define affect in a further step as something that is at odds with the figure of the other: "The later Deleuze is more 'Sartrean' in the sense that he conceives affect as more disruptive, more murderous than murmuring; it is less a mantle surrounding perception than perception's inner division, its dislocation from itself."[95] And then Copjec utters the famous "I'm already here!" from Grimm's fairytale "The Hare and the Hedgehog", conjuring up Freud's definition of affect as the phase of movement in which a slippage occurs between representation and affect. As in the fairytale, Freud was there the whole time, and Copjec makes it clear that affect can be understood in this way as the essential "out-of-phaseness"[96] peculiar to representation. Subjective perception becomes detached from the individual for a moment, causing this moment to become the difference of affect. In this argument, affect becomes a movement of thought, as both Freud and Lacan allegedly understood it: "That Freud tried to theorize this movement of thought by insisting on affect's displacement is a truth nearly lost on his readers, mainly because he reserved the much-maligned word 'discharge' to describe the process."[97]

In a section entitled "Anxiety: Sister of Shame",[98] Copjec adapts Freud's definition to her own ends insofar as it is now not the repressed that returns and creates fear, but the disconnect (between perception and slippage) that opens up for a moment. According to Copjec, anxiety arises when the subject's shameful relationship to its existence opens up, when anxiety attacks the suture of the subject and stops, for a moment, the flight into being (Lacan's understanding of shame).[99]

The striking focus on shame in the current reception of Tomkins returns inadvertently to an old theme, as shame also occupies a central place in Lacan's work, although without dominating his theoretical concepts to the same degree. For Lacan, shame constitutes the fundamental link to existence insofar as it prevents the subject from becoming absorbed in being, thus imposing the distance to the world and others that is necessary for survival. More than one definition of *shame* exists, then, but the symptom is always enjoyment at the same time as obstruction or prevention. Or have we lost sight of who was trying to catch up with whom in the race between the hare and the hedgehog? Are we back where the others were waiting the whole time? Is all the hype surrounding affect a pretext to make us believe that a shift in the "analytic of man" toward the "posthuman" and the "transhuman" actually involves a meaningful step forward? Or has affect perhaps merely made it clear that the real, the unconscious, the body, the organism, are jokers that can take on a charge or that can undergo slippage?

Even if Freud and Lacan (like a pair of hedgehogs) have always been where the hare of affect is now trying to overtake them, the resulting shift in the *dispositif* (of sex) cannot be stopped.

What can be diagnosed is a shift of sexuality toward its possible extinction in a comprehensively psychoanalytical sense. As one of the grand narratives of the nineteenth and twentieth centuries, it is losing its benchmark status and breaking down into many little rivulets that flow alongside and against one another. Queerness, asexuality, patchwork families, childlessness and population ageing, the redefinition of family relations, the commercialization of sex, the trade in human organs, movements of migration, and the spiral of capitalist development are interrelated signs forming a matrix within which the genealogical power of sexuality is visibly breaking down.[100]

Like the discovery of sexuality in the nineteenth century, the current desire for affect is certainly not a liberation. Instead, it is an unloading (of the ship that has now arrived).

NOTES

1. Rosi Braidotti, *Transpositions: On Nomadic Ethics* (Cambridge, UK: Polity, 2006), 9.
2. According to this theory of evolution, one cell survives inside another, to the advantage of both, leading to mutual dependence. This theory was made famous from the 1970s onward by Lynn Margulis in particular. See Lynn Margulis and Dorion Sagan, *What Is Life?* (London: Weidenfeld and Nicholson, 1995); and Lynn Margulis and Dorion Sagan, *What Is Sex?* (New York: Simon & Schuster, 1997).
3. See Luciana Parisi, *Abstract Sex: Philosophy, Bio-Technology and the Mutations of Desire* (London: Bloomsbury Academic, 2004), vii.
4. William J. T. Mitchell, "The Pictorial Turn," in *Artforum* (March 1992); and William J. T. Mitchell, *What Do Pictures Want? The Lives and Loves of Images* (Chicago: University of Chicago Press, 2005).
5. Rosalind Krauss has developed the emphatic concept of a "post-medium condition" for today's art. In the postmodern age, she writes, the desire for "purity" and the "essence" of art often evoked by modernism can no longer be upheld. Not only have media become "multimedia", but the various forms of artistic praxis can also no longer be distinguished from capitalist strategies. From this she concludes the need for a concept of artistic praxis that does justice to this postmedium condition and that articulates the specific medium in question in its "differentiating peculiarity". Rosalind Krauss, *A Voyage on the North Sea* (London: Thames & Hudson, 2000).
6. One example here is the development of machines that can see, process, decide, and kill without the involvement of a human individual. Other examples include animals and machines replacing or augmenting human skills with their superior competence (e.g., dogs whose acute sense of smell is deployed in early cancer detection).
7. Brian Massumi, "Navigating Moments," in *21C Magazine* (2003).
8. See Stefan Rieger, *Kybernetische Anthropologie* (Frankfurt, Germany: Suhrkamp, 2003), 214.
9. J. G. Ballard, *Crash* (London: Jonathan Cape, 1973). *Crash* is the first volume in the Technoscape Trilogy and was filmed by David Cronenberg in 1996.
10. A term borrowed from Anthony Vidler's *The Architectural Uncanny: Essays in the Modern Unhomely* (Cambridge, MA: MIT Press, 1994).
11. Matt Smith, "The Work of Emotion: Ballard and the Death of Affect," in *Adventure thru Inner Space: Essays & Articles*, http://www.jgballard.ca/criticism/death_of_affect.html (retrieved 19 May 2014).

12. Karl Clausberg and Cornelius Weiller, "Wie Denken aussieht. Zu den bildgebenden Verfahren der Hirnforschung," in Christian Geyer (ed.), *Hirnforschung und Willensfreiheit* (Frankfurt: Suhrkamp, 2004), 245–49, here 245.

13. Ernst Mach, *The Analysis of Sensations, and the Relation of the Physical to the Psychical* (Chicago: Open Court, 1914).

14. Sigmund Freud, "A Note on the Unconscious in Psychology," in *Standard Edition, Vol. 12* (London: Hogarth Press, 1955), 255–66, here 264.

15. Mai Wegener, "Unbewußt/das Unbewusste", in Karlheinz Barck, Martin Fontius, Dieter Schlenstedt, Burkhart Steinwachs, and Friedrich Wolfzettel (eds.), *Ästhetische Grundbegriffe , Vol. 6* (Stuttgart, Germany: J. B. Metzler, 2005), 202–40.

16. Gustav Theodor Fechner, *Elements of Psychophysics* (1860) (New York: Holt, Rinehart, and Winston, 1966).

17. Gustav Theodor Fechner, *Vorschule der Ästhetik*, 2 vols. (Leipzig, Germany: Breitkopf & Härtel, 1876).

18. Hermann von Helmholtz, *Treatise on Physiological Optics* (1856–1866) (Rochester, NY: The Optical Society of America, 1924).

19. Friedrich Nietzsche, "Nachgelassenes Fragment 5" [89] (1870–1871), in Friedrich Nietzsche, *Kritische Gesamtausgabe, series 3, vol. 3* (Berlin: de Gruyter, 1975–1984), 120.

20. Sigmund Freud, *The Interpretation of Dreams* (1900) (New York: Basic Books, 1955).

21. Joan Copjec, *Imagine There's No Woman: Ethics and Sublimation* (Boston: Beacon Press, 2002), 180.

22. "It originates in an elsewhere, and has to be understood as belonging to Being." [Paul Verhaeghe, *Beyond Gender: From Subject to Drive* (New York: Other Press, 2001), 102.]

23. Jacques Lacan, "The Mirror Stage as Formative of the I Function," in *Écrits: The First Complete Edition in English*, trans. Bruce Fink in collaboration with Héloïse Fink and Russell Grigg (New York: Norton, 2006), 75–81; and Jacques Lacan, *The Four Fundamental Concepts of Psychoanalysis: The Seminar XI* (New York: Norton, 1998), 67–78.

24. Annette Bitsch, "Kybernetik des Unbewußten, das Unbewußte der Kybernetik," in Claus Pias (ed.), *Cybernetics|Kybernetik, The Macy Conferences 1946–1953, Essays & Dokumente, Vol. II* (Zurich, Switzerland: diaphanes, 2003), 153–68, here 156.

25. Ibid.

26. Verhaeghe, *Beyond Gender*, 81.

27. Ibid., 96.

28. Ibid., 97.

29. "Llanguage [*lalangue*]," Lacan explains, "serves purposes that are altogether different from that of communication." This llanguage "presents all sorts of affects that remain enigmatic. Those affects are what result from the presence of llanguage insofar as it articulates things by way of knowledge (*de savoir*) that go much further than what the speaking being sustains (*supporte*) by way of enunciated knowledge." Jacques Lacan, *The Seminar of Jacques Lacan XX: On Feminine Sexuality, the Limits of Love and Knowledge (Encore)* (New York: Norton, 1999), 138–39.

30. Jacques Lacan, *The Seminar of Jacques Lacan VII: Ethics of Psychoanalysis* (New York: Norton, 1992), 102.

31. Teresa Brennan, *The Transmission of Affect* (Ithaca, NY: Cornell University Press, 2004), 164.

32. Lacan, *Four Fundamental Concepts*, 218.

33. Ibid.

34. Ibid., 218–19.

35. See Verhaeghe, *Beyond Gender*, 131.

36. Sigmund Freud, *The Ego and the Id* (1923) (New York: Norton, 1960), 26. This puts Freud close to Bergson, who also defines the body's boundary as acting both inward and outward: "And that is why [the body's] surface, the common limit of the external and the internal, is the only portion of space which is perceived and felt." [Henri Bergson, *Matter and Memory* (New York: Cosimo, 2007), 58].

37. Lacan, *Four Fundamental Concepts*, 270.

38. Verhaeghe, *Beyond Gender*, 118.
39. The concept of "partial objects" was promoted by Melanie Klein in particular, who used it to attribute independent psychical functions to a person's various body parts and physical processes, with key roles being played by the breasts, the penis, excrements/secretions, and so on.
40. Slavoj Žižek, *Organs without Bodies: Deleuze and the Consequences* (London: Routledge, 2012), 31.
41. Ibid., 20.
42. See ibid., 19.
43. Ibid., 79.
44. Ibid.
45. See ibid., 80.
46. Ibid., 81.
47. Gilles Deleuze, *Difference and Repetition* (New York: Columbia University Pess, 1994), xxi.
48. Žižek, *Organs without Bodies*, 84.
49. As well as the cuts of cosmetic surgery, affective regulation is a standard part of entertainment media. The most lasting impact of talk shows and other mass media formats lies in their conversion of psychical fixations into states of affective tension. We have already spoken of artistic practices designed to induce states of happiness in the audience. In this context, the imperative to enjoy is misunderstood as the right to enjoyment, while at the same time its "obscene underside" is overlooked, the constant self-monitoring and permanent comparison with others, their bodies, their performance.
50. Braidotti, *Transpositions*, 270.
51. Ibid., 253.
52. Ibid.
53. Ibid.
54. Ibid.
55. See Elizabeth Grosz, *Volatile Bodies: Toward a Corporeal Feminism* (Bloomington: Indiana University Press, 1994), 209.
56. Braidotti, *Transpositions*, 269.
57. Luce Irigaray, *An Ethics of Sexual Difference* (New York: Cornell University Press, 1993).
58. Grosz, *Volatile Bodies*, 191.
59. Moira Gatens, *Imaginary Bodies: Ethics, Power, and Corporeality* (London: Routledge, 1996).
60. The fact that Žižek is only now making fun of Genevieve Lloyd suggests that he has not been aware of (or not taken seriously) a development that has been going on for years: "not to mention feminists like Genevieve Lloyd who propose to decipher a mysterious third kind of knowledge in the *Ethics* as feminine intuitive knowledge." (Žižek, *Organs without Bodies*, 29).
61. Elizabeth Grosz tried to define sexual difference ontologically with reference to Derridas "new choreography of sexual difference". (Jacques Derrida, "Geschlecht: Sexual Difference, Ontological Difference," in *Research in Phenomenology*, 13 (1983), 65–83). In this model, Derrida stresses that it can no longer be a matter of bringing women and men into line with each other, thus tacitly preserving the male as the norm. In addition, the peculiarities of the two sexes no longer provide a legitimate point of departure. Instead, a radical plurality is called for in the sense of a "supplementary logic", a logic that breaks through binary opposition. On this "supplementary logic", see Jacques Derrida, *Writing and Difference* (Chicago: University of Chicago Press, 1978), 196–231.
62. Besides Genevieve Lloyd, the idea that sexual difference does not manifest itself per se, expressed instead in all cognitive, moral, and political activity, has also been stated in similar terms by Moira Gatens and Elizabeth Grosz. See Braidotti, *Transpositions*, 186.
63. Ibid., 148.
64. Vita Sackville-West, a friend of Woolf's and the model for the figure of Orlando in her novel of that name.
65. Braidotti, *Transpositions*, 196.
66. Ibid., 197.
67. Ibid.

68. "Pastnesses opening onto a future, but with no present to speak of. For the present is lost with the missing half-second, passing too quickly to be perceived, too quickly, actually, to have happened." [Brian Massumi, "The Autonomy of Affect," in Paul Patton (ed.), *Deleuze: A Critical Reader* (Cambridge, MA: Blackwell, 1996), 217–39, here 224].

69. See Braidotti, *Transpositions*, 137.

70. Volkmar Sigusch, "Gibt es Asexuelle?" in *Frankfurter Rundschau*, 12 October 2005.

71. See Volkmar Sigusch, *Neosexualitäten. Über den kulturellen Wandel von Liebe und Perversion* (Hamburg, Germany: Campus, 2005), 20–26.

72. In her *Countersexual Manifesto*, Beatriz Preciado calls for the natural contract between the sexes and society to be replaced by a "contra-sexual contract" that installs sexuality as a technical issue rather than a natural one. This program is neither new nor does the "philosophy of the dildo" proclaimed by Preciado open up a perspective that can be taken seriously. The dildo, she claims, will create a new democracy of the sexes; as well as subverting the rule of the phallus, the dildo also causes genital sexuality to forfeit its hegemonic status, opening up new options for pleasure. The question here, however, is what is Preciado's countersexual manifesto campaigning against? Against another sexual manifesto? Or against sexuality as a whole? Beatriz Preciado, *Manifesto Contra-Sexual/Countersexual Manifesto* (Madrid: Opera Prima, 2002).

73. See Keith Ansell Pearson, *Viroid Life: Perspectives on Nietzsche and the Transhuman Condition* (London: Routledge, 1997), 34f.

74. In the nineteenth century, Hartmann proposed a division of the unconscious into the levels of corporeality, the mind, and actual metaphysics. See Angus Nicholls and Martin Liebscher (eds.), *Thinking the Unconscious: Nineteenth-Century German Thought* (Cambridge, MA: Cambridge University Press, 2010).

75. See Parisi, *Abstract Sex*, vii. On the biophysical level, she argues, sex consists in bacterial exchange and cell division, corresponding on the biodigital level to cloning and cybernetic sex.

76. Matthew Fuller, "Luciana Parisi Interview," (28 October 2004), http://www.nettime.org/Lists-Archives/nettime-l-0410/msg00054.html (retrieved 16 May 2014).

77. Parisi, *Abstract Sex*, 11.

78. Ibid., 12.

79. Donna J. Haraway, *The Companion Species Manifesto: Dogs, People, and Significant Others* (Chicago: Prickly Paradigm Press, 2003).

80. Parisi, *Abstract Sex*, 102–10.

81. Ulrich Bröckling, Susanne Krasmann, and Thomas Lemke (eds.), *Governmentality: Current Issues and Future Challenges* (London: Routledge, 2011), 4.

82. Ibid.

83. Thomas Lemke, "Die Regierung der Risiken. Von der Eugenik zur genetischen Gouvernementalität," in Ulrich Bröckling, Susanne Krasmann, and Thomas Lemke (eds.), *Gouvernementalität der Gegenwart. Studien zur Ökonomisierung des Sozialen* (Frankfurt, Germany: Suhrkamp, 2000), 227–64, here 228.

84. Freely adapted from Thomas Lemke's concept of "genetification," see ibid., 230.

85. Ibid., 234.

86. Ibid., 240.

87. Jean Baudrillard, *The Vital Illusion* (New York: Columbia University Press, 2000).

88. Ernesto Laclau, *On Populist Reason* (London: Verso, 2005), 227f.

89. Maurizio Lazzarato, *Videophilosophie. Zeitwahrnehmung im Postfordismus* (Berlin: Merve, 2002), 177.

90. Ibid., 10 (italics in the original).

91. Michael Hardt and Antonio Negri, *Empire* (Cambridge, MA: University of Harvard Press, 2000); Michael Hardt and Antonio Negri, *Multitude, War and Democracy in the Age of Empire* (New York: Penguin, 2004).

92. Hardt and Negri, *Empire*, 65.

93. But Deleuze, too, stressed that affects cannot be simply accessed but that they show thinking its limits and limitations. See Gilles Deleuze, *Difference and Repetition*, 144f.

94. Freud draws attention to affect as a signal several times, as in his lecture on "Anxiety", where he relates anxiety, signal and affect to each other: when the emergence of anxiety is reduced to a signal, then affect comes into play. See Sigmund Freud, "XXV: Anxiety" (1916–1917), in *Introductory Lectures on Psychoanalysis* (London: Hogarth Press, 1963), 392–411, here 405.

95. Joan Copjec, "May '68, The Emotional Month", in Slavoj Žižek (ed.), *Lacan: The Silent Partners* (London: Verso, 2006), 90–114, here 94.

96. Ibid.

97. Ibid., 95.

98. The allusion to the title of the Tomkins reader edited by Eve Kosofsky Sedgwick and Frank Adam (*Shame and Its Sisters*) is unmistakable here—or is it just pure coincidence?

99. Joan Copjec: "Flight into being [. . .] which protects us from the ravage of anxiety." (Copjec, "May '68", 111).

100. One sign of this breakdown is the closure in 2006 of the Institute for Sexology at the University of Frankfurt with the retirement of its director, Volkmar Sigusch.

SIX

Postscript: A New Affective Organization

Life as such "lurks in the interstices of every living cell, and in the interstices of the brain".[1]

In the preceding chapters, I have outlined the discussions of affect and its exploitation within various disciplines of the humanities, the media and the arts, stressing the degree to which this is linked to developments in media technology. By way of a summary and conclusion, I would now like to discuss the implementation of affect as a comprehensive reorganization of what "desire after affect" means under the conditions of today's media technology.

Two fields are particularly relevant here. First, an approach based on media ecology culminating in a definition of affect as something detached from the body as a ubiquitous technology—as "radical relationality". And second, a new definition, or rather location, of affect in brain research, where talk of neuroplasticity by writers including Catherine Malabou not only reformulates the unconscious but also declares the replacement of the *dispositif* of sex by that of affect as final. As what I would like to call a "relational organizing power", affect thus takes on a new task: both auto-affectively controlling brain movement and setting in motion a politico-economically decentralized organization of the emerging biomediated bodies.[2]

MEDIA TECHNOLOGY MEETS BIOLOGY

Up to the present, technical and living processes developed more or less separately. Until well into the twentieth century, life and technology trod separate paths and were also kept separate in the field of theory. But media analyses, such as Donna Haraway's from the early 1980s, elaborated on since by writers including N. Katherine Hayles, Alexander Galloway and Eugene Thacker,[3] agree first that media can no longer be defined as prostheses that amplify the senses, having instead attained a new immersive dimension, replacing our senses, making them more intense and subjective, more intimate and technical; and second that perception, memory, and affect have become technical modalities.

Today, neocybernetic approaches address a question posed by Georges Canguilhem in his "Machine and Organism", an essay where he advocates an understanding of technology as a universal biological phenomenon. In 1946 to 1947, when Canguilhem was giving his lecture, he would conclude by saying that, for some years now, tests had been underway—at MIT under the name *bionics*—to research biological models and structures that could be used as models in technology. "Bionics is the extremely subtle art of information", writes Canguilhem, "that has taken a leaf from natural life."[4] Today, media are put on a level with insects, rays, instincts, stimuli, and reflexes,[5] and theories of imitation from the animal kingdom are applied to our understanding of human social and political crowd/swarm formations. Not that comparisons between the animal and human are anything particularly novel; what is new is the fact that today they are meant seriously—the anthropological supremacy of the human can no longer be upheld in our current technical-organic structure.

When Canguilhem articulated his appeal immediately after World War II, warning against the reductionism of a rapidly expanding hegemony of cybernetics à la Norbert Wiener, it fell on deaf ears. Technology and biology, or technology as biology, was not a possible equation for many reasons. Today, by contrast, one may observe a new liaison based on linking approaches from (neuro-) biology and information technology, a link established via an original deferral or the inscription of a missing time gap.

Before being introduced into cultural studies by Brian Massumi as the zone of affect, this original deferral, time lapse, or "missing half-second" (described in more detail in chapter 3) was the subject of a research tradition that goes back a long way. Jimena Canales has reconstructed this tradition,[6] documenting a huge interest within the disciplines of experimental psychology, astronomy, physics and metrology during the nineteenth century. Sigmund Freud was taken with it, as was Wilhelm Wundt at his Institute of Psychology in Leipzig. Others, like Frances Galton, saw the study of the missing split-second as a continuation of craniometry on a different level: those who react slowly have a sensitive personality, those who react quickly are aggressive and more intelligent. Gradually, this interest in measuring individual reaction times, "personal equating" or "personal error", also began to appear in film experiments, with noteworthy early examples including Marey's chronophotography and Muybridge's proto-cinematography. All this began with Hermann von Helmholtz, who wrote in 1850: "I have found that a measurable amount of time passes as the stimulus exerted by a momentary electrical current on the lumbar plexus of a frog is propagated to the place where the femoral nerve enters the calf muscle."[7] But what Helmholtz had discovered with his measurements was not only the disappearance of time but also and above all the delay of energy—the energy in a muscle is not exerted completely at the moment of the stimulus "but to a large extent only after that stimulus has already ceased".[8] Between stimulation and contraction, then, time (and energy) passes—not much but enough to be clearly identifiable. The immediacy on which previous assumptions had been based turned out to be an "interval, a period, a space of time both circumscribed and empty—an interim, *du temps perdu*".[9]

This missing half-second has long since arrived in the laboratories of neuroscience, where it is making a comeback as "short delay"[10] and "affective cognition"[11]—as well as in discussions of the plasticity of the brain.

BIOMEDIA AND THE COSHAPING OF BODIES

The debate surrounding affect and its possible links to (new) media technology at the end of the last century led to a rediscovery of Henri Bergson. As described in chapter 1, Mark Hansen (among others) drew on Bergson to define the body as a central filter for the (immersive) world of images that surrounds us, acting as one big sensory organ that guides our perception and orientation in this visual universe. Within this model, affect is seen as something that both goes beyond the body and, at the same time, amplifies it. In the spirit of Spinoza ("we don't know what the body is able to do"), the body performs the activity of organizing our being-in-the-world.

In the course of extensive industrialization since the nineteenth century, this body has increasingly come to be viewed as a thermodynamic organism, an autopoietic body of reproduction, "trained to work",[12] that is open to energy (including sensory stimuli and other signals) but isolated from its surroundings in terms of information. Today, this view is proving obsolete. Deleuze and Guattari's "body without organs" is already a departure from this intense linking of matter and information, conceived of more in virtual terms as an imaginary body beyond the apparatus of media technology. What we have today is a strong focus on the "biomediated body" (Clough). Biotechnology, information technology and cognitive science are striving to fuse living matter and computer programming to define the initial parameters of a body that is no longer a cyborg, its biology no longer distinguishable from its technology.[13] But just as Haraway made clear in her *Cyborg Manifesto* in the early 1980s that we are all cyborgs (equipped with glasses, pacemakers and other prostheses), in 2003 her *Companion Species Manifesto*[14] once again emphasized that crossing and mixing of bodies on many different levels has always taken place.

A few years later, in *When Species Meet*, she presents an analysis of her coexistence with her dog Cayenne, in which she shows not only how human and animal make themselves understood to one another but also, above all, the extent to which human and animal bodies adjust to one another, become attuned, and "infect" each other in complex ways:

> In recent speaking and writing on companion species, I have tried to live inside the many tones of regard/respect/seeing each other/looking back at/meeting/optic-haptic encounter. Species and respect are in optic/haptic/affective/cognitive touch: they are at table together; they are messmates, companions. [. . .] *Companion species*—coshapings all the way down, in all sorts of temporalities and corporealities—is my awkward term for a not-humanism in which species of all sorts are in question.[15]

This reshaping or coshaping of bodies is understood by Haraway as a permanent meeting and mutual affecting, comparable with the relationship between horse and rider described by the French behaviorist Jean-Claude Barrey: "Who influences and who is influenced, in this story, are questions that can no longer receive a clear answer. Both, human and horse, are cause and effect of each other's movements. Both induce and are induced, affect and are affected."[16]

This transfer, also known as "isopraxis" or "synchronous isopraxis", drew renewed interest in neuroscience, in particular following Giacomo Rizzolatti's discovery of mirror neurons in 1992. But in his reading of Spinoza, Deleuze, too, refers explicitly to ethology, which, as he writes, deals with the affects, a capacity that is equally unforeseeable in animals and humans.[17] Ethology examines the mimetic, empathic and imitative behaviour of animals and humans and explores the question of how an imitated movement becomes a movement of one's own. While communication and language were long considered as the main factor in mutual learning, the focus has now shifted to the body, to affective competences, and to the resulting movements that are not controlled by consciousness and that reinforce or create synaptic connections in the brain (neuroplasticity). This new focus on a different form of knowledge production is also mentioned by Isabelle Stengers, who, with reference to Haraway's dog tales, stresses "that we need other kinds of narratives, narratives that populate our worlds and imaginations in a different way". These other narratives are needed because the "great NBIC convergence—the convergence between Nanotechnology, Biotechnology, Information Technology and Cognitive Science [. . .] is not about understanding but about transforming."[18]

THE BLIND FEELING

All of these points underpin the current interest in defining perception as subjective but also subcutaneous and above all as not linked to an a priori subject. In this view, not only do humans and animals perceive in the same way, but human perception is also figured in organological terms.

Brian Massumi and Erin Manning,[19] Steven Shaviro,[20] Mark Hansen[21] and Luciana Parisi[22] are just a few of the writers currently citing Alfred N. Whitehead's process philosophy in their attempts to conceive of perception and sensation without the category of a conscious subject. According to Whitehead, perception is first and foremost a physical process that he defines as emotional, a "blind emotion" that is "received as felt elsewhere in another occasion".[23] This involves not an accumulation of data but always a data relationship. The perceiving subject does not preexist the perceived world but emerges through and in the process of perception. For Whitehead, the tradition of metaphysical theories of perception is marked by a fundamental misunderstanding whose root he sees in their privileging of the visual. The classical description or basic theory—"I see something, so I simply perceive it"—is criticized by Whitehead, who points out that this seeing must always already be preceded by a process of abstraction ("prehension"), as a result of which the "feeling is subjectively rooted in the immediacy of the present occasion: it is what the occasion feels for itself, as derived from the past and as merging into the future".[24] We encounter this "feeling for itself" again later in this chapter in the concept of the auto-affection of the brain. For Whitehead, the process of perception leads to a "superject" that generates itself via the intake of data (sensory perceptions). In contrast to Kant, for whom experience also begins with affected contemplation that sets the activity of reason in motion, Whitehead assumes that consciousness is a negligible aspect of subjective experience. As constant perception, experience takes place for the most part below the threshold of consciousness, as the physical sensation that precedes every subject. In this "theory of sensation" the subject as superject is the "purpose of the process originating the feelings".[25] This process of "superjectification" centres on (physical) sensation, on (always already abstract) prehension or grasping, and on processes of affection by which matter becomes form and form becomes data.

While Mark Hansen takes Whitehead's "blind feeling" as the basis for his notion of expanded experience, I would like to think blind feeling together with affect, focusing not so much on an expanded asubjective-technical experience and more on processes of affecting that move and organize human beings and others, as affective modulations. The question of whether one can speak of these as unconscious processes is one I will return to. In the following discussion of neuroplasticity, we encounter this affective modulation as auto-affection or auto-modulation, raising the question of how the movements of the brain can be translated into what Whitehead called "blind feeling" as the basic movement of an everlasting automodelling process.

LIVED TIME IN THE AGE OF FABRICATED AFFECTS

Bernard Stiegler has written that Freud's psychoanalysis lacked one crucial thing—a theory of tertiary retention as a "theory of the materialization of spatialized time and [. . .] of hypermatter". According to Stiegler, this hypermateriality developed with quantum mechanics and denotes a "complex of energy and information in which matter can no longer be distinguished from its form".[26] A process can be described as hypermaterial if the form (as embodied information) is an actual sequence of material states resulting from an overall set of devices and programmes. But at the precise moment when the distinction between form and matter becomes meaningless, what Stiegler calls a psycho-power comes into play—psychopower instead of psychoanalysis.

Stiegler's treatise on the present in terms of media theory and a philosophy of technology is framed by the concepts of *Technics and Time*.[27] (Media) technologies are viewed as a constitutive, disciplinary, formative power exerting a key influence on the relationship between nature-culture-technology-society and the individual. Stiegler can be seen as a spokesman for the organology presented or imagined by writers from Kapp to Canguilhem to Simondon. A central role is played here by Stiegler's concept of "pharmacological knowledge". As a critique of Foucault's blind spots, Stiegler formulates elements of a new programme of the "care of the self". How, he asks, can good technologies of the self be distinguished from the negative "pharmakon" of the programming industries and viral marketing? How can the materiality of technical objects with their potential for both individuation and deindividuation be grasped as a "production machine"[28] now that Foucault's biopower no longer offers a satisfactory explanation, formulated as it was with a view of the old Europe and of practices that have now been rendered obsolete by viral marketing strategies and other capitalist methods of appropriation? Now that state biopower has given way to a "psycho-power of the market",[29] how are the three organological levels—the psychosomatic organs of the physical individual, the technical and artificial organs of the technical individual, and the organs of society (institutions and organizations)—to be studied in their transductive relations?[30] In Stiegler's view, then, an organology that understands psychical, technical and collective individuals as specific "*dispositifs* of individuation" must take into account the "psycho-powers of the markets" in order to arrive at an understanding of technology and media that does justice to the material-mental complex of individuation today.

It is against the background of these models (blind feeling, technics and time) that we must consider subsequent approaches that push a (new) theory of media and subjectivization in terms of environment, atmosphere or radical relationality,[31] where affect takes on a kind of self-organizing function that ignores the borders of the body and of consciousness. As discussed previously, this is precisely the task assigned to affect by Antonio Damasio: to perform a self-regulating function between the organism and its surroundings. Into this function, however, are inscribed increasingly (media-) technological implementations that (are intended to) provide control, self-surveillance and self-regulation in the sense of maintaining a homeostasis (of bodies). As Natasha Schüll has shown, affect modulation and self-regulation are now also a focus in the development of game designs,[32] where the original economic interest has visibly mutated into a perverted form of Foucault's "care of the self". It is also worth remembering here that in immersive media art (and to an extent in early theories of computer games), affect was understood as "felt seeing" or somatic body reactions and not in the sense of (self-) control as is the case today. This development thus clearly reflects the diverse and contradictory interest in affect, which, as I have stressed, means not a liberation of the emotions from logos or language but a transition to seamless integration (of the biomediated body) into the overall technical-economic structure.

ON THE SHAPING OF AN AFFECTIVE NONCONSCIOUS

In brain research, media technologies as (new) "discourse networks"[33] play a key role by giving access to neural processes and translating them into simulations, constituting a "plastic" counterpart to the media-technical implementation of virtuality.

In *What Should We Do with Our Brain?* Catherine Malabou introduces the concept of plasticity into the discussion as the "hermeneutic motor scheme of the new age".[34] Plasticity is understood here as a singular scheme or motive that opens the door to the current epoch by enabling the interpretation of phenomena and major events as they arise. In this way, Malabou argues, plasticity has displaced the previous motor scheme of writing (*écriture*), championed from Roland Barthes to Jacques Derrida as *the* inscription model in the era of structures and language. As we have seen, Derrida introduced writing and difference as the mode and central authority of thought and knowledge production, using as his basic example psychoanalysis, which he viewed as a science of the trace, of facilitation, and of engrams. According to Derrida, Freud first described the work of facilitations in his *Project*, pursuing the question of the translation of energy into memory in *The Interpretation of Dreams*.[35] This work of quantitative inscription and its switching into qualitative memory traces is understood today—against the backdrop of a general return to materialism[36]—as the plastic (self-) shaping of the brain.

In *Mythologies*, Roland Barthes gives free reign to his love of plastic, qualifying it less as a substance and more as the "very idea of its endless transformation"—"it is less a thing than the trace of a movement".[37] This plasticity also appears in Simondon's theory of the "mode of existence of technical objects". Only a few years after Barthes's celebration of plastic, the French techno-philosopher made a distinction between the plasticity of the machine and that of the human brain. While the first refers to the plasticity of the carrier, in the case of humans it refers to the plasticity of content, of memory, as Simondon emphasizes: "The memory of the machine triumphs in the multiple and the disordered: human memory triumphs in the unity of forms and in order."[38] The reason for this is the machine's lack of integrative plasticity, a vital aspect of the human. Whereas human memory reforms with every new input so that every new content means a new formatting code, the form of the machine is stable/static, with plasticity limited to its software. At this point Simondon refers to Bergson, who also thought about this capacity for recording and archiving, specifically in terms of its temporal intensity (condensation) as the main cause for any modulation (change). For Simondon, human and other living species are primarily shifters and converters, they are modulations and not a reservoir of energy.[39]

It should be noted here that this plasticity is conceived of together with temporality, which in turn is conceived of together with intensity. And in the debate on neuroplasticity, precisely this combination becomes the complex of a new "cerebral *non*conscious affectivity".[40] The parallels between the affective interval (described in detail in chapters 1 and 3) and the interval in the context of neural plasticity are hardly surprising. Around 1900, Bergson already described the brain as a "zone of indetermination",[41] going so far as to call it a place where the interval resides. Going against the scientific wisdom of his time, he declared the brain a tabula rasa, a temporal gap, a span of time between stimulus and response.[42] For Bergson, the brain was comparable in media terms with a telephone exchange, its task being to establish or postpone connections, thus mediating or dividing movement.[43] Freud, too, spoke of this interposed quality when he noted the impossibility of actual localization: "We can avoid any possible abuse of this method of representation by recollecting that ideas, thoughts and psychical structures in general must never be regarded as localized *in* organic elements of our nervous system but rather, as one might say, *between* them, where resistances and facilitations provide the corresponding correlates."[44]

Today, the brain is described as a network of billions of neurons that are responsible for every movement, performing this task thanks to cuts, gaps and leaps inscribed in the plasticity of the brain—gaps that open up between the synapses. The neural circuits, as Jean Pierre Changeux writes, consist of neurons lying unconnected in the synapses.[45] Thus we even find gaps within the synapses themselves—"synaptic gaps".[46] The term *synaptic plasticity* was introduced in 1949 by the Canadian neuroscientist Donald Olding Hebb.[47] According to his model, the plasticity of the brain is manifested by the fact that when one neuron drives the activity of another neuron, the connection between these neurons is reinforced. In this context Changeux speaks of the "coactivation of two cells" that creates "cooperation at the level of their contacts".[48] William James already spoke of this plasticity in his *Principles of Psychology* (1890), stating that "organic matter, especially nervous tissue, seems endowed with a very extraordinary degree of plasticity", so that he stressed, as one of his first basis assumptions, "that *the phenomena of habit in living beings are due to the plasticity of the organic materials of which their bodies are composed.*"[49] Pathways are thus either reinforced, deepened or created by the constant performance of life. For a long time, however, this view received little attention, and until far into the twentieth century, the research hypothesis stated that the brain lost its plasticity at birth or, at the very latest, when adulthood was reached. Nikolas Rose and Joelle Abi-Rached tell this same story, stressing that this view changed radically by the close of the twentieth century. Today, they write, the brain is "envisaged as mutable across the whole of life, open to environmental influences, damaged by insults, and nourished and even reshaped by stimulation—in a word, *plastic*."[50]

Against this backdrop, Catherine Malabou introduces the concept of plasticity into a new philosophical debate on the nature of the brain in which neuroscience and cultural studies (in particular the study of psychoanalysis) are viewed as equal partners. She, too, begins by stressing the degree to which models of the brain reflect the politics of their time: today, there is no more talk of brains as telephone exchanges or computers; instead, the preferred models are based on flexibility and plasticity, metaphors that now dominate the spheres of politics and economics. Like earlier models, talk of the brain's plasticity has an agenda, articulating a claim not only to produce knowledge about the brain but also to see how much this knowledge shapes its object. Malabou distinguishes between three forms of plasticity: one of development, one of modulation, and one of recovery (now discussed under the term *resilience*).[51] Taking these changes as her point of departure, she examines the work of the brain (as Freud examined the work of the psyche) in order to understand why and how the brain changes, giving rise to the "persona of the brain" as something radically different. And she finds that the activity of the brain (like that of the unconscious before it) leads a life of its own, whose movements the subject can neither feel nor situate within its self-image—a paradoxical blindness of the subject with regard to its own brain: "*An inability of the subject to feel anything as far as it is concerned*."[52] So although the brain is the reason we touch ourselves, the brain itself does not appear as part of our body image: "*The brain absents itself at the very site of its presence to self*. It is only accessible by means of cerebral imaging technology."[53] One might of course object that the unconscious as defined by psychoanalysis can also be neither felt nor integrated into any part of the body image—revealing itself instead in the famous Freudian slips, in dreams, as displacement and condensation. Freud also used the example of the Mystic Writing Pad to explain the functioning of the unconscious: every trace ever scratched or inscribed on the pad is preserved, even if it is no longer visible, revealed only when light shines on the wax from a particular angle. With this image, Freud described the unconscious as something that is atemporal, beyond time. The new unconscious entity, however, the "cerebral unconscious" or, as Malabou calls it, the "cerebral nonconscious", does the opposite, operating as pure time.

THE SELF-TIMING OF THE BRAIN

It should be clear by now that the brain has been conquered not only by affect but also by time as duration and interval. As I have shown, the time of the brain, of cerebral duration (in Bergson's sense), has gaps, voids and interruptions where something happens: either nothing (in Hertha Sturm's view) or too much (in Brian Massumi's).

Malabou introduces affect in a way that corresponds to this cerebral temporality, in the process placing an emotional self at the centre of a new libidinal economy. "Within the brain," she writes, "affect does not detach from itself; it does not deprive itself of its own energy."[54] In the brain, then, affect comes to itself (the missing time and energy are gathered) and is declared as the "core self" that manifests itself as pure temporality.

This notion of self-affection in time, originating in Kant, is defined by Heidegger as the "essential structure of subjectivity", positing the relationship between this selfhood and time-as-pure-intuition as one of affection.[55] At every moment of this self-referentiality, change takes place; that is, the subject can only grasp itself in its permanent alterity after the fact. This definition of auto-affection as pure time and of time as the essential structure of subjectivity as complete immanence of auto-affection prompts Malabou to ask another question: "Can we think of affects outside autoaffection, affects without subjects, affects that do not affect 'me'?"[56]

On the one hand, this question takes us back to an older description of the brain and its activities. At the end of the nineteenth century, Pierre Janet cited Alexandre Herzen and his remarks on the brain and its cerebral activities: "It is psychic nothingness, the total absence of consciousness; then one begins to have a vague, unlimited, infinite feeling, a feeling of existence in general, without any delimitation of one's own individuality, without the slightest trace of any distinction between the I and the non-I."[57] But this definition can also be found in a description by Merleau-Ponty, who speaks of an "untouchable" quality in self-touching[58] that lacks the entity that contains the self-affection (an I or whatever one wishes to call it). In the context of his concept of the unconscious, Freud never spoke of detached self-touching, making the question of touching all the more central in our discussion of auto-affection. For if the unconscious and its memories have been understood from Freud to Derrida as traces, this raises the question of how these traces are to be understood today when they are attached to a thinking based not on *écriture* but on plasticity, modulation and modelling.[59]

In *Of Grammatology*, Derrida defines *the voice* as a "hearing-oneself-speak" that foregoes a "signifier interrupting self-presence", thus defining "consciousness as pure auto-affection".[60] This voice is contrasted with writing as an inscription that always already marks a difference. In his later work, however, Derrida swung toward touching, dealing with it via the philosophy of Jean-Luc Nancy as a moment between activity and passivity: "Touching situates the locus of equilibrium between action and passion. [. . .] Touch at the same time fulfils it and covers the entire field of experience, every interval, and every degree between passivity and activity. [. . .] Touch, as such, occupies a median and ideal region of effort poised between passivity and activity."[61] Touching oneself as a first movement without touching anything[62]—this primal form of a self-moving (self-) desire (life as self-affirmation) takes the place of the trace as *différance*.

Over recent years, "affective" brain activity has also been much discussed in neuroscience, where it has been stressed that the way we think and act is guided not so much by cognitive processes as by deep-seated, ancient affects. Jaak Panksepp, who coined the term *affective neuroscience* in the early 1990s,[63] distinguishes between affective feelings and cognitive processes. Affective feelings are

> distinct neurobiological processes in terms of anatomical, neurochemical, and various functional criteria. [. . .] Emotional and motivational feelings are unique experientially valenced 'state spaces' that help organisms make cognitive choices—e.g., to find food when hungry, water when thirsty, warmth when cold, and companionship when lonely or lusty. If affective organic processes [. . .] are to a substantial degree distinct from those that mediate cognitive deliberation, [. . .] then we must develop special strategies to understand them in neural terms.[64]

This interpretation sounds comparable with that of Antonio Damasio, who has defined *affects* as tuning elements that are responsible for keeping the body in a state of constant exchange with its surroundings. But Panksepp goes one step further by pinpointing that these affects are largely subcortical processes allegedly revealing an old evolutionary history. He thus argues that "we should remain open to the possibility that the fundamental ability of neural tissue to elaborate primary-process forms of affective experience evolved long before human brain evolution allowed us to think and to talk about such things".[65]

John Protevi, on the other hand, speaks of "affective cognition" and insists that cognitive and affective processes must be understood not as separate but as a single process. With reference to Deleuze and Spinoza, *affects* are defined here as a kind of resonator forming "somatic markers" (Damasio) that define the affective cognition profile of bodies as "embodied and historical".[66]

Malabou, too, borrows from Deleuze und Damasio for her concept of an "affective autocerebrality" but with one key difference:

her concept of auto-affection leads, as we have seen, via Jacques Derrida and Jean-Luc Nancy to a nonconscious, bringing it closer to Panksepp's notion of distinct affective processes and Massumi's previously mentioned "autonomy of affect".

While in psychoanalytical theory the ego is engaged in an imaginary (mirror) relationship, in Malabou's model this becomes an auto-affective relationship structured by time: in the brain nothing is centralized, affect and core-self are equalized in a temporal dimension. As a result, the famous cut in psychoanalysis between unconscious desire and a narcissistic imaginary has shifted to become a split between cerebral auto-affection and emotional self.

In order to oppose the tendency within neuroscience to merge the productive power of this split into a monistic neural energy, Malabou refers to a fundamental divide rooted in Freud's thinking of the sexual—between ego drives and sexual drives, between ego and object drives, and finally the all-encompassing distinction between life and death drives. In Freud's version the sexual (as opposed to sexuality) is always structurally divided, which (put in very simple terms) prompts Lacan to postulate the structurally endless movement of desire. As Malabou notes, Freud strongly resisted any monistic theory of libido (such as that proposed by C. G. Jung), always maintaining the other of (or rather within) the sexual. The same applies to the monistic neuronal energy model of today's neuroscience that Freud, she argues, would also have rejected. With the help of psychoanalytic drive theory, then, Malabou formulates a model of a cerebral nonconscious that posits cerebral auto-affection as the "unconscious of subjectivity".[67]

MODULATION AND SELF-MODELLING

How does Malabou's "affective nonconscious" relate to my remarks on a *dispositif* of affect? By substituting the brain for sexuality, by replacing sexual eventality with a future psychopathology in cerebral eventuality, Malabou confirms my theory that the *dispositif* of sex has been shifting to one of affect, involving a whole range of reorderings that impact on mental self-reference, the definition of sexuality, and desire.

The way affect is now credited with the revolutionary potential to found a new libidinal economy must of course be viewed against the backdrop of this shift. Whereas in the twentieth century, with reference to Freud, every uprising, revolt, emancipation and liberation was understood as the breaking-out of a repressed sexual energy, the same kind of power is now attributed to affect, both politically and in terms of brain activity. As I have emphasized in my analysis of psychoanalytical affect and the time-based models of affect in philosophy and neuroscience, the latter do not merely translate or rewrite the psychoanalytical model but actually transform what is at stake: whereas desire was formerly (and for a long time) attributed to an unconscious, it has now become an auto-affective energy that is described not as unconscious but as nonconscious.

How are we to imagine a desire that is not linked (as in psychoanalysis) to a subject's lack of being and (as in Marxist theory) to an economy of added value? Whereas Lacan inserted desire into a Möbius strip where thinking and being cannot be had at the same time, this irresolvable break can be seen to have shifted: in "blind feeling", this break is not between thinking and being, or between physical labour and added value, but a matter of autonomous movements of the body whose work of prehension shapes a subject capable of consciousness. Haraway defines this prehension as a "concrescence of prehensions", meaning that everything is constituted only in a mutual grasping, with nothing existing before its respective relatings: "Prehensions have consequences. The world is a knot in motion. [. . .] There are no pre-constituted subjects and objects, and no single sources, unitary actors, or final ends."[68] The movement of a desire conceived of in this way no longer operates as a force of interpellation (as posited by Althusser in his definition of ideology drawing on Spinoza) but as movement and (self-) touching, which is why I would also propose that it should rather be referred to here as an "imitation of desire".

In *A Thousand Plateaus*, Deleuze and Guattari describe imitation as a "flow" that moves through beliefs and desires:

> Beliefs and desires are the basis of every society, because they are flows and as such are 'quantifiable'; they are veritable social Quantities, whereas sensations are qualitative and representations are simple resultants. Infinitesimal imitation, opposition, and invention are therefore like flow quanta marking a propagation, binarization, or conjugation of beliefs and desires.[69]

Understood in the humanities and social sciences as a psychosocial process, since the 1970s imitation has been increasingly rejected by psychoanalytically orientated media and film theory on the grounds that it is based on an overly rigid role model. The sociological term was replaced by the more psychoanalytical concept of identification that placed more emphasis on the dimension of the unconscious. Today, amid a general decline of interest in psychoanalysis, the question of imitation (always conceived of as movement!) is also beginning to play a conspicuous part in discussions of affect. Not least because this imitation, as introduced into sociology by Gabriel Tarde, has been charged, via the interpretation of Deleuze and Guattari, with a structure of desire that is connected in many ways with current trends. According to Christian Borch and Urs Stäheli, Tarde's "sociology of desire" or "affect sociology" is so important to theoretical debate today because, rather than reducing desire to a "psychoanalytical case history of identification",[70] it takes the idea of "mimetic repetition" and shows how imitation is driven or hindered by the forces of desire and belief.

At present, this "imitation of desire", as I would like to call it, plays a prominent role in two fields: in studies of movement (especially in dance) and in the development of surveillance technologies. With this notion of an "imitation of desire", I would like to draw attention to a basic shift. This concept of imitation no longer has any psychoanalytical connotation in the sense of an identificatory charge, added to which it is no longer defined in terms of an existential lack. Instead, a desire is imitated (adopted) insofar as it is transformed, via deferral and interval, into movement in time. But once imitation is freed of such "psychoanalytical ballast", we are not far removed from desire as mere exercise (in the sense of a self-training or a slightly misunderstood technology of the self).

As Bruno Latour has repeatedly stressed in his work, the issue of self-training intersects here with questions of "existence" as media design. In a lecture at the Design History Society in 2008,[71] Latour focused on Peter Sloterdijk, who, he says, has excelled in translating Heidegger's definition of *Dasein* back into its repressed, ignored materiality.[72] In this light, Latour transposes his "plasma of the social" into a design-based model of the life-world, in which technical artifacts, nonhuman and human agencies, enter into new relationships. As nature and society are permeated by media and technology, leading to a profusion of quasi-objects and quasi-subjects, the distinction between function and form becomes obsolete: "To define humans is to define envelopes, the life support systems, the *Umwelt* that make it possible for them to breathe. This is exactly what humanism has always missed."[73]

It is no surprise then, that current media theory has a tendency to understand twenty-first-century media in terms of an environment, atmosphere, or ecology that is elementary to the modulations of human beings (Galloway/Thacker). In his "Postscript for the Societies of Control", Deleuze also speaks of modulation in a double sense: first, as a deterritorializing liberation (the surfer riding the wave), and second, as self-modulation in the sense of the post-Fordist demand for a flexible, adaptive working subject. Controls are a "*modulation,* like a self-transmuting molding continually changing from one moment to the next, or like a sieve whose mesh will transmute from point to point."[74] This contrasts with the "spaces of enclosure" (family, school, church) that functioned via sexuality and its productive suppression and that have long since lost their integrity, undergoing an endless series of crises. Today's logic of control imposes itself via limitless postponement, characterized by constant movement (in the form of further training, services, etc.), never attaining and never sufficing, always working on oneself and everything else. Whereas disciplinary man was a "discontinuous producer of energy", the "man of control undulates".[75]

This resonates with a more widespread transition from a body conceived of in thermodynamic terms to a biomediated body, including a shift from mental depth to affective surface (in the sense of interfaces, gaps, friction and touch). The view of neuroplasticity and affect as the new centre of a libidinal economy fits very snugly into this model.

DESIRE FOR DISAFFECTION

In 2007, I concluded the German version of this book by comparing psychoanalysis and Deleuze's philosophy of becoming with Grimm's tale of "The Hare and The Hedgehog", describing the affective turn as a battle for interpretative hegemony. Today, I would describe it not as a contest but as a powerful reinterpretation of what desire is capable of under the conditions of media technology, brain research, and turbo-capitalism. But this also means that the desire *for* affect has since turned into desire *after* affect.

Whereas Deleuze claimed that Spinoza had given the body back to philosophers, a body whose capabilities were unknown, this idea can be paraphrased for today by saying that the body has now arrived at the centre of a *dispositif* of affect, where it is truth and added value in one.

In this same context, I have written elsewhere of the interest currently being focused on movement in general and dance in particular, referring to "affective modulations"[76] that operate below the threshold of visual perception and outside symbolic networks, like waves, like traffic, like the movement of many, like the cells in an organism, like animal bodies, like media networks. When approaches based on media ecology claim that media technologies operate beyond consciousness and that—as Bernard Stiegler has stressed—there seems to be no escaping this capitalist grammatization machine, then in this context desire might manifest itself by disturbing this all-encompassing modulation, by deviating from the great wave, even if only by a tiny amount, leading to what Louis Althusser once called a radically contingent encounter—or a nonencounter? And might we then modify Massumi's "affective modulation [meets] affective modulation",[77] into a "disaffective modulation"?

With her subtitle *From Neurosis to Brain Damage*, Catherine Malabou points to the possibility of mental illnesses being rediagnosed as types of brain damage. In the context of the auto-affection of neural processes, traumatic events, head injuries, ageing processes, Alzheimer's and dementia could be read as affective withdrawal, as a withdrawal of cathexis: not auto-affection but a radical withdrawal or a subjective miscathexis. This can also be interpreted as her attempt to understand how a person becomes someone else as a result of brain damage, switching to a different level of being where experience is organized differently, no longer communicating with or affecting consciousness.

As well as speaking of the radical contingency of the encounter, Althusser also described Spinoza as the philosopher of the "void" who simply refers to God as *only nature*, in which everything exists in two potencies, as extension and as thought. But this thinking refers not to a subject but, in the sense of a random encounter between mind and body, "to the succession of the modes of the attribute 'extension'."[78] If we take a leap here to the interval of affect (described by Deleuze as being filled by affect but not entirely) and if we think this gap together with the random encounter, then a figure of disaffection becomes visible that is not based on pathological deviations and disorders, instead acquiring an existential function. With the help of this figure, it is possible to conceive of *desire after affect* as a movement that hinders the smooth integration of the biomediated body by deferring it for the *moment of a half-second*.

NOTES

1. Alfred N. Whitehead, *Process and Reality: An Essay in Cosmology* (New York: The Free Press, 1978), 105.
2. According to Catherine Malabou, the connection between neuronal and political can be easily established via the metaphor of the network. Paraphrasing the French neurologist Marc Jeannerod, she writes: "The representation of the center collapses into the network." Catherine Malabou, *What Should We Do with Our Brain?* (New York: Fordham University Press, 2008), 35.
3. N. Katherine Hayles, *How We Became Posthuman: Virtual Bodies in Cybernetics, Literature, and Informatics* (Chicago: University of Chicago Press, 1999); Alexander R. Galloway and Eugene Thacker, *The Exploit: A Theory of Networks* (Minneapolis: University of Minnesota Press, 2007).
4. Georges Canguilhem, "Machine and Organism," in Jonathan Crary and Sanford Kwinter (eds.), *Incorporations* (New York: Zone Books, 1992), 45–69.
5. See Jussi Parikka, *Insect Media: An Archaeology of Animals and Technology* (Minneapolis: University of Minnesota Press, 2009).
6. Jimena Canales, *A Tenth of a Second: A History* (Chicago: University of Chicago Press, 2009).
7. Quoted in Henning Schmidgen, *Die Helmholtz-Kurven. Auf der Spur der verlorenen Zeit* (Berlin: Merve, 2009), 74.
8. Ibid., 93.
9. Ibid.
10. "Libet's Short Delay," in *Conscious Entities*, (2 June 2005), http://www.consciousentities.com/libet.htm (retrieved May 17 2014).

11. John Protevi, "Ontology, Biology, and History of Affect," in Levi Bryant, Nick Srnicek, and Graham Harman (eds.), *The Speculative Turn* (Melbourne: Re:press, 2011), 393–405, here 395f.

12. Patricia T. Clough, "The Affective Turn: Political Economy, Biomedia and Bodies," in *Theory, Culture & Society*, 25.1 (2008), 1–22, here 2.

13. As a counterpart to this, attempts are being made to develop affective computing; i.e., programming machines that are capable of understanding and correctly responding to emotions, which are expressed primarily via the muscles of the face. See Rosalind Picard, *Affective Computing* (Cambridge, MA: MIT Press, 2000). It is no coincidence that a major role is played here by the Ekman-Tomkins paradigm that has been heavily criticized by Ruth Leys (among others). See Ruth Leys, *From Guilt to Shame: Auschwitz and After* (Princeton, Oxford: Princeton University Press, 2007), 137f.

14. Donna J. Haraway, *The Companion Species Manifesto: Dogs, People, and Significant Others* (Chicago: Prickly Paradigm Press, 2003).

15. Donna J. Haraway, *When Species Meet* (Minneapolis: University of Minnesota Press, 2008), 164.

16. Ibid., 229.

17. See Gilles Deleuze, *Spinoza: Practical Philosophy* (San Francisco: City Lights, 1988), 126.

18. Isabelle Stengers, "Wondering about Materialism," in Levi Bryant, Nick Srnicek, and Graham Harman 368-380. (eds.), *The Speculative Turn* (Melbourne: Re:press, 2011), 368–80, here 371.

19. Erin Manning and Brian Massumi, *Thought in ACT: Passages in the Ecology of Experience* (Minnesota: University of Minnesota Press, 2014).

20. Steven Shaviro, *Without Criteria: Kant, Whitehead, Deleuze, and Aesthetics* (Cambridge, MA: MIT Press, 2012).

21. Mark B. N. Hansen, "Feeling without Feelers, or Affectivity as Environmental Force," in Marie-Luise Angerer, Bernd Bösel, and Michaela Ott (eds.), *Timing of Affect: Epistemologies, Politics, Aesthetics* (Zurich, Switzerland: diaphanes and University of Chicago Press, forthcoming).

22. Luciana Parisi, *Contagious Architecture: Computation, Aesthetics, and Space* (Cambridge, MA: MIT Press, 2013).

23. Whitehead, *Process and Reality*, 162.

24. Ibid.

25. Ibid., 222.

26. Bernard Stiegler, *Hypermaterialität und Psychomacht* (Berlin: diaphanes, 2010), 119.

27. Bernard Stiegler, *Technics and Time 1: The Fault of Epimetheus* (Stanford, CA: Stanford University Press, 1998); Bernard Stiegler, *Technics and Time 2: Disorientation* (Stanford, CA: Stanford University Press, 2009).

28. Bernard Stiegler, *Von der Biopolitik zur Psychomacht* (Frankfurt, Germany: Suhrkamp, 2009), 50.

29. Ibid., 53.

30. Bernard Stiegler, "Allgemeine Organologie und positive Pharmakologie (Theorie und Praxis)," in Erich Hörl (ed.), *Die technologische Bedingung. Beiträge zur Beschreibung der technischen Welt* (Berlin: Suhrkamp, 2011), 110–46.

31. With his concept of "expanded experience", Mark Hansen refers not only to Whitehead but also and in particular to Gilbert Simondon's concept of transindividuality. On transindividuality, see Arne de Boever, Alex Murray, Jon Roffe, and Ashley Woodward (eds.), *Gilbert Simondon: Being and Technology* (Edinburgh, UK: Edinburgh University Press, 2012), 230.

32. Natasha Dow Schüll, *Addiction by Design: Machine Gambling in Las Vegas* (Princeton, NJ: Princeton University Press, 2012). Here she develops the theory that it is no longer a matter of the pleasure of playing and winning but of compulsion, tracking players, intensification—of players becoming accustomed to routine repetitions, whose interruption is to be avoided. In this context, one might also mention the current focus on autistic people, who are considered to be equipped with special competences (fast, precise pattern recognition; capacity for sustained repetition) that are already being exploited by IT companies. According to *Der Spiegel* (21 May 2013), the international company SAP has employed hundreds of autistic people in order to integrate their special skills in its production processes.

33. Friedrich A. Kittler, *Discourse Networks, 1800/1900* (Stanford, CA: Stanford University Press, 1992).
34. See Richard Iveson, "Plasticity and the Living Dead: Malabou Reading Freud," in *Zoogenesis: Thinking Animals, Encounter, and Other Stuff*, (23 March 2013), http://zoogenesis.wordpress.com/2013/03/23/plasticity-and-the-living-dead-malabou-reading-freu (retrieved 5 May 2014).
35. See chapter 3.
36. See Stacey Alaimo and Susan Hekman (eds.), *Material Feminisms* (Bloomington: Indiana University Press, 2008); Diana Coole and Samantha Frost (eds.), *New Materialisms: Ontology, Agency, and Politics* (Durham, NC: Duke University Press, 2010); and Rick Dolphijn and Iris van der Tuin (eds.), *New Materialism: Interviews & Cartographies* (Ann Arbor, MI: Open Humanities Press, 2012).
37. Roland Barthes, *Mythologies* (1957) (New York: Hill and Wang, 1972), 97.
38. Gilbert Simondon, *Du mode d'existence des objets techniques* (1958) (Paris: Aubier, 1989), 122.
39. Ibid., 123f.
40. The concept of plasticity is also being rediscovered in art. On plasticity's long tradition in the twentieth century, see Dietmar Rübel, *Plastizität. Die Kunstgeschichte des Veränderlichen* (Munich, Germany: Verlag Silke Schreiber, 2012). One might also recall Joseph Beuys's concept of the "social sculpture."
41. Henning Schmidgen, "Leerstellen des Denkens. Die Entdeckung der physiologischen Zeit," in Bernhard J. Dotzler and Henning Schmidgen (eds.), *Parasiten und Sirenen. Zwischenräume als Orte der materiellen Wissensproduktion* (Bielefeld, Germany: Transcript, 2008), 107–24, here 108; and Henri Bergson, *Matter and Memory* (New York: Cosimo, 2007), 23, 28.
42. Schmidgen, "Leerstellen des Denkens," 109.
43. Bergson, *Matter and Memory*, 19.
44. Sigmund Freud, *The Interpretation of Dreams* (1900) (New York: Basic Books, 1955), 572.
45. "Nerve circuits consist of neurons juxtaposed at the synapses; there is a *break* between one neuron and the other." Pierre Changeux, *Neuronal Man: The Biology of Mind* (1985) (Princeton, NJ: Princeton University Press, 1997), 83.
46. Malabou, *What Should We Do*, 36.
47. Donald Olding Hebb, *The Organization of Behaviour: A Neuropsychological Theory* (New York: John Wiley & Sons, 1949).
48. Changeux, *Neuronal Man*, 142.
49. William James, *The Principles of Psychology, Vol. 1* (New York: Henry Holt, 1890), 105.
50. Nikolas Rose and Joelle M. Abi-Rached, *Neuro: The New Brain Sciences and the Management of Mind* (Princeton, NJ: Princeton University Press, 2013), 48.
51. Malabou, *What Should We Do*, 68f.
52. Catherine Malabou, *The New Wounded: From Neurosis to Brain Damage* (New York: Fordham University Press, 2012), 42.
53. Ibid., 43.
54. Ibid., 44.
55. Martin Heidegger, *Kant and the Problem of Metaphysics* (Bloomington, IN: Bloomington University Press, 1997), 132f.
56. Catherine Malabou and Adrian Johnston, *Self and Emotional Life* (New York: Columbia University Press, 2013), 6.
57. Pierre Janet, quoted in Daniel Heller-Roazen, *The Inner Touch: Archaeology of a Sensation* (New York: Zone Books, 2009), 281.
58. Maurice Merleau-Ponty, quoted in Heller-Roazen, *The Inner Touch*, 296.
59. See also my remarks on the different concepts of the trace in Freud and Massumi in chapter 3.
60. Jacques Derrida, *Of Grammatology* (1967) (Baltimore, MD: Johns Hopkins University Press, 1997), 98.
61. Jacques Derrida, *On Touching, Jean-Luc Nancy* (Stanford, CA: Stanford University Press, 2005), 155.
62. Jean-Luc Nancy, *Corpus* (New York: Fordham University Press, 2008).
63. Jaak Panksepp, *Affective Neuroscience* (New York: Oxford University Press, 1998).

64. Jaak Panksepp, "At the Interface of the Affective, Behavioral, and Cognitive Neurosciences: Decoding the Emotional Feelings of the Brain," in *Brain and Cognition*, 52 (2003), 4–14, here 6.

65. Ibid., 7.

66. Protevi, "Ontology, Biology, and History of Affect," 402.

67. Malabou, *New Wounded*, 43.

68. Haraway, *Companion Species Manifesto*, 6

69. Gilles Deleuze and Félix Guattari, *A Thousand Plateaus: Capitalism and Schizophrenia* (1980) (Minneapolis: University of Minnesota Press, 1987), 219.

70. Christian Borch and Urs Stäheli (eds.), *Soziologie der Nachahmung und des Begehrens—Materialien zu Gabriel Tarde* (Frankfurt, Germany: Suhrkamp, 2009), 11.

71. Bruno Latour, "A Cautious Prometheus? A Few Steps toward a Philosophy of Design (with Special Attention to Peter Sloterdijk)," keynote lecture for the *Networks of Design* meeting of the Design History Society, Falmouth, Cornwall, UK, 3 September 2008, http://www.bruno-latour.fr/sites/default/files/112-DESIGN-CORNWALL-GB.pdf (retrieved 3 July 2014).

72. See chapter 2.

73. See also my comments in chapter 1 on Olafur Eliasson, described by Latour in 2003 as a new artist dealing with questions of our survival as a member of a laboratory.

74. Gilles Deleuze, "Postscript on the Society of Control," in Gilles Deleuze, *Negotiations* (New York: Columbia University Press, 1995), 177–82, here 178f.

75. Ibid., 180.

76. In the new discourse on affect and dance, too, autistic people are cited as an example, emphasizing not their integration into industrial workflows (as mentioned earlier) but their especially affective relationship with their environment. See Marie-Luise Angerer, "Affective Modulations in Politics, Theory and Art," in Gabriele Brandstetter, Gerko Egert, and Sabine Zubarik (eds.), *Touching and Being Touched* (Berlin: De Gruyter, 2013), 235–48; and Erin Manning, *Always More Than One: Individuation's Dance* (Durham, NC: Duke University Press, 2013).

77. Brian Massumi, "Navigating Moments," in *21C Magazine* (2003).

78. See Louis Althusser, "The Underground Current of the Materialism of the Encounter," in Louis Althusser, *Philosophy of the Encounter: Later Writings, 1978–87* (London: Verso, 2006), 178.

Bibliography

Adams, Parveen, *The Emptiness of the Image* (London: Routledge, 1996).
Agamben, Giorgio, *Homo Sacer: Sovereign Power and Bare Life* (Stanford, CA: Stanford University Press, 1998).
Ahmed, Sara, *The Cultural Politics of Emotions* (Edinburgh, UK: Edinburgh University Press, 2004).
Alaimo, Stacey; and Hekman, Susan (eds.), *Material Feminisms* (Bloomington: Indiana University Press, 2008).
Althusser, Louis, "Ideology and Ideological State Apparatuses," in Louis Althusser, *On Ideology* (London: Verso, 2008).
Althusser, Louis, "The Underground Current of the Materialism of the Encounter," in Louis Althusser, *Philosophy of the Encounter: Later Writings, 1978–87* (London: Verso, 2006).
Angerer, Marie-Luise, "Affective Modulations in Politics, Theory and Art," in Gabriele Brandstetter, Gerko Egert, and Sabine Zubarik (eds.), *Touching and Being Touched* (Berlin: De Gruyter, 2013), 235–48.
Angerer, Marie-Luise, *Body Options. Körper.Spuren.Medien.Bilder* (Vienna: Turia & Kant, 1999).
Angerer, Marie-Luise, "Cybertroubles: The Question of the Subject in Cyberfeminism," in Claudia Reiche and Verena Kuni (eds.), *Cyberfeminism: Next Protocols* (New York: Autonomedia, 2002), 18–31.
Angerer, Marie-Luise, "Expanded Thoughts. Zu Valie EXPORT," in *LAB, Jahrbuch für Künste und Apparate* (Cologne, Germany: Art Academy of Media, 2006), 11–25.
Angerer, Marie-Luise; Bösel, Bernd; and Ott, Michaela (eds.), *Timing of Affect: Epistemologies, Politics, Aesthetics* (Zurich, Switzerland: diaphanes and University of Chicago Press, forthcoming).
Ansermet, François; and Magistretti, Pierre, *Biology of Freedom: Neural Plasticity, Experience and the Unconscious* (London: Karnac, 2007).
Armstrong, Rachel, "Cyborg Film Making in Great Britain," in Andrea B. Braidt (ed.), *[Cyborgs.Nets/z]*, catalog accompanying the film *Dandy Dust* (Vienna: Eigenverlag, 1999).
Aronowitz, Stanley, "Technology and the Future of Work," in Gretchen Bender and Timothy Druckrey (eds.), *Culture on the Brink: Ideologies of Technology* (Seattle: New Press, 1998), 15–30.
Badiou, Alain, *The Adventure of French Philosophy* (New York: Verso, 2012).
Badiou, Alain, *The Century* (New York: Polity, 2007).
Ballard, J. G., *Crash* (London: Jonathan Cape, 1973).
Barthes, Roland, *Camera Lucida—Reflections on Photography* (New York: Hill and Wang, 1981).
Barthes, Roland, *Mythologies* (1957) (New York: Hill and Wang, 1972).
Baudrillard, Jean, *The Vital Illusion* (New York: Columbia University Press, 2000).
Baudry, Jean-Louis, "The Apparatus: Metapsychological Approaches to the Impression of Reality in Cinema," in *Camera Obscura*, 1 (1976), 104–26.
Baudry, Jean-Louis, "Ideological Effects of the Basic Cinematographic Apparatus," in *Film Quarterly*, 28.2 (1974), 39–47.
Bennett, Jill, *Empathic Vision: Affect, Trauma and Contemporary Art* (Stanford, CA: Stanford University Press, 2005).
Bennington, Geoffrey; and Derrida, Jacques, *Jacques Derrida* (Chicago: University of Chicago Press, 1993).

Bergermann, Ulrike, "Morphing. Profile des Digitalen," in Petra Löffler and Leander Scholz (eds.), *Das Gesicht ist eine starke Organisation* (Cologne, Germany: DuMont, 2004), 250–74.
Bergson, Henri, *Matter and Memory* (New York: Cosimo, 2007).
Bitsch, Annette, "Kybernetik des Unbewussten, das Unbewusste der Kybernetik," in Claus Pias (ed.), *Cybernetics|Kybernetik, The Macy Conferences 1946–1953, Essays & Dokumente, Vol. II* (Zurich, Switzerland: diaphanes, 2003), 153–68.
Boever, Arne de, Alex Murray, Jon Roffe, and Ashley Woodward (eds.), *Gilbert Simondon: Being and Technology* (Edinburgh, UK: Edinburgh University Press, 2012.
Borch, Christian; and Stäheli, Urs (eds.), *Soziologie der Nachahmung und des Begehrens—Materialien zu Gabriel Tarde* (Frankfurt, Germany: Suhrkamp, 2009).
Bordwell, David; and Thompson, Kristin, *Film History: An Introduction* (New York: Columbia University Press, 1994).
Braidotti, Rosi, "Between No Longer and the Not Yet: On Bios/Zoë-Ethics," in *Filozofski vestnik*, 23.2 (2002), 9–26.
Braidotti, Rosi, *Metamorphosis: Towards a Materialist Theory of Becoming* (Cambridge, UK: Polity, 2002).
Braidotti, Rosi, *Transpositions: On Nomadic Ethics* (Cambridge, UK: Polity, 2006).
Brennan, Teresa, *The Transmission of Affect* (Ithaca, NY: Cornell University Press, 2004).
Bröckling, Ulrich; Krasmann, Susanne; and Lemke, Thomas (eds.), *Governmentality: Current Issues and Future Challenges* (London: Routledge, 2011).
Brütsch, Matthias; Hediger, Vinzenz; Keitz, Ursula von; Schneider, Alexandra; and Margrit Tröhler (eds.), *Kinogefühle. Emotionalität und Film* (Marburg, Germany: Schüren Verlag, 2005).
Butler, Judith, *Bodies That Matter: On the Discursive Limits of "Sex"* (New York: Routledge, 1993).
Butler, Judith, *Gender Trouble: Feminism and the Subversion of Identity* (New York: Routledge, 1999).
Butler, Judith, *The Psychic Life of Power: Theories in Subjection* (Stanford, CA: Stanford University Press, 1997).
Canales, Jimena, *A Tenth of a Second: A History* (Chicago: University of Chicago Press, 2009).
Canguilhem, Georges, "Machine and Organism," in Jonathan Crary and Sanford Kwinter (eds.), *Incorporations* (New York: Zone Books, 1992), 45–69.
Cartwright, Lisa, *Moral Spectatorship: Technologies of Voice and Affect in Postwar Representations of the Child* (Durham, NC: Duke University Press, 2008).
Changeux, Pierre, *Neuronal Man: The Biology of Mind* (1985) (Princeton, NJ: Princeton University Press, 1997).
Chodorow, Nancy J., *The Power of Feelings* (New Haven, CT: Yale University Press, 1999).
Clausberg, Karl; and Weiller, Cornelius, "Wie Denken aussieht. Zu den bildgebenden Verfahren der Hirnforschung," in Christian Geyer (ed.), *Hirnforschung und Willensfreiheit* (Frankfurt, Germany: Suhrkamp, 2004), 245–49.
Clough, Patricia T., "The Affective Turn: Political Economy, Biomedia and Bodies," in *Theory, Culture & Society*, 25.1 (2008), 1–22.
Clough, Patricia T.; Goldberg, Greg; Schiff, Rachel; Weeks, Aaron; and Willse, Craig, "Notes Towards a Theory of Affect-Itself," *Ephemera*, 7.1 (2007), 60–77.
Coole, Diana; and Frost, Samantha (eds.), *New Materialisms. Ontology: Agency, and Politics* (Durham, NC: Duke University Press, 2010).
Copjec, Joan, *Imagine There's No Woman: Ethics and Sublimation* (Boston: Beacon Press, 2002).
Copjec, Joan, "May '68, The Emotional Month," in Slavoj Žižek (ed.), *Lacan: The Silent Partners* (London: Verso, 2006), 90–114.
Crary, Jonathan, *24/7: Late Capitalism and the End of Sleep* (London: Verso, 2014).
Crary, Jonathan, *Techniques of the Observer: On Vision and Modernity in the Nineteenth Century* (Cambridge, MA: MIT Press, 1992).
Crary, Jonathan, "Your Colour Memory: Illuminations of the Unforeseen," in Olafur Eliasson and Gitte Ørskou (eds.), *Olafur Eliasson: Minding the World* (Aarhus, Denmark: ARoS Aarhus Kunstmuseum, 2004), 209–25 (exhibition

catalog), http://www.olafureliasson.net/publications/download_texts/Your_colour_memory.pdf(retrieved 3 July 2014).

Cubitt, Sean, *Digital Aesthetics* (London: Sage, 1998).

Damasio, Antonio R., *The Feeling of What Happens: Body and Emotion in the Making of Consciousness* (New York: Harcourt Brace, 1999).

Damasio, Antonio R., *Looking for Spinoza: Joy, Sorrow, and the Feeling Brain* (New York: Houghton Mifflin, 2003).

Daston, Lorraine; and Galison, Peter, "The Image of Objectivity," in *Representations*, 40 (1992), 81–128.

Davies, Char, "Immersence," www.immersence.com (retrieved 22 May 2014).

Dean, Tim, *Beyond Sexuality* (Chicago: University of Chicago Press, 2000).

Deleuze, Gilles, *Bergsonism* (New York: Zone, 1988).

Deleuze, Gilles, *Cinema 1: The Movement-Image* (Minneapolis: University of Minnesota Press, 1986).

Deleuze, Gilles, *Cinema 2: The Time-Image* (Minneapolis: University of Minnesota Press, 1989).

Deleuze, Gilles, *Difference and Repetition* (New York: Columbia University Pess, 1994).

Deleuze, Gilles, *Foucault* (London: Continuum, 1999).

Deleuze, Gilles, "Postscript on the Society of Control," in Gilles Deleuze, *Negotiations* (New York: Columbia University Press, 1995), 177–82.

Deleuze, Gilles, *Spinoza: Practical Philosophy* (San Francisco: City Lights, 1988).

Deleuze, Gilles; and Guattari, Félix, *Anti-Oedipus: Capitalism and Schizophrenia* (1972) (Minneapolis: University of Minnesota Press, 1983).

Deleuze, Gilles; and Guattari, Félix, *A Thousand Plateaus: Capitalism and Schizophrenia* (1980) (Minneapolis: University of Minnesota Press, 1987).

Deleuze, Gilles; and Guattari, Félix, *What Is Philosophy?* (London: Verso, 1994).

Derrida, Jacques, "Freud and the Scene of Writing," in Jacques Derrida, *Writing and Difference* (Chicago: University of Chicago Press, 1978), 196–231.

Derrida, Jacques, "Geschlecht: Sexual Difference, Ontological Difference," in *Research in Phenomenology*, 13 (1983), 65–83.

Derrida, Jacques, *Of Grammatology* (1967) (Baltimore, MD: Johns Hopkins University Press, 1997).

Derrida, Jacques, *On Touching, Jean-Luc Nancy* (Stanford, CA: Stanford University Press, 2005).

Derrida, Jacques, "Signature Event Context," in Jacques Derrida, *Limited Inc.* (Evanston, IL: Northwestern University Press, 1977), 1–21.

Derrida, Jacques, *Writing and Difference* (Chicago: University of Chicago Press, 1978).

Deuber-Mankowsky, Astrid, "Das virtuelle Geschlecht. Gender und Computerspiele, eine diskursanalytische Annäherung," in Claus Pias and Christian Holtorf (eds.), *Escape! Computerspiele als Kulturtechnik* (Cologne, Germany: Böhlau, 2007), 85–104.

Deuber-Mankowsky, Astrid, *Lara Croft: Cyberheroine* (Minneapolis: University of Minnesota Press, 2005).

Dolphijn, Rick; and van der Tuin, Iris (eds.), *New Materialism: Interviews & Cartographies* (Ann Arbor, MI: Open Humanities Press, 2012).

Dornes, Martin, "Wahrnehmen, Fühlen, Phantasieren," in Gertrud Koch (ed.), *Auge und Affekt. Wahrnehmung und Interaktion* (Frankfurt, Germany: Fischer, 1995), 15–38.

Elsaesser, Thomas, "Zu spät, zu früh? Körper, Zeit und Aktionsraum in der Kinoerfahrung," in Matthias Brütsch, Vinzenz Hediger, Ursula von Keitz, Alexandra Schneider, and Margrit Tröhler (eds.), *Kinogefühle. Emotionalität und Film* (Marburg, Germany: Schüren Verlag, 2005), 415–39.

Ernst, Wolfgang, "Temporalizing Presence and 'Re-Presencing' the Past: The Techno-Traumatic Affect," in Marie-Luise Angerer, Bernd Bösel, Michaela Ott (eds.), *Timing of Affect: Epistemologies, Politics, Aesthetics* (Zurich, Switzerland: diaphanes and University of Chicago Press, forthcoming).

EXPORT, VALIE, "womans art. manifest zur Ausstellung MAGNA" (arbeitstitel frauenkunst) eine ausstellung, an der nur frauen teilnehmen, in *Neues Forum*, 228 (1972).

Fechner, Gustav Theodor, *Elements of Psychophysics* (1860) (New York: Holt, Rinehart, and Winston, 1966).

Fechner, Gustav Theodor, *Vorschule der Ästhetik*, 2 vols. (Leipzig, Germany: Breitkopf & Härtel, 1876).
Feher, Michel, "Self-Appreciation; or, The Aspirations of Human Capital," in *Public Culture: Bulletin of the Project for Transnational Cultural Studies*, 21.1 (2009), 21–42.
Foerster, Heinz von, *Short Cuts 5* (Frankfurt, Germany: Zweitausendeins, 2001).
Foster, Hal, "Polemics, Postmodernism, Immersion, Militarized Space," in *Journal of Visual Culture*, 3.3 (2004), 320–35.
Foucault, Michel, *The Birth of the Clinic* (1963) (London: Tavistock, 1973).
Foucault, Michel, *The History of Sexuality, Vol. 1: The Will to Knowledge* (1976) (London: Penguin, 1998).
Foucault, Michel, *On the Government of the Living: Lectures at the Collège de France, 1979–1980* (Basingstoke, UK: Palgrave Macmillan, 2014).
Foucault, Michel, *The Order of Things: An Archaeology of the Human Sciences* (New York: Routledge, 2005).
Freud, Sigmund, "XXV: Anxiety" (1916–1917), in *Introductory Lectures on Psychoanalysis* (London: Hogarth Press, 1963), 392–411.
Freud, Sigmund, "Beyond the Pleasure Principle" (1920), in *The Standard Edition of the Complete Psychological Works of Sigmund Freud, Vol. 18* (London: Hogarth Press, 1955), 7–66.
Freud, Sigmund, "Civilization and Its Discontents" (1930) (New York: Norton, 1989).
Freud, Sigmund, "The Dissection of the Psychical Personality" (1933), in Sigmund Freud, *New Introductory Lectures on Psycho-Analysis* (New York: Norton, 1989), 71–100.
Freud, Sigmund, *The Ego and the Id* (1923) (New York: Norton, 1960).
Freud, Sigmund, *Inhibitions, Symptoms and Anxiety* (1926) (New York: Norton, 1989).
Freud, Sigmund, *The Interpretation of Dreams* (1900) (New York: Basic Books, 1955).
Freud, Sigmund, "A Note on the Unconscious in Psychology," in *The Standard Edition of the Complete Psychological Works of Sigmund Freud, Vol. 12* (London: Hogarth Press, 1955), 255–66.
Freud, Sigmund, *An Outline of Psycho-Analysis* (1938) (New York: Norton, 1989).
Freud, Sigmund, "Project for a Scientific Psychology" (1895), in *The Standard Edition of the Complete Psychological Works of Sigmund Freud, Vol. 1* (London: Hogarth Press, 1950), 281–391.
Freud, Sigmund, *Three Essays on the Theory of Sexuality* (1905) (New York: Basic Books, 2000).
Freud, Sigmund, "The Uncanny" (1919), in *The Standard Edition of the Complete Psychological Works of Sigmund Freud, Vol. 17* (London: Hogarth Press, 1955), 219–52.
Frohne, Ursula, "That's the only now I get—Immersion and Participation in Video-Installations by Dan Graham, Steve McQueen, Douglas Gordon, Doug Aitken, Eija-Liisa Ahtila, Sam Taylor-Wood," www.medienkunstnetz.de (retrieved 4 July 2014).
Fuller, Matthew, "Luciana Parisi Interview," (28 October 2004), http://www.nettime.org/Lists-Archives/nettime-l-0410/msg00054.html (retrieved 16 May 2014).
Galloway, Alexander R., *The Interface Effect* (Cambridge, MA: Polity Press, 2012).
Galloway, Alexander R.; and Thacker, Eugene, *The Exploit: A Theory of Networks* (Minneapolis: University of Minnesota Press, 2007).
Garbner, Marjorie, "Some Like It Haute," interview with Hannah J. L. Feldman in *World/Art*, 1 (1995), 30–33.
Gatens, Moira, *Imaginary Bodies: Ethics, Power, and Corporeality* (London: Routledge, 1996).
Gerson, Samuel, "The Enlivening Transference and the Shadow of Deadliness," paper delivered to a meeting of the Boston Psychoanalytic Society and Institute, 3 May 2003.
Gibson, William, *Neuromancer* (New York: Ace, 1984).
Grau, Oliver; and Keil, Andreas (eds.), *Mediale Emotionen. Zur Lenkung von Gefühlen durch Bild und Sound* (Frankfurt, Germany: Fischer, 2005).

Green, André, "Against Lacanism: A Conversation with Sergio Benvenuto," in *Journal of European Psychoanalysis*, 2 (Fall 1995–Winter 1996).
Green, André, *The Chains of Eros: The Sexual in Psychoanalysis* (London: H. Karnac, 2001).
Green, André, *Le discours vivant. La conception psychanalytique de l'affect* (Paris: PUF, 1973).
Green, André, *Life Narcissism and Death Narcissism* (London: Free Association Books, 2001).
Gregg, Melissa; and Seigworth, Gregory J. (eds.), *The Affect Theory Reader* (Durham, NC: Duke University Press, 2010).
Grewenig, Tobias, *Emotion's Defibrillator*, 2005, http://www.tobiasgrewenig.com/emotions_defibrillator/index.html (retrieved 23 May 2014).
Grosz, Elizabeth, *Time Travels: Feminism, Nature, Power* (Durham, NC: Duke University Press, 2005).
Grosz, Elizabeth, *Volatile Bodies: Toward a Corporeal Feminism* (Bloomington: Indiana University Press, 1994).
Guertin, Carolin, "Queer Hybrids: Cosmopolism and Embodied Arts," in Gerfried Stocker and Christine Schöpf (eds.), *Hybrid: Living in Paradox: Ars Electronica 2005* (Ostfildern-Ruit, Germany: Hatje Cantz, 2005), 166–69.
Gumbrecht, Hans Ulrich, *Production of Presence: What Meaning Cannot Convey* (Stanford, CA: Stanford University Press, 2004).
Habermas, Jürgen, *Knowledge and Human Interests* (London: Polity, 1987).
Hagen, Wolfgang, "Die Entropie der Fotografie. Skizzen einer Genealogie der digital-elektronischen Bildaufzeichnung," in Herta Wolf (ed.), *Paradigma Fotografie. Fotokritik am Ende des fotografischen Zeitalters, Vol. 1* (Frankfurt, Germany: Suhrkamp, 2002), 195–238.
Hall, Stuart. "On Postmodernism and Articulation: An Interview with Stuart Hall," in David Morley and Kuan-Hsing Chen (eds.), *Stuart Hall* (London: Routledge, 1996), 131–50.
Hansen, Mark B. N., "Beyond Affect? Technical Sensibility and the Pharmacology of Media," paper presented at *Critical Themes in Media Studies*, NYU, 2013.
Hansen, Mark B. N., "Embodying Virtual Reality: Touch and Self-Movement in the Work of Char Davies," in *Critical Matrix: The Princeton Journal of Women, Gender and Culture*, 12 (2004), 112–47.
Hansen, Mark B. N., "Feeling without Feelers, or Affectivity as Environmental Force," in Marie-Luise Angerer, Bernd Bösel, and Michaela Ott (eds.), *Timing of Affect: Epistemologies, Politics, Aesthetics* (Zurich, Switzerland: diaphanes and University of Chicago Press, forthcoming).
Hansen, Mark B. N., *New Philosophy for New Media* (Cambridge, MA: MIT Press, 2004).
Haraway, Donna J., *The Companion Species Manifesto: Dogs, People, and Significant Others* (Chicago: Prickly Paradigm Press, 2003).
Haraway, Donna J., "A Cyborg Manifesto: Science, Technology, and Socialist-Feminism in the Late Twentieth Century" (1983), in Donna J. Haraway, *Simians, Cyborgs, and Women: The Reinvention of Nature* (New York: Routledge, 1991), 149–81.
Haraway, Donna J., *When Species Meet* (Minneapolis: University of Minnesota Press, 2008).
Hardt, Michael; and Negri, Antonio, *Empire* (Cambridge, MA: University of Harvard Press, 2000).
Hardt, Michael; and Negri, Antonio, *Multitude, War and Democracy in the Age of Empire* (New York: Penguin, 2004).
Hayles, N. Katherine, *How We Became Posthuman: Virtual Bodies in Cybernetics, Literature, and Informatics* (Chicago: University of Chicago Press, 1999).
Hebb, Donald Olding, *The Organization of Behaviour: A Neuropsychological Theory* (New York: John Wiley & Sons, 1949).
Heidegger, Martin, *Kant and the Problem of Metaphysics* (Bloomington, IN: Bloomington University Press, 1997).
Heidegger, Martin, "Letter on 'Humanism'" (1949), in William McNeill (ed.), *Martin Heidegger: Pathmarks* (Cambridge, MA: Cambridge University Press, 1998), 239–76.
Heiser, Jörg, "Imagination: The Making Of," in exhibition catalog, *The Secret Hotel* (Bregenz, Austria: Kunsthaus Bregenz, 2005).

Heller-Roazen, Daniel, *The Inner Touch: Archaeology of a Sensation* (New York: Zone Books, 2009).
Helmholtz, Hermann von, *Treatise on Physiological Optics* (1856–1866) (Rochester, NY: The Optical Society of America, 1924).
Hemmings, Clare, "Invoking Affect," in *Cultural Studies*, 19.5 (2005), 548–67.
Holl, Ute, *Kino, Trance & Kybernetik* (Berlin: Brinkmann & Bose, 2002).
Irigaray, Luce, *An Ethics of Sexual Difference* (New York: Cornell University Press, 1993).
Irigaray, Luce, *Speculum of the Other Woman* (1974) (Ithaca, NY: Cornell University Press, 1985).
Irigaray, Luce, *This Sex Which Is Not One* (1977) (Ithaca, NY: Cornell University Press, 1985).
Iveson, Richard, "Plasticity and the Living Dead: Malabou Reading Freud," in *Zoogenesis: Thinking Animals, Encounter, and Other Stuff*, 23 March 2013, http://zoogenesis.wordpress.com/2013/03/23/plasticity-and-the-living-dead-malabou-reading-freu (retrieved 5 May 2014).
Jaeger, Frédéric, "The Now in Pure Intensity," www.critic.de/film/mommy-6705 (retrieved 23 May 2014).
James, William, *The Principles of Psychology, Vol. 1* (New York: Henry Holt, 1890).
Kaufer, Stefan, "Leg dich hin und sei still. Olafur Eliasson hat in der Galerie Tate Modern in London ein überwältigendes Szenario installiert," *Frankfurter Rundschau* online, 4 January 2004.
Keil, Andreas; and Eder, Jens, "Audiovisuelle Medien und neuronale Netzwerke," in Oliver Grau and Andreas Keil (eds.), *Mediale Emotionen. Zur Lenkung von Gefühlen durch Bild und Sound* (Frankfurt, Germany: Fischer, 2005), 224–41.
Kittler, Friedrich A., *Discourse Networks, 1800/1900* (Stanford, CA: Stanford University Press, 1992).
Kittler, Friedrich A., *Short Cuts* (Frankfurt, Germany: Zweitausendeins, 2002).
Kochinka, Alexander, *Emotionstheorien. Begriffliche Arbeit am Gefühl* (Bielefeld, Germany: Transcript, 2004).
Kosofsky Sedgwick, Eve, *Epistemology of the Closet* (Berkeley: University of California Press, 1990).
Kosofsky Sedgwick, Eve, *Touching Feeling: Affect, Pedagogy, Performativity* (Durham,NC: Duke University Press, 2003).
Kosofsky Sedgwick, Eve; and Frank, Adam (eds.), *Shame and Its Sisters: A Silvan Tomkins Reader* (Durham, NC: Duke University Press, 1995).
Krauss, Rosalind, *A Voyage on the North Sea* (London: Thames & Hudson, 2000).
Kristeva, Julia, *New Maladies of the Soul* (New York: Columbia University Press, 2005).
Kristeva, Julia, *Revolution in Poetic Language* (New York: Columbia University Press, 1984).
Lacan, Jacques, *Anxiety: The Seminar of Jacques Lacan, Book X* (Cambridge, UK: Polity, 2014).
Lacan, Jacques, *The Four Fundamental Concepts of Psychoanalysis: The Seminar XI* (New York: Norton, 1998).
Lacan, Jacques, "The Freudian Thing, or the Meaning of the Return to Freud in Psychoanalysis" (1955), in Jacques Lacan, *Écrits: The First Complete Edition in English* (New York: Norton, 2006), 334–63.
Lacan, Jacques, "The Mirror Stage as Formative of the I Function," in *Écrits: The First Complete Edition in English* (New York: Norton 2006), 75–81.
Lacan, Jacques, *The Seminar of Jacques Lacan: Book II: The Ego in Freud's Theory and in the Technique of Psychoanalysis* (Cambridge: Cambridge University Press, 1988).
Lacan, Jacques, *The Seminar of Jacques Lacan VII: The Ethics of Psychoanalysis* (New York: Norton, 1992).
Lacan, Jacques, *The Seminar of Jacques Lacan XX: On Feminine Sexuality, the Limits of Love and Knowledge (Encore)* (New York: Norton, 1999).
Laclau, Ernesto, *On Populist Reason* (London: Verso, 2005).
Laclau, Ernesto, "Subject of Politics, Politics of the Subject," in Ernesto Laclau, *Emancipation(s)* (London: Verso, 1996), 47–65.

Laplanche, Jean; and Pontalis, Jean-Bertrand, "Fantasy and the Origins of Sexuality," in Victor Burgin, James Donald, and Cora Kaplan (eds.), *Formations of Fantasy* (London: Routledge, 1986), 5–34.

Laplanche, Jean; and Pontalis, Jean-Bertrand, *The Language of Psychoanalysis* (London: Karnac, 1988).

Latour, Bruno, "Atmosphère, Atmosphère," in Susan May (ed.), *The Weather Project* (London: Tate, 2004).

Latour, Bruno, "A Cautious Prometheus? A Few Steps toward a Philosophy of Design (with Special Attention to Peter Sloterdijk)," keynote lecture for the *Networks of Design* meeting of the Design History Society, Falmouth, Cornwall, UK, 3 September 2008, www.bruno-latour.fr/sites/default/files/112-DESIGN-CORNWALL-GB.pdf (retrieved 3 July 2014).

Lazzarato, Maurizio, *Videophilosophie. Zeitwahrnehmung im Postfordismus* (Berlin: Merve, 2002).

Lem, Stanisław, "Golem IV," in *Imaginary Magnitude* (San Diego: Harvest, 1985).

Lemke, Thomas, "Die Regierung der Risiken. Von der Eugenik zur genetischen Gouvernementalität," in Ulrich Bröckling, Susanne Krasmann, and Thomas Lemke (eds.), *Gouvernementalität der Gegenwart. Studien zur Ökonomisierung des Sozialen* (Frankfurt, Germany: Suhrkamp, 2000), 227–64.

Lenoir, Tim, foreword, in Mark B. N. Hansen, *New Philosophy for New Media* (Cambridge, MA: MIT Press, 2004), xiii–xxvii.

Leys, Ruth, *From Guilt to Shame: Auschwitz and After* (Princeton, NJ: Princeton University Press, 2007).

"Libet's Short Delay," in *Conscious Entities*, 2 June 2005, http://www.consciousentities.com/libet.htm (retrieved May 17 2014).

Lippard, Lucy, "Vorwort," in *Valie EXPORT: MAGNA. Feminismus: Kunst und Kreativität* (exhibition catalogue) (Vienna: Galerie Nächst St. Stephan, 1975).

Lorenzer, Alfred, *Die Wahrheit der psychoanalytischen Erkenntnis. Ein historisch-materialistischer Entwurf* (Frankfurt, Germany: Suhrkamp, 1976).

Lyotard, Jean-François, *The Postmodern Condition: A Report on Knowledge* (Minneapolis: University of Minnesota Press, 1984).

Mach, Ernst, *The Analysis of Sensations, and the Relation of the Physical to the Psychical* (Chicago: Open Court, 1914).

Mahrenholz, Simone, "Derrick de Kerckhove—Medien als Psychotechnologien," in Alice Lagaay and David Lauer (eds.), *Medien-Theorien. Eine philosophische Einführung* (Frankfurt, Germany: Campus, 2004).

Malabou, Catherine, *The New Wounded: From Neurosis to Brain Damage* (New York: Fordham University Press, 2012).

Malabou, Catherine, *What Should We Do with Our Brain?* (New York: Fordham University Press, 2008).

Malabou, Catherine; and Johnston, Adrian, *Self and Emotional Life* (New York: Columbia University Press, 2013).

Manning, Erin, *Always More Than One: Individuation's Dance* (Durham, NC: Duke University Press, 2013).

Manning, Erin; and Massumi, Brian, *Thought in ACT: Passages in the Ecology of Experience* (Minneapolis: University of Minnesota Press, 2014).

Manovich, Lev, "image_future" (spring 2004), in www.manovich.net (retrieved 4 July 2014).

Margulis, Lynn; and Sagan, Dorion, *What Is Life?* (London: Weidenfeld and Nicholson, 1995).

Margulis, Lynn; and Sagan, Dorion, *What Is Sex?* (New York: Simon & Schuster, 1997).

Marks, Laura U., *The Skin of the Film: Intercultural Cinema, Embodiment, and the Senses* (Durham, NC: Duke University Press, 2000).

Marks, Laura U., *Touch: Sensuous Theory and Multisensory Media* (Minneapolis: University of Minnesota Press, 2002).

Massumi, Brian, "The Autonomy of Affect," in Paul Patton (ed.), *Deleuze: A Critical Reader* (Cambridge, MA: Blackwell, 1996), 217–39.

Massumi, Brian, "The Bleed: Where the Body Meets Image," in John C. Welchman (ed.), *Rethinking Borders* (Minneapolis, MN: Macmillan, 1996), 18–40.

Massumi, Brian, "Navigating Moments," in *21C Magazine* (2003).

Massumi, Brian, *Parables for the Virtual: Movement, Affect, Sensation* (Durham, NC: Duke University Press, 2002).

Massumi, Brian, *A User's Guide to Capitalism and Schizophrenia: Deviations from Deleuze and Guattari* (Cambridge, MA: MIT Press, 1993).
Maturana, Humberto; and Varela, Francisco, *Autopoiesis and Cognition: The Realization of the Living* (Dordrecht, Netherlands: Reidel, 1980).
McLuhan, Marshall, *Understanding Media: The Extensions of Man* (New York: McGraw Hill, 1964).
Metz, Christian, "The Imaginary Signifier," in *Screen*, 16.2 (1975), 14–76.
Michalka, Mathias (ed.), *X-SCREEN* (Vienna: Museum Moderner Kunst, 2004).
Minh-Ha, Trinh T., *Framer Framed: Film Scripts and Interviews* (New York: Routledge, 1992).
Mitchell, William J. T., "The Pictorial Turn," in *Artforum* (March 1992).
Mitchell, William J. T., *What Do Pictures Want? The Lives and Loves of Images* (Chicago: University of Chicago Press, 2005).
Moss, David, "Memories of Being: Orlan's Theatre of the Self," in *Art + Text*, 54 (1996), 67–72.
Mulvey, Laura, "Visual Pleasure and Narrative Cinema," in *Screen*, 16.3 (1975), 6–18.
Nancy, Jean-Luc, *Corpus* (New York: Fordham University Press, 2008).
Nathanson, Donald L., *Shame and Pride: Affect, Sex, and the Birth of the Self* (New York: Norton, 1992).
Neitzel, Britta; Bopp, Matthias; and Nohr, Rolf F. (eds.), *"See? I'm real . . ." Multidisziplinäre Zugänge zum Computerspiel am Beispiel von "Silent Hill"* (Münster, Germany: LIT, 2005).
Nicholls, Angus; and Liebscher, Martin (eds.), *Thinking the Unconscious: Nineteenth-Century German Thought* (Cambridge, MA: Cambridge University Press, 2010).
Nietzsche, Friedrich, "Nachgelassenes Fragment 5" [89] (1870–1871), in Friedrich Nietzsche, *Kritische Gesamtausgabe, Series 3, Vol. 3* (Berlin: de Gruyter, 1975–1984).
Oliveira, Carlos, "Global Algorithm 1.7: The Silence of the Lambs: Paul Virilio in Conversation," in *CTheory.net* (12 June 1996), http://www.ctheory.net/articles.aspx?id=38 (retrieved May 19, 2014).
Ott, Michaela, *Affizierung. Zu einer ästhetisch-epistemischen Figur* (Munich, Germany: edition text + kritik, 2010).
Panksepp, Jaak, *Affective Neuroscience* (New York: Oxford University Press, 1998).
Panksepp, Jaak, "At the Interface of the Affective, Behavioral, and Cognitive Neurosciences: Decoding the Emotional Feelings of the Brain," in *Brain and Cognition*, 52 (2003), 4–14.
Parikka, Jussi, *Insect Media: An Archaeology of Animals and Technology* (Minneapolis: University of Minnesota Press, 2009).
Parisi, Luciana, *Abstract Sex: Philosophy, Bio-Technology and the Mutations of Desire* (London: Bloomsbury Academic, 2004).
Parisi, Luciana, *Contagious Architecture: Computation, Aesthetics, and Space* (Cambridge, MA: MIT Press, 2013).
Pearson, Keith Ansell, *Viroid Life: Perspectives on Nietzsche and the Transhuman Condition* (London: Routledge, 1997).
Pias, Claus (ed.), *Cybernetics/Kybernetik, The Macy Conferences 1946–1953, Essays & Dokumente, Vol. 1* (Zurich, Switzerland: diaphanes, 2003).
Picard, Rosalind, *Affective Computing* (Cambridge, MA: MIT Press, 2000).
Piercy, Marge, *He, She and It* (New York: Random House, 1991).
Plant, Sadie, "The Future Looms: Weaving Women and Cybernetics," in *Body & Society*, 1.3–4 (1995), 45–64.
Plant, Sadie, "The Virtual Complexity of Culture," in George Robertson, Melinda Mash, Lisa Tickner, Jon Bird, Barry Curtis, and Tim Putnam (eds.), *FutureNatural, Nature/Science/Culture* (New York: Routledge, 1996), 203–17.
Preciado, Beatriz, *Manifesto Contra-Sexual/Countersexual Manifesto* (Madrid: Opera Prima, 2002).
Probyn, Elspeth, *Blush: Faces of Shame* (Minneapolis: University of Minnesota Press, 2005).
Protevi, John, "Ontology, Biology, and History of Affect," in Levi Bryant, Nick Srnicek, and Graham Harman (eds.), *The Speculative Turn* (Melbourne: Re:press, 2011), 393–405.

Rabinow, Paul, *Anthropos Today: Reflections on Modern Equipment* (Princeton, NJ: Princeton University Press, 2003).

Rabinow, Paul, *Essays on the Anthropology of Reason* (Princeton, NJ: Princeton University Press, 1996).

Regis, Edward, *Great Mambo Chicken and the Transhuman Condition: Science Slightly over the Edge* (Harmondsworth, UK: Penguin, 1992).

Reiche, Claudia, *Digitaler Feminismus* (Hamburg, Germany: Thealit, 2006).

Revonsuo, Antti, *Inner Presence: Consciousness as a Biological Phenomenon* (Cambridge, MA: MIT Press, 2006).

Rieger, Stefan, *Kybernetische Anthropologie* (Frankfurt, Germany: Suhrkamp, 2003).

Rose, Jacqueline, *Sexuality in the Field of Vision* (London: Verso 1985).

Rose, Nikolas; and Abi-Rached, Joelle M., *Neuro: The New Brain Sciences and the Management of Mind* (Princeton, NJ: Princeton University Press, 2013).

Rübel, Dietmar, *Plastizität. Die Kunstgeschichte des Veränderlichen* (Munich, Germany: Verlag Silke Schreiber, 2012).

Salecl, Renata, "Sexuelle Differenz als Einschnitt in den Körper," in Jörg Huber and Martin Heller (eds.), *Inszenierung und Geltungsdrang, Interventionen* (Zurich, Switzerland: Museum für Gestaltung, 1998), 165–85.

Salter, Chris, "Atmospheres of Affect," in Marie-Luise Angerer, Bernd Bösel, and Michaela Ott (eds.), *Timing of Affect: Epistemologies, Politics, Aesthetics* (Zurich, Switzerland: diaphanes and University of Chicago Press, forthcoming).

Saussure, Ferdinand de, *Course in General Linguistics* (1916) (Glasgow, UK: Fontana/Collins, 1977).

Schmidgen, Henning, *Das Unbewusste der Maschinen, Konzeptionen des Psychischen bei Guattari, Deleuze und Lacan* (Munich, Germany: Fink, 1997).

Schmidgen, Henning, *Die Helmholtz-Kurven. Auf der Spur der verlorenen Zeit* (Berlin: Merve, 2009).

Schmidgen, Henning, "Leerstellen des Denkens. Die Entdeckung der physiologischen Zeit," in Bernhard J. Dotzler and Henning Schmidgen (eds.), *Parasiten und Sirenen. Zwischenräume als Orte der materiellen Wissensproduktion* (Bielefeld, Germany: Transcript, 2008), 107–24.

Schüll, Natasha Dow, *Addiction by Design: Machine Gambling in Las Vegas* (Princeton, NJ: Princeton University Press, 2012).

Schulze, Holger, "Klang Erzählungen. Zur Klanganthropologie als einer neuen, empfindungsbezogenen Disziplin," in Oliver Grau and Andreas Keil (eds.), *Mediale Emotionen. Zur Lenkung von Gefühlen durch Bild und Sound* (Frankfurt, Germany: Fischer, 2005), 215–23.

Searle, John R., *Freedom and Neurobiology* (New York: Columbia University Press, 2007).

Searle, John R., *Intentionality: An Essay in the Philosophy of Mind* (Cambridge, UK: Cambridge University Press, 1983).

Searle, John R., *The Rediscovery of the Mind* (Boston: MIT Press, 1992).

Shaviro, Steven, *Cinematic Body* (Minneapolis: University of Minnesota Press, 1993).

Shaviro, Steven, *Post-Cinematic Affect* (New Alresford, UK: John Hunt Publishing, 2010).

Shaviro, Steven, *Without Criteria: Kant, Whitehead, Deleuze, and Aesthetics* (Cambridge, MA: MIT Press, 2012).

Shepherdson, Charles, "The Gift of Love and the Debt of Desire," in *Differences*, 10 (1998).

Shepherdson, Charles, "The Role of Gender and the Imperative of Sex," in Joan Copjec (ed.), *Supposing the Subject* (London: Verso, 1994), 158–84.

Shusterman, Richard, *Performing Live: Aesthetic Alternatives for the Ends of Art* (Ithaca, NY: Cornell University Press, 2000).

Sigusch, Volkmar, "Gibt es Asexuelle?" in *Frankfurter Rundschau*, 12 October 2005.

Sigusch, Volkmar, *Neosexualitäten. Über den kulturellen Wandel von Liebe und Perversion* (Hamburg, Germany: Campus, 2005).

Simondon, Gilbert, *Du mode d'existence des objets techniques* (1958) (Paris: Aubier, 1989).

Simpson, Mark, "The Metrosexual Is Dead. Long Live the 'Spornosexual,'" in *The Telegraph*, (10 June 2014), http://www.telegraph.co.uk/men/fashion-and-style/10881682/The-metrosexual-is-dead.-Long-live-the-spornosexual.html (retrieved 10 June 2014).

Sloterdijk, Peter, *Bubbles: Spheres Vol. 1: Microspherology* (Los Angeles: Semiotext(e), 2011).

Sloterdijk, Peter, "Rules for the Human Zoo: A Response to the Letter on Humanism," in *Society and Space*, 27 (2009), 12–28.

Smith, Matt, "The Work of Emotion: Ballard and the Death of Affect," in *Adventure thru Inner Space: Essays & Articles*, http://www.jgballard.ca/criticism/death_of_affect.html (retrieved May 19, 2014).

Sobchak, Vivian, "The Scene of the Screen: Envisioning Cinematic and Electronic Presence," in Hans Ulrich Gumbrecht and K. Ludwig Pfeiffer (eds.), *Materialities of Communication* (Stanford, CA: Stanford University Press, 1994), 83–106.

Sofoulis, Zoë, "Contested Zones: Artists, Technologies, and Questions of Futurity," in *Leonardo*, 29.1 (1996), 59–66.

Spinoza, Benedictus de, *A Spinoza Reader: The Ethics and Other Works* (Princeton, NJ: Princeton University Press, 1994).

Stengers, Isabelle, "Wondering about Materialism," in Levi Bryant, Nick Srnicek, and Graham Harman (eds.), *The Speculative Turn* (Melbourne: Re:press, 2011), 368–80.

Stiegler, Bernard, "Allgemeine Organologie und positive Pharmakologie (Theorie und Praxis)," in Erich Hörl (ed.), *Die technologische Bedingung. Beiträge zur Beschreibung der technischen Welt* (Berlin: Suhrkamp, 2011), 110–46.

Stiegler, Bernard, *Hypermaterialität und Psychomacht* (Berlin: diaphanes, 2010).

Stiegler, Bernard, "Relational Ecology and the Digital *Pharmakon*," in *Culture Machine*, 13 (2012), 1–19, http://www.culturemachine.net/index.php/cm/article/view/464/501.

Stiegler, Bernard, *Technics and Time 1: The Fault of Epimetheus* (Stanford, CA: Stanford University Press, 1998).

Stiegler Bernard, *Technics and Time 2: Disorientation* (Stanford, CA: Stanford University Press, 2009).

Stiegler, Bernard, *Von der Biopolitik zur Psychomacht* (Frankfurt, Germany: Suhrkamp, 2009).

Stiegler, Bernd, *Theoriegeschichte der Photographie* (Munich, Germany: Wilhelm Fink, 2006).

Sturm, Hertha; Altstötter-Gleich, Christine; Groebel, Jo; and Grewe-Partsch, Marianne, *Fernsehdiktate. Die Veränderung von Gedanken und Gefühlen. Ergebnisse und Folgerungen für eine rezipientenorientierte Mediendramaturgie* (Gütersloh, Germany: Bertelsmann, 1991).

Sturm, Hertha; and Brown, J. Ray (eds.), *Wie Kinder mit dem Fernsehen umgehen. Nutzen und Wirkung eines Mediums* (Stuttgart, Germany: Klett-Cotta, 1979).

Tan, Ed S., *Emotion and the Structure of Narrative Film: Film as an Emotion Machine* (Mahwah, NJ: Lawrence Erlbaum Associates, 1996).

Tomkins, Silvan, *Affect, Imagery, Consciousness*, 2 vols. (New York: Springer, 1962/1963).

Tournier, Michel, *Friday or The Other Island* (1967) (London: Penguin, 1984).

Transmediale, *Smile Machines: Humor Kunst Technologie* (exhibition catalog, transmediale 06, Berlin 2006).

Tröhler, Margit; and Hediger, Vinzenz, "Ohne Gefühl ist das Auge der Vernunft blind," in Matthias Brütsch, Vinzenz Hediger, Ursula von Keitz, Alexandra Schneider, and Margrit Tröhler (eds.), *Kinogefühle. Emotionalität und Film* (Marburg, Germany: Schüren Verlag, 2005), 7–22.

Turkle, Sherry, *Alone Together: Why We Expect More from Technology and Less from Each Other* (New York: Basic Books, 2011).

Turkle, Sherry, *Life on the Screen: Identity in the Age of the Internet* (New York: Simon & Schuster, 1995).

Turkle, Sherry, *The Second Self: Computers and the Human Spirit* (Cambridge, MA: MIT Press, 1984).

Tuschling, Anna, "The Age of Affective Computing," in Marie-Luise Angerer, Bernd Bösel and Michaela Ott (eds.), *Timing of Affect: Epistemologies, Politics,*

Aesthetics (Zurich, Switzerland: diaphanes and University of Chicago Press, forthcoming).

Verhaeghe, Paul, *Beyond Gender: From Subject to Drive* (New York: Other Press, 2001).

Verhaeghe, Paul, *Love in a Time of Loneliness: Three Essays on Drive and Desire* (New York: Other Press, 1999).

Vidler, Anthony, *The Architectural Uncanny: Essays in the Modern Unhomely* (Cambridge, MA: MIT Press, 1994).

Viola, Bill, "Viola on How Technology Has Influenced Our Perception of the World," from a conversation with Bill Viola, Peter Sellers and David Ross, San Francisco Museum of Modern Art, 26 June 1999, www.sfmoma.org/media/features/viola/inter04.html (retrieved 22 May 2014).

Volkart, Yvonne, "Physicalization in Networked Space: Melinda Rackham—Visualization of Identity and Subjectivity in Cyberspace," in *Springerin*, 1 (2000), http://www.springerin.at/dyn/heft_text.php?textid=868&lang=en&pos=1 (retrieved 20 June 2014).

Vrhunc, Mirjana, *Bild und Wirklichkeit. Zur Philosophie Henri Bergsons* (Munich, Germany: Fink, 2002).

Weber, Samuel, *Return to Freud: Jacques Lacan's Dislocation of Psychoanalysis* (Cambridge, UK: Cambridge University Press, 1991).

Wegener, Mai, "Unbewußt/das Unbewusste" in Karlheinz Barck, Martin Fontius, Dieter Schlenstedt, Burkhart Steinwachs and Friedrich Wolfzettel (eds.), *Ästhetische Grundbegriffe, Vol. 6* (Stuttgart, Germany: J. B. Metzler, 2005), 202–40.

Weigel, Sigrid, "Phantombilder," in Oliver Grau and Andreas Keil (eds.), *Mediale Emotionen. Zur Lenkung von Gefühlen durch Bild und Sound* (Frankfurt, Germany: Fischer, 2005), 242–76.

Wetherell, Margaret, *Affect and Emotion: A New Social Science Understanding* (London: Sage, 2012).

Whitehead, Alfred N., *Process and Reality: An Essay in Cosmology* (New York: The Free Press, 1978).

Wittgenstein, Ludwig, *Philosophical Investigations*, revised 4th ed. (Chichester, UK: Blackwell, 2009).

Wirth, Uwe (ed.), *Performanz* (Frankfurt, Germany: Suhrkamp, 2002).

Žižek, Slavoj, "Class Struggle or Postmodernism? Yes, Please!" in Judith Butler, Ernesto Laclau, and Slavoj Žižek, *Contingency, Hegemony, Universality* (London: Verso, 2000), 90–135.

Žižek, Slavoj, *Enjoy Your Symptom! Jacques Lacan in Hollywood and Out* (New York: Routledge, 2001).

Žižek, Slavoj, "Four Discourses, Four Subjects," in Slavoj Žižek, (ed.), *Cogito and the Unconscious* (Durham, NC: Duke University Press, 1998), 74–116.

Žižek, Slavoj, "Is It Possible to Traverse the Fantasy in Cyberspace?" in Elizabeth Wright and Edmond Wright (eds.), *The Žižek Reader* (Oxford, UK: Blackwell, 1999), 102–24.

Žižek, Slavoj, "Lacan with Quantum Physics," in George Robertson, Melinda Mash, Lisa Tickner, Jon Bird, Barry Curtis, and Tim Putnam (eds.), *FutureNatural, Nature/Science/Culture* (New York: Routledge, 1996), 270–92.

Žižek, Slavoj, *On Belief* (London: Routledge, 2003).

Žižek, Slavoj, *Organs without Bodies: Deleuze and the Consequences* (London: Routledge, 2012).

Žižek, Slavoj, *The Parallax View* (Cambridge, MA: MIT Press, 2006).

Žižek, Slavoj, *The Plague of Fantasies* (London: Verso, 1997).

Žižek, Slavoj, *The Ticklish Subject* (London: Verso, 2000).

Index